the STEELERS EXPERIENCE

EXPERIENCE

A YEAR-BY-YEAR CHRONICLE OF **THE PITTSBURGH STEELERS**

Abby Mendelson and David Aretha

MVP
BOOKS

First published in 2014 by MVP Books, an imprint of Quarto Publishing Group USA Inc., 400 First Avenue North, Suite 400, Minneapolis, MN 55401 USA

MVP Books titles are also available at discounts in bulk quantity for industrial or sales-promotional use. For details write to Special Sales Manager at Quarto Publishing Group USA Inc., 400 First Avenue North, Suite 400, Minneapolis, MN 55401 USA.

To find out more about our books, visit us online at www.mvpbooks.com.

Library of Congress Cataloging-in-Publication Data Available

ISBN-13: 978-0-7603-4576-4

Text compiled, edited, and fact-checked by Facts That Matter, Inc.

Front cover: Associated Press
Frontis: Joe Robbins/Getty Images
Contents page: Justin K. Aller/Getty Images

Acquiring editor: Josh Leventhal
Design manager: James Kegley
Layout: Rebecca Pagel

Printed in China

CONTENTS

INTRODUCTION

A Town, Its Team, and Its Fans

Dogged perseverance by the Rooney family resulted in astonishing success and the rise of Steelers Nation, whose powerful support inspired the team to further glory.

They've gone from an afterthought, an enterprise barely in business, to the standard bearer for a city. Once operated out of a pocket notebook, they've become not only their own brand but also synonymous with strength, resilience, and victory.

Along an 80-year-old rutted road, the Pittsburgh Steelers have transformed the experience, not only of football but of Pittsburgh itself, in ways wholly unimaginable.

In retrospect, they were made for each other: a team born of brawn and bone-jarring hits, of power backs and rifle arms; a town conceived in coal and steel, open-hearth furnaces, and Bessemer converters. Tough, loyal, and gritty, in mill towns all up and down the Three Rivers, they lived for shots and beers, hardhats and lunch buckets, punch palaces over prom nights.

This is still fertile soil for football, and Western Pennsylvania remains a highly recruited area. With its pride in physical labor—and fear of failure—the region has produced the nation's highest number of Hall of Fame quarterbacks: Jim Kelly to Danny Marino, Joe Namath to Joe Montana. You never come home from the gridiron on your shield. You send the other guy home on *his* shield.

If the local culture is now more Carnegie Mellon than Jones and Laughlin, transplant surgeons more than soot-stained steelworkers, the legacy lives on. When wide receiver Hines Ward was dubbed the dirtiest player on the planet, these fans—this self-styled Steelers Nation—loved it. The way they loved James Harrison spearing *anybody*. Jack Lambert dumping Cliff Harris after the Cowboy had taunted errant-footed kicker Roy Gerela.

"Mean" Joe Greene sacking Dan Pastorini four times.

Donnie Shell fracturing Earl Campbell's sternum.

Mike Wagner nearly busting Kenny Anderson in half.

Troy Polamalu hitting so hard that other teams have to scratch new game plans in the dirt.

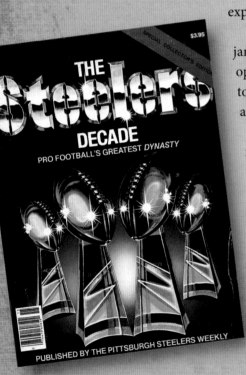

The four Super Bowl trophies that the Steelers won in the 1970s set the gold standard for modern sports dynasties.
MVP Books Collection

The Pittsburgh Steelers have a storied tradition going back 80 years. The current crop of players honors that tradition by wearing "throwback" jerseys for two games each season, as displayed by Ben Roethlisberger and the rest of the team at this 2008 contest at Heinz Field. *George Gojkovich/Getty Images*

They're integral parts of the single most remarkable turnaround in American sports history, a team transformed from decades of not-so-lovable losers into perennial champions, with a nationwide—if not global—cadre of intensely loyal fans who *expect* them to win.

Steelers Nation, self-created, self-branded, appreciates the Steelers in large part because the same Rooney family that opened the doors in 1933 appreciates them. Never denigrating the town or the fans, three generations of North Side Irishmen have always put the town ahead of the team, the fans ahead of both.

Steelers fans clattered around in cavernous Forbes Field, were exposed to the elements in Pitt Stadium, bonded together in Three Rivers Stadium, and now bask in the Great Hall and luxury boxes in Heinz Field. The Steelers Experience typically has reflected Pittsburgh's core values, with the players relying more on smarts and skill than stuff-strutting or trash talk.

The Steeler Nation always comes out in full support of its team, waving their "Terrible Towels." In 2005, they cheered their way to a fifth Super Bowl title for the Steelers. *MVP Books Collection*

That Experience helped forge Steelers Nation and caused the fans in turn to coax, cajole, and cheer the team into champions—and to celebrate itself as a growing, leaderless, wholly democratic entity.

"Whether you're a stockbroker or 7-Eleven clerk," offered fan Amy Michalic, "you're equal in Steelers Nation. There's a commonality that allows you to take part without fear of discrimination. Steelers Nation brings Pittsburghers together. Always has, always will."

Steelers Nation dresses babies in Steelers bibs, gives jerseys as treasured gifts, paints faces black and gold on Game Day.

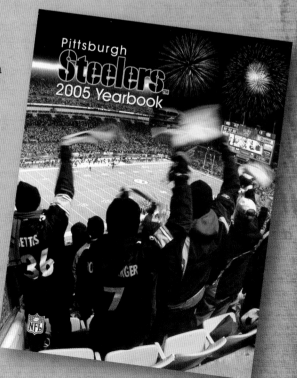

"Isn't it exciting?" asked Dr. Audrey Guskey, Duquesne University marketing professor and consumer trends expert. "Steelers Nation—the whole Steelers Experience—has given Pittsburgh such life and energy. It's unified the whole community—all demographic groups. The great thing is, Steelers Nation wasn't created by marketers. Steelers Nation comes from the heart of the people. *This* is the true Steelers Experience—and *we're* dreaming it."

—A. M.

THE 1930s

ROONEY, BLOOD, AND WHIZZER WHITE

A Pittsburgh sports promoter lays out $2,500 for a franchise in the NFL. But amid the Depression and global uncertainty, will fans support the team?

Depression-era Pittsburgh was something to see. Shuttered steel mills. Bread lines. Newspaper stories about war raging in Asia, civil war in Spain, and Hitler's consolidation of power in Germany, all of which presaged worse things to come.

Big-time football was Pitt and Carnegie Tech, an autumn game for college boys. They had the big stadiums, the big crowds. Pitt, since the 1910s, had been a perennial national champion, always in the hunt.

Semipro football, like the kind that semipro athlete, small-time sports promoter, and world-class horse player Art Rooney ran—his J. P. Rooneys and Hope Harveys— well, it wasn't much more than a bunch of aging athletes getting muddy and knocking leatherheads. You could count the paying customers on the fingers of one hand.

In 1933, as Pennsylvania's notoriously restrictive Sunday Blue Laws were being relaxed, Rooney—looking for a bit of cachet—ponied up the $2,500 entrance fee for a franchise in the new National Football League. He then transformed his rough-and-tumble Majestics into the Pittsburgh Pirates (the name cribbed from the two-time World Series champions), thinking the name might pump up the gate.

Still . . . *football?* Didn't the man know there was a Depression going on? Who could afford to watch football?

Who *wanted* to?

And the so-called *National* Football League? It was just a handful of cities; not much national about it. An 11-game card. These Pirates were men who couldn't afford to quit their day jobs but didn't mind getting beat up. Little more than pickup squads, they each got a C-note for their Sunday pains—busted noses and bruised backs. It was good money when workmen's wages were $40 a week.

The money was good enough to attract John McNally from Notre Dame. The only problem was that, in 1934, John McNally was still enrolled at Notre Dame. In fact, he even played for Notre Dame.

No problem! On Saturdays, he was demur collegian John McNally. On Sundays, he was dashing, hell-for-leather Johnny Blood, the Pirates' first true gate attraction. Although the few fans loved him, Blood lasted but a single season, then returned in 1937 as player and coach.

Oh, the coaches. Who *were* those guys? Pirates coaches were a decidedly mixed bag. Behind the bench, Jap Douds gave way to Luby DiMeolo (whom the ex-pugilist owner actually decked one day in the office), who in turn passed the playbook (such as it was) to Knute Rockne acolyte Joe Bach, who gave way to Johnny Blood, fired in favor of Walt Kiesling.

So much for patience and consistency.

In 1938, his sole season with Pittsburgh, Byron "Whizzer" White did his best to earn his eye-popping $15,000 salary, as he led the NFL in rushing. *Sporting News Archive/ Getty Images*

Of course, a major-league franchise needed a major-league arena, regardless of the fact that it was never filled. The Pirates experience in the '30s was to sit in cavernous Forbes Field, which autumn rains turned into a quagmire, frozen by December.

In '38, Rooney decided to jack the gate. Paying the unheard-of salary of $15,000, he brought in All-American Byron "Whizzer" White. Gibraltar solid at the box office, playing tailback in the then-stylish single-wing offense, and hating his nickname, White led the league in both rushing and income.

That lasted a year, and then the Pirates petered out. Although war was ginning up steel production, times were still tough. Discretionary dollars did not go to pro football. Crib the baby's milk money? For *this*?

It was neither the time nor the town for this newfangled thing.

It'll never last, fans said, not when the faithful flocked to Forbes Field in the low four figures.

Let Mr. Arthur Rooney and his five sons go back to playing the ponies and promoting boxing.

Future of the football Pirates? With war looming on the American horizon, I wouldn't give you a plugged nickel for it, bub.

—A. M.

In the franchise's second season, the Steelers (Pirates) adopted horizontal-striped jerseys and socks. Although they look like a team of convicts when pictured in black-and-white, the design was reintroduced by the team in 2012 for the "throwback" uniforms. *MVP Books Collection*

The Chief:
Art Rooney

The fact that Art Rooney oversaw a losing NFL team for four decades, and yet was the most beloved figure in Pittsburgh, says something about the man's charms and character. Andy Russell recalled feeling dejected after losing the season finale in 1963: "But I remember vividly how Mr. Rooney, despite that devastating loss, shook everyone's hand, praising our effort, wishing us good luck in the off-season, and, being the classy man that he was, caring about his players."

"His real thing was dealing with people," said Art's son Dan. "He made you feel as if the most important thing he had to do was to talk to you. He made you feel as if you were a friend. It wasn't planned, and it wasn't calculated."

Art Rooney was the founder of the Steelers franchise in 1933 and remained with the organization until his death in 1988. *NFL Photos/AP Images*

Steelers fans loved Art Rooney largely because he was one of them. His father's family had worked as steelworkers, and his mother's family had toiled in the coal mines. The oldest of ninc children, Arthur Joseph Rooney was born in 1901. He grew up in Old Allegheny section of Pittsburgh, and he lived with his family above his father's saloon. Three Rivers Stadium would be built on the land where the saloon once stood.

An Irish Catholic, Art attended St. Peter's Parochial School and Duquesne University Prep School. Though his brother Dan would become a priest, Art found his calling in the world of sports. He played semipro football and minor-league baseball, and he became a champion amateur boxer.

Though he would attend three colleges, Rooney preferred the sporting life—promoting boxing matches and football teams, playing cards, and betting on horses. Baseball would remain his lifelong passion, but he became increasingly involved in football. When he had the chance to transform his semipro Majestics into an NFL franchise in 1933, he went for it. He submitted his fee of $2,500, and the Pittsburgh Pirates (who would be renamed the Steelers in 1940) were born.

The Pirates would struggle financially during the Great Depression and war years, and they likely would have gone the way of the St. Louis Gunners and Portsmouth Spartans had Rooney not accumulated a fortune at the track in 1936. As reported in *Newsweek* in 1939, Rooney ran $300 to $21,000 at the Empire City racetrack. Two days later at Saratoga, the lucky Irishman plopped $2,000 on Quel Jeu, at 8-to-1, and collected his winnings. Race after race, Rooney prevailed, amassing a fortune of—according to the magazine—$260,000.

Newsweek writer John Lardner, who wrote that the Irishman "speaks only six words a month in a good year," reported that Rooney triumphed in one race in which four horses were involved in a photo finish. While he waited for the photo to be developed, Rooney—who stood to win $80,000 on the race—lit a cigar and went to the men's room. "When I brought him the good news there," said friend Joseph Madden, "he was telling the colored groom the difference between the single wingback and [Pop] Warner's double wing."

After his epic day at Saratoga, Rooney went home and told his wife, Kathleen, who was pregnant, "We don't have to worry about money again."

Rooney, known affectionately as "The Chief," initially ran the Steelers out of a hotel office. His "files" were a pocket notebook held together with rubber bands. As his staff grew, Rooney treated everyone like family. Unfortunately, cronyism contributed to his losing ways, as he tended to hire people, including head coaches, whom he knew and trusted instead of taking the time to find the right person. His son Dan, who would assume more control of the team in the 1960s and '70s, fixed that situation.

Despite his sunny disposition, Art Rooney hated those Sunday losses as much as anybody. "We had a standing rule in my house: Nobody was allowed to mention the Steelers for two days after we lost," he once said. "That's how much it bothered me."

Despite his well-known penchant for cigars, Rooney lived to enjoy all of the Steelers' Super Bowl victories in the 1970s and died at the age of 87. "He was a man who belonged to the entire world of sports," NFL Commissioner Pete Rozelle said upon his death. "It is questionable whether any sports figure was more universally loved and respected."

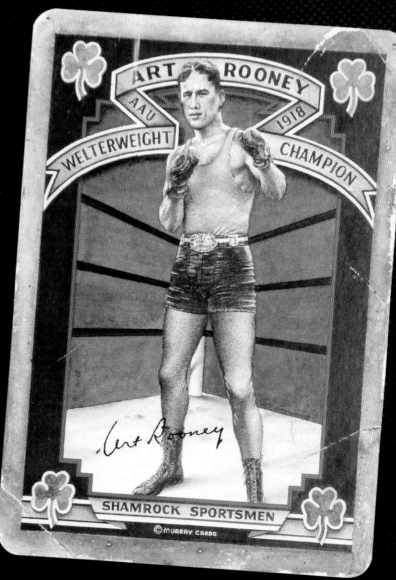

As an undefeated AAU boxer, Rooney likely would have made the 1920 U.S. Olympic team. He did not attend the trials, however, believing he would be disqualified due to the payments he had received for playing semipro sports. *MVP Books Collection*

Rooney, with his signature cigar in hand, is honored with a statue outside of Heinz Field. *Shutterstock.com*

Game-by-Game

9/20	**L, 2–23,** vs. New York Giants
9/27	**W, 14–13,** vs. Chicago Cardinals
10/4	**L, 6–21,** vs. Boston Redskins
10/11	**W, 17–0,** vs. Cincinnati Reds
10/15	**L, 47–0,** at Green Bay Packers
10/22	**T, 0–0,** at Cincinnati Reds
10/29	**W, 16–14,** at Boston Redskins
11/5	**T, 3–3,** at Brooklyn Dodgers
11/12	**L, 0–32,** vs. Brooklyn Dodgers
11/19	**L, 6–25,** at Philadelphia Eagles
12/3	**L, 3–27,** at New York Giants

Team Scoring

67 points scored
208 points allowed

WEDNESDAY NIGHT LIGHTS

Pirates Win Three Games in Inaugural Campaign

On September 20, 1933, the Pittsburgh Pirates played their first game in the National Football League—under flood lights on a Wednesday night. Pennsylvania's "blue laws" prohibited Sunday games, but those laws would be repealed in November. On this evening, a curious crowd of nearly 20,000 flocked to Forbes Field—home of the baseball Pirates—to play the New York Giants.

As expected, it was all New York, as rookie Giants tailback Harry Newman led his team to a 23–2 victory. But, Chester L. Smith of the *Pittsburgh Press* wrote the next day, the home team produced "enough savage and spectacular football to insure the professional league a permanent home here if it continues to furnish as much entertainment in the future."

NFL President Joe Carr told Pirates coach Forrest "Jap" Douds, "You're not going to win any championship, but you have a fine foundation to build on." If Carr meant that the team would not win a championship in 1933 . . . or even in the next 40 years . . . he would have been correct. Pittsburgh's first win came the following week at Forbes Field, as Butch Kottler picked off a pass and returned it 99 yards for a touchdown in a 14–13 win over the Chicago Cardinals.

The Pirates finished their inaugural season at 3–6–2. They were shut out three times, including 47–0 against the Green Bay Packers and 0–0 versus the Cincinnati Reds. The statistics weren't pretty. The Pirates ranked near the bottom of the league with 2.7 yards per rush, while leading passer Tony Holm completed just 30 tosses—13 of them to the other teams.

These inaugural uniforms included Pittsburgh's coat of arms on the front of the jersey. *MVP Books Collection*

FIRING BLANKS

Pirates' Passing Grade? Incomplete

As late as the 1970s, many of football's old-school coaches still didn't like to pass the ball. Maybe they were haunted by the memory of the 1934 Pirates, or at least teams that resembled them. In '34, the Pirates aired it out 186 times, among the most in the NFL, but completed just 31 percent of their passes for four touchdowns and 23 interceptions. They exemplified the expression that "when you throw, three things can happen, and two of them are bad."

Despite their pass-happy ways, the 1934 Pirates scored an average of 4.3 points per game. En route to a 2–12 record, they were shut out six times, including twice by the Boston Redskins. Rookie tailback Warren Heller, a local boy out of Pitt, did well as a ground-gainer (528 yards) but completed just 27.7 percent of his passes while leading the NFL with 15 interceptions.

In 1934, future Pro Football Hall of Famer John McNally joined the Steelers. Back in 1925, McNally had turned pro under the secret alias "Johnny Blood" (taken from the Rudolph Valentino movie *Blood and Sand*) so that he could maintain his college eligibility. McNally could flat-out fly, but he played only five games with Pittsburgh in 1934. He would return to the team in 1937 as a player/coach.

At least the Pirates looked fashionable. Their jerseys included black and yellow horizontal stripes, and each digit of their uniform number was in its own box. Their leather helmets included a unique vertical striping pattern. When the Steelers prepared for their 80th season in 2012, they selected the 1934 design for their "throwback" jerseys.

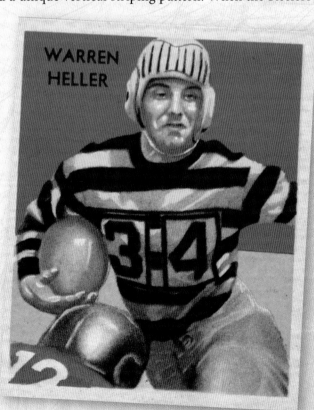

In 1934, Pirates fans kept their eyes on tailback Warren Heller, who ranked second in the NFL in passing yards (511) and fifth in rushing yards (528). *MVP Books Collection*

Game-by-Game

9/9	**W**, 13–0,	vs. Cincinnati Reds
9/16	**L**, 0–7,	vs. Boston Redskins
9/26	**L**, 0–17,	vs. Philadelphia Eagles
10/3	**L**, 12–14,	vs. New York Giants
10/7	**W**, 9–7,	at Philadelphia Eagles
10/10	**L**, 0–28,	vs. Chicago Bears
10/14	**L**, 0–39,	at Boston Redskins
10/21	**L**, 7–17,	at New York Giants
10/28	**L**, 3–21,	at Brooklyn Dodgers
11/4	**L**, 7–40,	at Detroit Lions
11/11	**L**, 0–6,	at St. Louis Gunners
11/18	**L**, 0–10,	vs. Brooklyn Dodgers

Team Scoring

51 points scored
206 points allowed

Game-by-Game

9/13   **W, 17–7,**
at Philadelphia Eagles

9/22   **L, 7–42,**
vs. New York Giants

9/29   **L, 7–23,**
vs. Chicago Bears

10/6   **L, 0–27,**
at Green Bay Packers

10/9   **L, 6–17,**
vs. Philadelphia Eagles

10/20   **W, 17–13,**
vs. Chicago Cardinals

10/27   **W, 6–0,**
vs. Boston Redskins

11/3   **L, 7–13,**
vs. Brooklyn Dodgers

11/10   **W, 16–7,**
at Brooklyn Dodgers

11/24   **L, 14–34,**
vs. Green Bay Packers

12/1   **L, 3–13,**
at Boston Redskins

12/8   **L, 0–13,**
at New York Giants

Team Scoring

100 points scored

209 points allowed

DOUBLED UP

Pirates Allow Twice as Many Yards as They Gain

A rt Rooney's failed attempts to find the right coach for Pittsburgh—a string of ineptitude that would last for 36 years—continued in 1935. After Jap Douds and Luby DiMeolo couldn't produce a winner in 1933 and '34, The Chief brought in a man who had played for legendary Notre Dame coach Knute Rockne.

Joe Bach, in fact, had helped lead the Fighting Irish to the 1924 national championship, the team that featured the fabled "Four Horsemen" backfield. Bach was one of the "Seven Mules" who blocked for the romping Horsemen. In 1935, he served as the head football coach at Duquesne University.

Unfortunately, none of the Four Horsemen graced the Pirates' roster in 1935. Pittsburgh's top four ground-gainers included Warren Heller (112 yards, 3.0 a carry), Art Strutt (111, 2.4), Cy Casper (102, 1.8), and Jim Levey, who carried the ball 42 times for 61 yards, or 1.5 per lug.

Leading passer Johnny Gildea went 28 for 105 (27 percent) with 20 interceptions, the most in the league. The Pirates were last in the NFL in both yards gained and yards allowed, coughing up more than twice as many attained. Pittsburgh's 42–7 loss to the New York Giants actually could have been a lot worse. Giants head coach Steve Owen would admit years later to shaving points in this game, as he ordered his players to fumble the ball three times inside Pittsburgh's 10-yard line.

Signed to a three-year contract, Bach would be back in 1936. Fortunately, many of his players would not.

Pirates head coach Joe Bach, for whom Art Rooney served as best man at his wedding, kept the team respectable (10–14) in 1935 and 1936. Bach is portrayed here on a Bowman card. *MVP Books Collection*

TO PLAY OR NOT TO PLAY

Shakespeare Passes on Steelers, Who Finish 6–6

6–6   2nd place

The NFL Draft began in 1936, and, boy, did Art Rooney pick a winner in the first round: William Valentine Shakespeare! That's right, with the third overall selection, the Pirates took the Notre Dame All-American halfback. Known as the "Bard of South Bend" and "The Merchant of Menace," Shakespeare had beaten Ohio State with a last-second touchdown pass on one of the greatest *plays* of his time.

Unfortunately, Shakespeare's pro career ended before Act I. Pro football didn't pay enough, so he opted for a career in business. Rooney's other draft picks that year included second-round selection Len Barnum, the first quarterback ever drafted. He would complete 38 of 120 passes in the NFL—none for Pittsburgh. The Pirates also selected All-American tackle Truman "Big Dog" Spain, who was compared to Clark Gable for his rugged good looks. Spain, who was drafted 30th overall, one spot ahead of Paul "Bear" Bryant, never played in the NFL.

Though he crapped out in the draft, Rooney won more than a quarter-million dollars at the racetrack in the summer of 1936 and rode the winning streak into the season. The Pirates won their first three games of the year, a feat they wouldn't accomplish again until 1973. Tailback Ed Matesic threw for 850 yards, second most in xthe league.

In early November, the Pirates stood at 6–3 and needed to win just one of their remaining games to take the East Division and play in the NFL Championship Game. They lost them all by a combined score of 72–9. After the season, Rooney fired coach Joe Bach.

William "Bill" Shakespeare was a triple-threat All-American at Notre Dame, but he opted not to play for Pittsburgh after the Pirates drafted him. *MVP Books Collection*

Game-by-Game

9/13	W, 10–0,	vs. Boston Redskins
9/23	W, 10–6,	at Brooklyn Dodgers
9/27	W, 10–7,	vs. New York Giants
10/4	L, 9–27,	vs. Chicago Bears
10/14	W, 17–0,	vs. Philadelphia Eagles
10/18	L, 7–26,	vs. Chicago Bears
10/25	L, 10–42,	at Green Bay Packers
11/1	W, 10–7,	vs. Brooklyn Dodgers
11/5	W, 6–0,	at Philadelphia Eagles
11/8	L, 3–28,	at Detroit Lions
11/15	L, 6–14,	at Chicago Cardinals
11/29	L, 0–30,	at Boston Redskins

Team Scoring

98 points scored
187 points allowed

1937

Game-by-Game

9/5	**W,** 27–14,	vs. Philadelphia Eagles
9/19	**W,** 21–0,	at Brooklyn Dodgers
9/26	**L,** 7–10,	vs. New York Giants
10/4	**L,** 0–7,	vs. Chicago Bears
10/10	**L,** 3–7,	at Detroit Lions
10/17	**L,** 20–34,	at Washington Redskins
10/24	**L,** 7–13,	vs. Chicago Cubs
10/31	**W,** 16–7,	vs. Philadelphia Eagles
11/7	**L,** 0–17,	at New York Giants
11/14	**W,** 21–13,	vs. Washington Redskins
11/21	**L,** 0–23,	vs. Brooklyn Dodgers

Team Scoring

122 points scored
145 points allowed

A Hall of Fame back with blistering speed, Johnny "Blood" McNally scored 49 touchdowns in his NFL career, including five in his three years with Pittsburgh. *AP Images*

FANS LOSE INTEREST

Pirates Sink Like a Stone After a Promising 2–0 Start

Though the Steelers currently boast a sellout streak that stretches back four decades, fans were not quite as loyal back in 1937. In fact, they were downright fickle. In Week 1 at Forbes Field, only 8,588 fans trudged to Forbes Field to see the Pirates take on the cross-state Philadelphia Eagles. Pittsburgh won 27–14, then prevailed in Brooklyn in its next game 21–0. Pirates fans were so excited that they showed up 33,095 strong the following Sunday. But on Halloween, by which time the Pirates had dropped five in a row, only 2,772 fans bothered to trek to Forbes Field.

The Pirates, apparently, were only fun when they were winning, which wasn't often in the late 1930s under coach John McNally, aka Johnny Blood.

The 34-year-old tailback still had a spring in his step in 1937, as he caught four touchdown passes as the player/coach. But McNally was no Pop Warner. He got the job largely because he was chummy with Rooney, which hadn't been the first time that The Chief had fallen victim to cronyism (nor would it be the last). While Pittsburgh had one of the league's best rushers in John "Bull" Karcis—a 5-foot-9, 223-pound battering ram who rumbled for 513 yards in just six games—Pittsburgh was subpar on both sides of the ball in '37.

The Pirates finished the season at 4–7. The fact that they lost to the Brooklyn Dodgers 23–0 in the season finale, after beating them so thoroughly in September, hinted at the direction that this team was headed.

The Forbes Field Experience

As old-time football fans settled into their seats at Forbes Field on September 20, 1933, to watch the first NFL game in Pittsburgh, they might have reminisced about the Forbes games of yore. In the 1910s, the University of Pittsburgh had gone undefeated five times while calling Forbes Field home, winning national championships each year. In 1910, the Panthers didn't allow a single point the entire season.

So much for the good old days. Reality set in on that September evening in '33, as the Pirates lost their inaugural contest 23–2. "The Giants won," Art Rooney stated after the game. "Our team looks terrible. The fans didn't get their money's worth."

In the Pirates' and Steelers' 31 seasons at Forbes Field, patrons rarely got their money's worth. From 1933 to '63, fans enjoyed only seven winning seasons and witnessed only one playoff game, a 21–0 home loss to Philadelphia in 1947.

Located in the Oakland neighborhood of Pittsburgh, Forbes Field was built for the MLB Pirates in 1909. It was billed as the world's first three-tiered concrete-and-steel stadium—appropriate, considering the city in which it was built. The stadium could seat well over 30,000, but rarely did fans fill the place on football Sundays. At the worst of times, Forbes was a cold, barren stadium in which shivering fans watched the go-nowhere Steelers slip and fall on a rock-hard baseball infield.

At least fans didn't have to worry about personal seat licenses or outrageous ticket prices. A second-tier ticket in 1936 cost $1.60, and in 1961 a first-tier box seat was just $5.00. Nor did fans have to deal with shoulder-to-shoulder crowding. "The place was ours," said longtime fan Joe Chiodo. "We sat anywhere we wanted."

This overhead shot shows Forbes Field's light towers, which were installed for baseball night games in 1940. *AP Images*

1938

Game-by-Game

9/9	**L**, 7–16, at Detroit Lions
9/11	**L**, 14–27, vs. New York Giants
9/16	**L**, 7–27, at Philadelphia Eagles
9/23	**W**, 17–3, at Brooklyn Dodgers
10/3	**W**, 13–10, at New York Giants
10/9	**L**, 7–17, vs. Brooklyn Dodgers
10/23	**L**, 0–20, at Green Bay Packers
11/6	**L**, 0–7, vs. Washington Redskins
11/20	**L**, 7–14, at Philadelphia Eagles
11/27	**L**, 0–15, at Washington Redskins
12/4	**L**, 7–13, at Cleveland Rams

Team Scoring

79 points scored

169 points allowed

GAMBLING ON THE WHIZZER

High-Salaried Rookie Leads the League in Rushing

During the Depression, Art Rooney's main goal was to simply keep the team afloat. But by 1938, the country was coming out of the Depression and Rooney had the urge to lay down a huge bet—just like he had at Saratoga two summers earlier. With the fourth pick in the NFL Draft, The Chief selected All-American halfback Byron "Whizzer" White out of Colorado and then paid him the outrageous-for-the-day salary of $15,000. Rooney justified the expense by claiming that White was a guaranteed gate attraction—much like Red Grange in the 1920s.

The Whizzer was indeed terrific in 1938, leading the NFL with 152 carries and 567 rushing yards—including a league-high 79-yard romp. "Of all the athletes I have known in my lifetime," Rooney would claim, "I'd have to say Whizzer White came as close to anyone to giving 100 percent of himself when he was in competition."

The Whizzer, however, should have kept the ball tucked under his arm; his 18 interceptions led all NFL passers. In the end, White did not improve the team—Pittsburgh finished at 2–9—or inflate attendance. The Pirates played only five home games in 1938 (down from seven a year earlier), and of the three home games for which attendance figures are known, they averaged just 14,000 fans.

After the season, White went to Oxford University in England on a Rhodes Scholarship. Though he would play two more NFL seasons, with Detroit in 1940 and '41, his true calling was in law. From 1962 to '93, White would serve as an associate justice on the U.S. Supreme Court.

Byron "Whizzer" White's 79-yard run on November 20 versus the Eagles was the NFL's longest rushing play in 1938. *New York Times Co./Getty Images*

A One-Win Effort

As War Brews, Pirates' Season Is Inconsequential

Huge books on Steelers history have been written without even mentioning 1939. Due to the burgeoning war in Europe, it was an inconsequential year for football in Pittsburgh. As the season began on September 14, Hitler's military juggernaut was advancing through Poland, killing, wounding, and capturing hundreds of thousands of Poles and causing panic and grief among the many Polish and Jewish immigrants in Pittsburgh. All the while, Pittsburgh's mills were in the midst of producing 95 million tons of steel for the war effort.

On the gridiron in 1939, the Pirates were absolutely wretched. In their first three games, they scored a total of seven points. The low point came in the third game, when George Halas's Bears whitewashed Pittsburgh 32–0 and outgaining the beleaguered team 441 yards to 54. After that embarrassment, Art Rooney replaced coach John McNally with Walt Kiesling, a former lineman who had concluded his 13-year NFL career with the Pirates in 1937–38.

The Pirates improved immediately under Kiesling, hanging tough with a powerful Giants team in his first game as head coach—but they still lost. The Pirates finished at 1–9–1, with their only win coming in the season finale against Philadelphia, which also finished at 1–9–1.

Many Pirates attempted to throw the ball during the season, and seven of them recorded interceptions—34 picks in all. Running back Boyd Brumbaugh could not fill the fleet cleats of Byron "Whizzer" White. He led the team with 282 yards rushing, but only at a 3.3-yard clip. End Sam Boyd was the only dangerous threat, catching 21 passes for 423 yards and two touchdowns. The Pirates concluded the decade with an overall record of 22–55–3.

Walt Kiesling, pictured on this Goal Line Art Card, made the Steelers at least competitive after taking over head coaching duties in October 1939. *MVP Books Collection*

1–9–1   4th place

Game-by-Game

9/14	**L**, 7–12,	at Brooklyn Dodgers
9/24	**L**, 0–10,	vs. Chicago Cardinals
10/2	**L**, 0–32,	vs. Chicago Bears
10/8	**L**, 7–14,	vs. New York Giants
10/15	**L**, 14–44,	at Washington Redskins
10/22	**L**, 14–21,	vs. Washington Redskins
10/29	**T**, 14–14,	at Cleveland Rams
11/5	**L**, 13–17,	at Brooklyn Dodgers
11/19	**L**, 7–23,	at New York Giants
11/23	**L**, 14–17,	at Philadelphia Eagles
11/26	**W**, 24–12,	Philadelphia Eagles

Team Scoring

114 points scored
216 points allowed

THE 1930s RECORD BOOK

Team Leaders

(**Boldface** indicates league leader)

Scoring Leaders (Points)

1933: Ed Westfall, 16
1934: Joe Skladany, 12
1935: Armand Niccolai, 28
1936: Armand Niccolai, 28
1937: John McNally, 30
1938: Byron White & Bill Sortet, 24
1939: Armand Niccolai, 24

Passing Leaders

(**Completions / Attempts / Yards**)

1933: Tony Holm, 17 / 52 / 406
1934: Warren Heller, 31 / 112 / 511
1935: Johnny Gildea, 28 / 105 / 529
1936: Ed Matesic, 64 / 138 / 850
1937: Max Fiske, 17 / 43 / 318
1938: Frank Filchock, 41 / 101 / 469
1939: Hugh McCullough, 32 / 100 / 443

Rushing Leaders

(**Carries / Yards / TDs**)

1933: Angelo Brovelli, 60 / 236 / 2
1934: Warren Heller, 132 / 528 / 1
1935: Art Strutt, 92 / 528 / 1
1936: Warren Heller, 106 / 332 / 0
1937: John Karcis, 127 / 513 / 3
1938: Byron White, **152 / 567** / 4
1939: Boyd Brumbaugh, 86 / 282 / 2

Receiving Leaders

(**Receptions / Yards / TDs**)

1933: Paul Moss, 13 / **283** / 2
1934: Ben Smith, 14 / 218 / 0
1935: Jim Levey, 7 / 112 / 2
1936: Wilbur Sortet, 14 / 197 / 1
1937: John McNally, 10 / 168 / 4
1938: Bill Davidson, 12 / 229 / 0
1939: Sam Boyd, 21 / 423 / 2

First-Team All-Pros

1937: Mike Basrak, C/K/KR/P/PR
1938: Byron Gentry, LG
1938: Byron White, TB

Pro Bowl Selections

1938: Byron Gentry, LG
1938: Stu Smith, FB
1939: Byron Gentry, LG

1st-Round Draft Picks

1936: Bill Shakespeare (3), Back, Notre Dame
1937: Mike Basrak (5), C, Duquesne
1938: Byron White (4), TB, Colorado

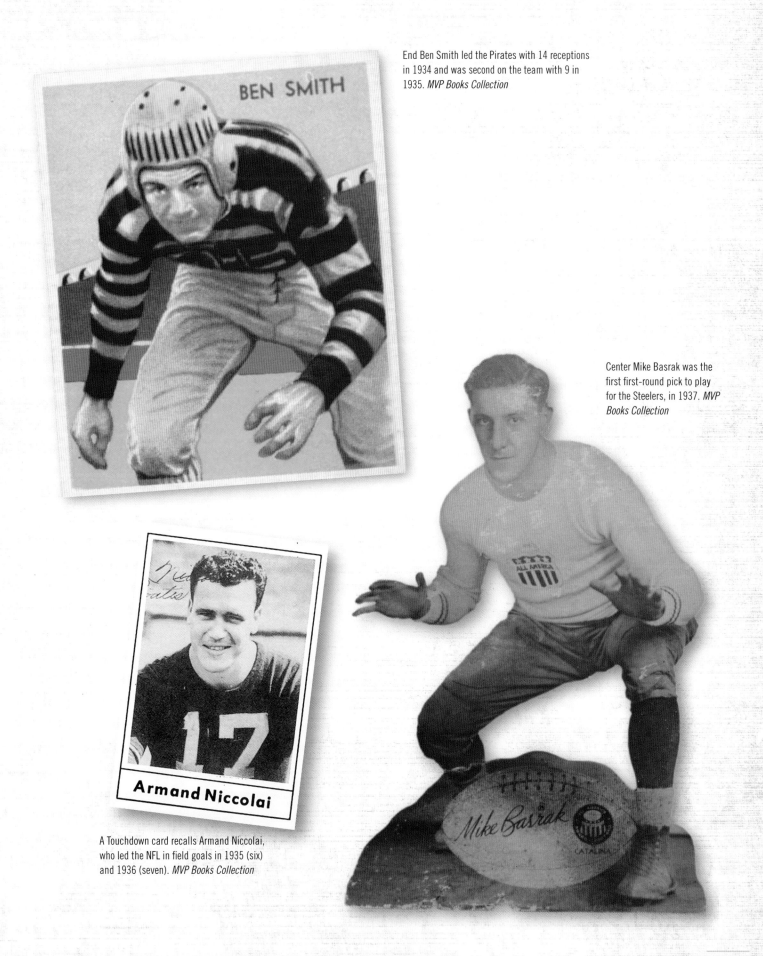

End Ben Smith led the Pirates with 14 receptions in 1934 and was second on the team with 9 in 1935. *MVP Books Collection*

Center Mike Basrak was the first first-round pick to play for the Steelers, in 1937. *MVP Books Collection*

BEN SMITH

Armand Niccolai

A Touchdown card recalls Armand Niccolai, who led the NFL in field goals in 1935 (six) and 1936 (seven). *MVP Books Collection*

THE 1940s

THE BULLET, THE WAR, AND THE LEGENDARY COACH

In a decade dominated by the war effort, speedy Bill Dudley and coach Jock Sutherland whip up some magic at Forbes Field.

This 1942 Steelers program features rookie halfback Curt Sandig and all-star center Chuck Cherundolo. It was Sandig's only season in Pittsburgh, but Cherundolo was a mainstay for most of the decade. *MVP Books Collection*

As war clouds gathered, Pittsburgh's mines, mills, and shipyards hummed 24/7, turning out everything from armor plate to landing craft. Gearing up for World War II, area manufacturing morphed into President Franklin Roosevelt's Arsenal of Democracy.

Smoke and sulfur clung to clothes, carpets, and drapes—even the family dog. There was soot aplenty, but nobody minded because the stuff that soiled two sets of shirts a day meant money. Millhands and barkeeps, housewives and shopkeepers all had handbags, back pockets, and bank balances choked with cash.

But at a time when football fans were men, the 1940s also meant that while some were pulling shifts, more were in the armed forces. When the vets came home, some signed up for football tickets. Others hedged their bets, cadged their coin, and put their lives back together.

So on cold, cut-up, wholly inadequate Forbes Field, the newly renamed Steelers continued to be a tough sell. To make matters worse, for the brave who made the trek to the old ballpark (the team wouldn't move to Pitt Stadium until '58), '40s-style football was little more than a vale of tears.

Pearl Harbor may have been bombed, and induction center lines may have stretched around the block, but in '42 the Steelers drafted Bill "The Bluefield Bullet" Dudley, the club's brightest star in its first 20 years. That year, the quadruple threat led the squad to a 7–4 record, the team's first winning season.

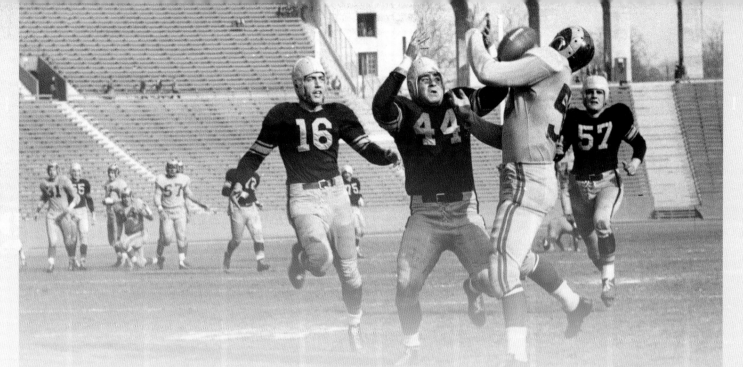

Then Dudley was gone, and the Steelers nearly followed. As the war geared up, and the able-bodied fought across the globe, teams merged to stay afloat. In 1943, the Steelers and cross-state Eagles became the Phil-Pitt Eagles—the Steagles. The following year, the Steelers ran the same play with the Chicago Cardinals, becoming Card-Pitt. The two-year record: 5–14–1.

Records hardly mattered, because nobody cared about professional sports—not with families battered and broken, war raging worldwide. When Johnny marched home—*finally!* —and Pittsburgh became the Renaissance City, the mills kept turning, money kept flowing, and fans started thinking sports again.

Dudley came back, too. *Damn*, that kid could run. It didn't matter that the Steelers went 2–8 in '45. Didn't matter that team gear was the pea coat that Cousin Herky brought home from the Navy. Smoke Control had cleared the skies, the Bullet could *fly*, and there was something to cheer about.

Then cheer louder. In 1946, the Steelers took their great leap forward, hiring championship Pitt coach Jock Sutherland. A brilliant football strategist and molder of talent, Sutherland had guided the Panthers to 111 wins from 1924 to '38 while winning five national championships. Adding sense and science to the Steelers, Sutherland used playbooks, game films, scouting reports. When razzle-dazzle Bill Dudley didn't fit the system, Sutherland traded him—without a peep from Art Rooney, who respected his coach too much to second-guess him. Sutherland seemed right on, as the next year, 1947, the Dudley-less Steelers went 8–4—the team's best finish until the 1970s—tying the Eagles for first place.

Fans naturally had high hopes for '48—until that spring, when Sutherland died unexpectedly. Young successor John Michelosen had all of his mentor's plays but none of his genius. Looking foursquare into the past, Michelosen favored the outdated, ineffective single-wing offense, guaranteeing losing seasons.

All Steelers fans could do was shrug their shoulders, tug their watch caps lower over their ears, hunch further into their coats, take another swig of rye stuffed in their pockets, and trudge off to the streetcars. Another hard workweek awaited.

—A. M.

Game-by-Game

9/8   **T, 7–7,**
vs. Chicago Cardinals

9/15   **T, 10–10,**
vs. New York Giants

9/22   **W, 10–7,**
at Detroit Lions

9/29   **L, 3–10,**
vs. Brooklyn Dodgers

10/6   **L, 10–40,**
vs. Washington Redskins

10/13   **L, 0–21,**
at Brooklyn Dodgers

10/20   **L, 0–12,**
at New York Giants

10/27   **L, 3–24,**
at Green Bay Packers

11/3   **L, 10–37,**
at Washington Redskins

11/10   **W, 7–3,**
vs. Philadelphia Eagles

11/28   **L, 0–7,**
at Philadelphia Eagles

Team Scoring

60 points scored
178 points allowed

THE "STEELERS" ARE BORN

Rooney Dumps "Pirates"; Fans Choose the New Name

Tired of the Pirates' losing ways, Art Rooney decided to make a fresh start in 1940. No longer would the club share a name with the baseball team. Rooney enlisted the editors of the *Pittsburgh Post-Gazette* to run a name-the-team contest. Readers responded with Wahoos, Triangles, and Bridgers as well as names that reflected the city's steel industry, including Millers, Tubers, and Smokers. But more than 20 readers suggested Steelers, and a panel—led by former Pirates coach Joe Bach—went with that. To this day, no NFL team name has reflected the theme of its city and/or the toughness of its players quite like Steelers.

Rooney rewarded those who suggested "Steelers" with season tickets to the 1940 campaign. They would have been better off staying home. The team opened the season with a pair of sister kisses (ties) at Forbes Field, then went 2–7 the rest of the way under coach Walt Kiesling. The Steelers scored only 60 points all season, or 5.5 per game, and averaged just 2.7 yards per rush. Lou Tomasetti led the team in rushing with just 246 yards. At least the Steelers didn't have to face quarterback Sid Luckman and the Chicago Bears, who went on to destroy the Washington Redskins 73–0 in that year's NFL Championship Game.

Steelers fans looking for some action would get it in the off-season, when Rooney sold the team but then brought it back again. Well, sort of. . . .

Helmetless New York Giants kicker Ward Cuff boots a 23-yard field goal against Pittsburgh in October 1940. The Steelers, who lost this game 12–0, scored 60 points the entire season. *AP Images*

THE PENNSYLVANIA POLKA

Rooney Sells Team, Buys Eagles, Renames Them Steelers

Game-by-Game

9/7	L, 14–17, at Cleveland Rams
9/21	L, 7–10, vs. Philadelphia Eagles
10/5	L, 10–37, vs. New York Giants
10/12	L, 20–24, vs. Washington Redskins
10/19	L, 7–28, at New York Giants
10/26	L, 7–34, at Chicago Bears
11/2	L, 3–23, at Washington Redskins
11/9	T, 7–7, at Philadelphia Eagles
11/16	W, 14–7, vs. Brooklyn Dodgers
11/23	L, 7–54, vs. Green Bay Packers
11/30	L, 7–35, at Brooklyn Dodgers

Team Scoring

103 points scored
276 points allowed

O n December 8, 1940, the day that the Chicago Bears routed the Washington Redskins 73–0 in the NFL Championship Game, Art Rooney made a heavy announcement: He had sold the Steelers. After losing money year after year, and with the war in Europe heating up, Rooney took the $160,000 that New York entrepreneur Alexis Thompson offered.

But The Chief wasn't ready to get out of football. With Thompson's money, Rooney bought a 50-percent stake in the struggling Philadelphia Eagles, owned by his friend Bert Bell. In a bizarre development, Rooney, Bell, and Thompson pooled all of the Steelers and Eagles players together and redistributed the talent on the two teams.

Thompson called his team the Iron Men, but he did not decide where they would play. Perhaps it would be Boston, which was near his home in New York. Then Rooney, who was regretting losing his team, made an offer to Thompson: Put the Iron Men in Philadelphia, which was close to New York, and the Eagles would move to Pittsburgh. Thompson agreed, but get this: The Iron Men would be known as the Philadelphia Eagles, and Bell's and Rooney's club would be called the Pittsburgh Steelers.

"To this day," Art's son Dan wrote in *My 75 Years with the Steelers and the NFL*, "the complexity of this crazy deal makes my head spin."

The deal has become known as the "Pennsylvania Polka." In 1941, both teams played as if their heads were still dizzy, with the Eagles going 2–8–1 and the Steelers finishing at 1–9–1— with Bell, Aldo Donelli, and Walt Kiesling (again) serving as head coaches. One week after the season ended, the Japanese bombed Pearl Harbor.

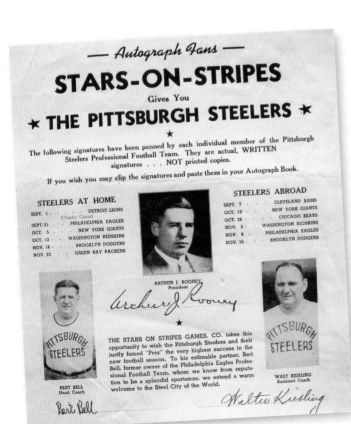

The 1941 Steelers were initially coached by Bert Bell (left), the team's co-owner, but he lasted just two games in that role. *MVP Books Collection*

1942

7–4 2nd place

Game-by-Game

9/13	**L**, 14–24,	vs. Philadelphia Eagles
9/20	**L**, 14–24,	at Washington Redskins
10/4	**W**, 13–10,	vs. New York Giants
10/11	**W**, 7–0,	at Brooklyn Dodgers
10/18	**W**, 14–0,	at Philadelphia Eagles
10/25	**L**, 0–14,	vs. Washington Redskins
11/1	**W**, 17–9,	at New York Giants
11/8	**W**, 35–7,	at Detroit Lions
11/22	**W**, 19–3,	vs. Chicago Cardinals
11/29	**W**, 13–0,	vs. Brooklyn Dodgers
12/6	**L**, 21–24,	at Green Bay Packers

Team Scoring

167 points scored
119 points allowed

Dudley Does Right

Rookie Sensation Sparks Team to First Winning Season

In their first few seasons, the Steelers made one regrettable pick after another in the NFL Draft. That all changed when they took Bill Dudley in the first round in 1942, followed by a bunch of married players. Guys with brides had a less likely chance of being drafted into the military, and were thus more likely to contribute on the gridiron.

A threat with his feet, arm, and kicking toe, Dudley rejuvenated the Steelers franchise. On his second carry in the opening game, the "Bluefield Bullet" ran 44 yards for a touchdown. The next week, he returned a kickoff 84 yards for a score. The Steelers, however, lost both games, dropping their record since 1938 to 6–36–4. A distraught Art Rooney considered selling the team again, but Redskins owner George Marshall convinced him to at least wait for the end of the season, when he likely would be able to sell it for more money.

Then an unusual thing happened: The Steelers actually started winning. A 13–10 home win over the Giants followed by road shutouts of Brooklyn and Philadelphia put Pittsburgh at 3–2. Steelers fans were so delirious over this "streak" that they came out 35,000 strong for the next game at Forbes Field. Although they lost that battle to Washington, the Steelers ripped off four straight wins after that, and they finished with their first-ever winning season: 7–4–0. In addition to Dudley's league-high 696 rushing yards, fullback Dick Riffle pounded out 467 yards. Unfortunately for Steelers fans, their team finished second in the East Division to the 10–1 Washington Redskins, who won the NFL Championship Game the following week.

As a first-team All-Pro in 1942, Bill Dudley led the NFL in rushing (696 yards), punt return yardage (271), and yards per kickoff return (27.1). He also threw for 438 yards. *AP Images*

The Bluefield Bullet

When Bill Dudley walked onto the football field as a high school freshman in Bluefield, Virginia, he weighed 105 pounds. "We haven't even got a suit that would fit you," the coach told him.

Young Bill was such a whiz in the classroom that he entered high school at 12 years old. Although he was short on stature, he used his intellect to become the savviest player on the roster. He developed into a star player in high school and an All-American at the University of Virginia—the school's first.

Drafted by the Steelers in the first round in 1942, Dudley showcased his unique skills, running back a kickoff in the season's second week. "He couldn't throw," Dan Rooney said. "He was not fast. He was not big. He couldn't kick. . . . [But] he was intelligent and explosive. He was a winner."

Nicknamed the "Bluefield Bullet," Dudley led the NFL in 1942 with 696 rushing yards—but that wasn't the half of it. He also led the team with six touchdowns and 438 passing yards, picked off three passes, boomed 18 punts, led the NFL in punt return yards (271), and posted the highest kickoff return average in the league (27.1). The only people who could stop him were Hitler and Hirohito, as Dudley missed the next two seasons serving in World War II.

When Dudley returned—for four games in 1945 and a full slate in '46—his maverick style clashed with the conservative nature of head coach Jock Sutherland. Dudley led the NFL in several categories in '46, including rushing yards (604), fumble recoveries (seven), and punt return yards (385), and he also intercepted nine passes. After the season, he was traded to Detroit, where he never recaptured his fabled success. Dudley was inducted into the Pro Football Hall of Fame in 1966.

Bill Dudley, showcased on this Goal Line Art Card, averaged 12.2 yards per punt return for his career, one of the best marks in NFL history. *MVP Books Collection*

5–4–1   3rd place

Game-by-Game

10/2   **W, 17–0,
vs. Brooklyn Dodgers

10/9   **W, 28–14,
vs. New York Giants

10/17   **L,** 21–48,
at Chicago Bears

10/24   **L,** 14–42, at New York
Giants

10/31   **W,** 34–13,
vs. Chicago Cardinals

11/7   **T, 14–14,
vs. Washington Redskins

11/14   **L,** 7–13,
at Brooklyn Dodgers

11/21   **W,** 35–34,
vs. Detroit Lions

11/28   **W,** 27–14,
at Washington Redskins

12/5   **L, 28–38,
vs. Green Bay Packers

*Combined with Philadelphia Eagles

**Home game played in Philadelphia

Team Scoring

225 points scored

230 points allowed

STEELERS + EAGLES = STEAGLES

Wartime Creation Includes Partially Blind, Deaf Players

Wartime shortages, in terms of money and manpower, prompted Steelers owners Art Rooney and Bert Bell to merge their team with the Philadelphia Eagles for the 1943 season. Known officially as the Phil-Pitt Combine, the club was commonly, and infamously, called the Steagles.

The Steagles included mostly Philadelphia Eagles, as only six Steelers were on the roster. Fans made players feel guilty for even playing football that season. If they were fit enough for the gridiron, fans reasoned, they were good enough for the battlefield. One Steagle, helmetless Bill Hewitt, felt so guilty that he quit in midseason.

In 1943, NFL players fell primarily into three groups: fathers, since they were among the last to be drafted into the military; men who worked in the defense industry, such as weapons plants; and 4-Fs, meaning those rejected by the Armed Forces due to a physical deficiency. The Steagles had a lot of those, including two guys who were largely blind and two others who suffered from partial deafness. Tony Bova was blind in one eye and nearly blind in the other. He led the Steagles with 17 receptions.

This collection of misfits had the misfortune of playing for two head coaches. The Eagles' Greasy Neale and the Steelers' Walt Kiesling detested each other so much that they both insisted on coaching the Steagles. Neale wound up leading the offense and Kiesling the defense.

In the diluted NFL of 1943, the Steagles were remarkably competitive, finishing at 5–4–1. At season's end, Philadelphia officials did away with the few Steelers on the roster and turned the team back to Eagles. Art Rooney would have to get creative again for the 1944 campaign.

The 1943 Philadelphia-Pittsburgh hodgepodge team was variably known as the Phil-Pitt Eagles, the Eagles-Steelers, and the Steagles. *MVP Books Collection*

DECEMBER 5, 1943
PHILADELPHIA, PA.

OFFICIAL 25¢ PROGRAM

Eagles-Steelers vs Green Bay Packers
THIS PROGRAM SPONSORED BY NAVY LEAGUE SERVICE

FROM STEAGLES TO CARD-PITT

Cardinals and Pittsburgh Join Forces, Go Winless

Sixty-five years before they met in Super Bowl XLIII, the Cardinals and Steelers had a more intimate encounter. In 1944, the Steelers merged with the Chicago Cardinals to form a club called Card-Pitt.

Blame NFL Commissioner Elmer Layden for this one. Entering 1944 with 11 teams in his circuit, the commish wanted an even number, so he asked Steelers owners Art Rooney and Bert Bell if they would merge with another team. Still short on quality players due to the war, the pair agreed. However, fans wondered, why did they choose the Cardinals—a team coming off a 0–10 season?

As with the Steagles, Card-Pitt was ruled by co-head coaches, Walt Kiesling of Pittsburgh and Phil Handler of Chicago—a duo of disciplinarians. When the players didn't meet their coaches' expectations, conflicts arose. The nastiest encounter occurred after the team dropped its third straight game to open the season, a 34–7 loss to the Bears. The coaches were so disgusted with the efforts of Johnny Butler, Eberle Schultz, and John Grigas that they fined them $200 apiece. That prompted their teammates to revolt, as they refused to practice until the fined players got a fair hearing. After Rooney got involved, Butler was suspended and then waived, while the fines of the other two were rescinded.

The "highlight" of Card-Pitt's season was a nasty brawl against the Redskins that required police intervention. The team finished at 0–10, losing the finale to the Bears 49–7. "Why don't they call themselves the Car-Pits?" a fan wrote to the *Pittsburgh Post-Gazette*. "I think it's very appropriate as every team in the league walks over them." Art Rooney agreed, calling his abomination "the worst team in NFL history."

1944

0–10 5th place

Game-by-Game

9/24	L, 28–30,	vs. Cleveland Rams
10/8	L, 7–34,	vs. Green Bay Packers
10/15	L, 7–34,	at Chicago Bears
10/22	L, 0–23,	at New York Giants
10/29	L, 20–42,	at Washington Redskins
11/5	L, 6–27,	vs. Detroit Lions
11/12	L, 7–21,	at Detroit Lions
**11/19	L, 6–33,	vs. Cleveland
**11/26	L, 20–35,	vs. Green Bay Packers
12/3	L, 7–49,	vs. Chicago Bears

*Combined with Chicago Cardinals
**Home game played in Chicago

Team Scoring

108 points scored
328 points allowed

1945

2–8   5th place

Game-by-Game

9/25   **L, 7–28,**
vs. at Boston Yanks

10/7   **L, 6–34,**
vs. New York Giants

10/14   **L, 0–14,**
vs. Washington Redskins

10/21   **W, 21–7,**
at New York Giants

10/28   **L, 6–10,**
vs. Boston Yanks

11/4   **L, 3–45,**
vs. Philadelphia Eagles

11/11   **W, 23–0,**
vs. Chicago Cardinals

11/18   **L, 6–30,**
at Philadelphia Eagles

11/25   **L, 7–28,**
at Chicago Bears

12/2   **L, 0–24,**
at Washington Redskins

Team Scoring

79 points scored
220 points allowed

It was no secret that Steelers founder Art Rooney still loved the horse track almost as much as his beloved football team. The 1945 losing season, however, convinced him it was time to hire a real coach. *Getty Images*

BACK TO THE STEELERS

The War Is Over, But the Losing Continues

After entering the 1940s as the Pirates, Art Rooney's club was subsequently called the Steelers, Steagles, Card-Pitt, and, in 1945 and forever after, the Steelers. With the war in Europe ending in May 1945 and Japan falling that August, NFL players returned to their teams—although some didn't arrive until later in the season.

Such was the case with Bill Dudley, the Steelers' rookie sensation of 1942. Dudley had experienced a relatively easy time in the Army, as he was stationed in Hawaii, played lots of football, and flew a couple supply missions in the Pacific. By the time he suited up with the Steelers in 1945, the team was 1–5 with just four games to play.

Dudley's first game on November 11 attracted an excited crowd to Forbes Field. The "Bluefield Bullet" didn't disappoint, as he ran for a pair of touchdowns and kicked two extra points in a 23–0 whitewashing of the woeful Chicago Cardinals. That was the last home game of the year, as the Steelers concluded the season with three blowout losses. Buzz Warren led the team in both rushing yards (292) and passing yards (368), but the numbers were paltry.

Many laid the blame on head coach Jim Leonard, a former Eagles star who served as a Holy Cross assistant before taking the Steelers job in '45. With the Depression and war over, Art Rooney realized that he could no longer hire "friends and cronies," as his son Dan put it, to run the team. "The 2–8 season," Dan wrote in *My 75 Years with the Pittsburgh Steelers and the NFL*, "convinced Dad that the team needed a real coach."

JOCK TAKES CHARGE

But Revered Coach Sutherland Clashes with Dudley

"Did you hear the news?" Steelers fans asked each other in 1946. The team hired Jock Sutherland. Art Rooney and Bert Bell had to give him a fat five-year contract and a share of team profits, but they were able to land the legendary coach to lead them in '46. Season ticket sales skyrocketed, from 1,500 the previous year to 22,000.

A native of Scotland with a degree in dentistry, Sutherland led the University of Pittsburgh to four undefeated seasons in 15 glorious years and turning around the Brooklyn Dodgers franchise in his two NFL campaigns (1940–41). Unlike previous Steelers coaches, Sutherland had a system and a vision. He was such a revered figure that equipment man Jack Scott freaked out one day when the coach's blackboard was missing. Scott instructed 14-year-old Dan Rooney to drive as fast as he could to the department store to buy a replacement board.

There was only one problem with Sutherland: His rigid coaching style clashed with the free-spirited play of superstar Bill Dudley. "This is the way things are going to be," Sutherland told Dudley. "No deviations."

In 1946, these two strong personalities managed to coexist. Dudley ran for an NFL-high 604 yards, picked off nine passes, and led the league in punt return yards (385) and all-purpose yards (1,378)—good enough to earn him league MVP honors. Dudley, in fact, amassed over 1,000 more all-purpose yards than the No. 2 guy on the team, fullback Tony Compagno.

The "Bluefield Bullet" impressed everyone in Pittsburgh except Sutherland, who was disappointed in the team's 5–5–1 record. After Dudley tore knee ligaments in the season finale, the coach shipped his maverick star and Jack Dugger to Detroit for three halfbacks and a first-round pick.

Jock Sutherland left the University of Pittsburgh in 1938 after the chancellor reduced the football team's budget. He moved on to the NFL, first with Brooklyn and then, after the war, the Steelers. *MVP Books Collection*

Game-by-Game

9/20	W, 14–7,	vs. Chicago Cardinals
9/29	T, 14–14,	at Washington Redskins
10/6	L, 14–17,	vs. New York Giants
10/13	W, 16–7,	vs. Boston Yanks
10/20	L, 7–17,	at Green Bay Packers
10/27	W, 33–7,	at Boston Yanks
11/3	W, 14–7,	vs. Washington Redskins
11/10	L, 7–17,	at Detroit Lions
11/17	W, 10–7,	vs. Philadelphia Eagles
11/24	L, 0–7,	at New York Giants
12/1	L, 7–10,	at Philadelphia Eagles

Team Scoring

136 points scored
117 points allowed

1947

8–4   2nd place

Game-by-Game

9/21	W, 17–10, vs. Detroit Lions
9/29	L, 7–48, vs. L.A. Rams
10/5	L, 26–27, at Washington Redskins
10/12	W, 30–14, at Boston Yanks
10/19	W, 35–24, vs. Philadelphia Eagles
10/26	W, 38–21, at New York Giants
11/2	W, 18–17, at Green Bay Packers
11/9	W, 21–14, vs. Washington Redskins
11/16	W, 24–7, vs. New York Giants
11/23	L, 7–49, at Chicago Bears
11/30	L, 0–21, at Philadelphia Eagles
12/7	W, 17–7, vs. Boston Yanks

Playoffs

12/21	L, 0–21, vs. Philadelphia Eagles

Team Scoring

240 points scored
259 points allowed

BEWARE OF DOUBLE ZERO

Clement Leads Steelers to First-Ever Playoff Appearance

In 1947, coach Jock Sutherland actually found a suitable replacement for Bill Dudley. It turned out that Johnny Clement, in his third year with the Steelers, could do nearly everything that Dudley could. Nicknamed "Zero" because of his 00 uniform number, Clement threw for a Steelers-record 1,004 yards in 1947—although it was good enough for only 10th in the suddenly pass-happy NFL. More impressively, he ranked second in the NFL in rushing with 670 yards, and his 5.2 yards per carry was the best in the league.

Nevertheless, the trade of Dudley to Detroit nearly came back to bite the Steelers. In the season opener against Pittsburgh, the "Bluefield Bullet" scored the first touchdown of the game on a 30-yard reception and also intercepted a pass. The Steelers needed to rally with two scores in the fourth quarter to defeat the Lions 17–10.

After two road losses, the Steelers began to steamroll opponents like they never had before, winning their next six battles while averaging 28 points a game. Left end Val Jansante was Clement's favorite target, catching 35 balls for 599 yards. Tony Compagno, Bob Davis, and Bill Garnaas caught just 19 passes altogether, but they averaged 25.2 yards per reception.

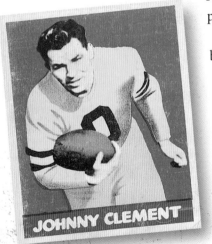

Injuries contributed to two late-season losses, but the Steelers finished at 8–4 and tied for first in the East Division. That set up something that Pittsburgh fans had never seen before: a real, live NFL playoff game—in Pittsburgh—on December 21. Christmas giftwrapping would have to wait until this Eagles-Steelers matchup was over.

An officer in the U.S. Army Air Corps during the war, Johnny Clement—pictured on this Leaf card—attacked the opposition on the ground and through the air in 1947. *MVP Books Collection*

The Playoff Debacle

Regret, disappointment, and tragedy. That's what greeted Steelers fans in 1947 as their team made the playoffs for the first time in their 14-year history.

Regret: Pittsburgh finished the 1947 season at 8–4 to tie Philadelphia for first place in the East Division, which necessitated a tiebreaking playoff between the two teams for the right to play in the NFL Championship Game. Unfortunately for the Steelers, they would have to play with an injured Johnny Clement, their leading rusher and passer, who had dislocated his elbow during a late-season 49–7 shellacking by the Bears. The only player who could have filled the shoes of Clement was Dudley, who, regrettably, had been traded prior to the season.

Disappointment: On December 21, Steelers fans packed Forbes Field to see their team face cross-state rival Philadelphia in the first-ever playoff game for either team.

The Eagles had finished a mediocre fifth in the NFL in points allowed, but with Clement playing hurt, Pittsburgh couldn't move the ball. "Zero" completed 4 of 16 passes for a meager 52 yards, and he ran for just 59 yards on 14 carries. While the Eagles scored a thrilling touchdown in each of the first three quarters—two on pass plays and one on a 79-yard Bosh Pritchard punt return—the Steelers mustered no points and just seven first downs. Philly prevailed 21–0.

Tragedy: While on a scouting trip the following spring, 59-year-old head coach Jock Sutherland began feeling disoriented. On April 11, he died following surgery to remove a malignant brain tumor. The sudden loss stunned the football community and left the Steelers with a void they couldn't possibly fill. "We respected him and feared his teams," said Bears owner/coach George Halas. "He was undoubtedly the best coach in the league."

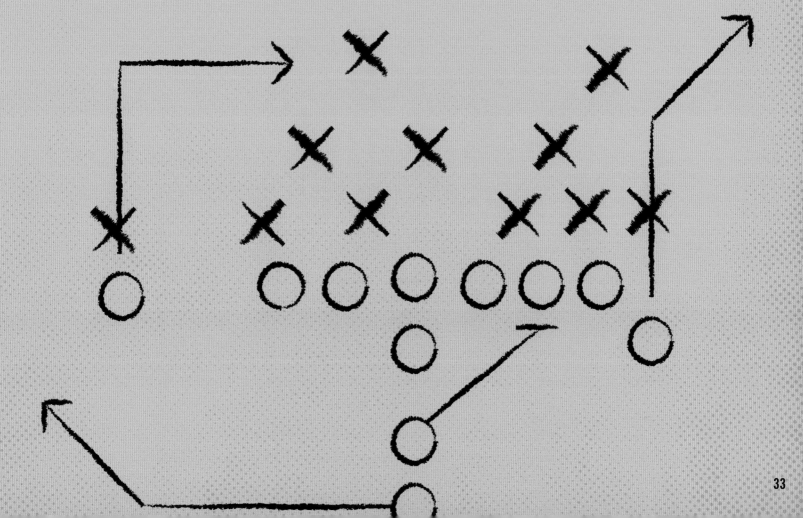

4–8   3rd place

Game-by-Game

9/26	**L, 14–17,** at Washington Redskins
10/3	**W, 24–14,** vs. Boston Yanks
10/10	**W, 10–7,** vs. Washington Redskins
10/17	**L, 7–13,** at Boston Yanks
10/24	**L, 27–34,** at New York Giants
10/31	**L, 7–34,** vs. Philadelphia Eagles
11/7	**W, 38–7,** vs. Green Bay Packers
11/14	**L, 7–24,** vs. Chicago Cardinals
11/21	**L, 14–17,** at Detroit Lions
11/28	**L, 0–17,** at Philadelphia Eagles
12/5	**W, 38–28,** vs. New York Giants
12/12	**L, 14–31,** at L.A. Rams

Team Scoring

200 points scored
243 points allowed

MICHELOSEN'S FATAL FLAW

Sutherland's Successor Insists on Using Mentor's Single-Wing

Despite his passing in April 1948, coach Jock Sutherland had a strong impact on the Steelers teams that followed. In the late '40s, the NFL Draft was held not in April but in the previous December, and Sutherland had a hand in a pair of smart selections. Halfback Jerry Nuzum would run for over 600 yards the following year, and defensive end Bill McPeak would become a three-time Pro Bowl defensive end with Pittsburgh.

More significantly, the Sutherland legacy continued with the promotion of 32-year-old John Michelosen to head coach. "You know as much football as I do," Sutherland had told his protégé. Michelosen had played for Sutherland at Pitt and had served as his assistant at the school as well as with the NFL's Dodgers and Steelers. In his four years as Steelers head coach (1948–51), Michelosen would follow his mentor's coaching techniques to at T—which would be his ironic fatal flaw. The young coach continued to use Sutherland's single-wing formation, which was considered archaic in a league that now embraced the more sophisticated T-formation.

Despite a solid defensive effort in 1948, the Steelers plummeted to 4–8 due to an offense that ranked seventh in the 10-team NFL. Ray Evans was among the lowliest passers in the league, throwing 17 interceptions compared to just five touchdown passes. Leading rusher Bob Cifers (361 yards) wasn't even close to cracking the league's top 10. While the rival Eagles soared to great heights in 1948—beating the Chicago Cardinals in the NFL Championship Game—the Steelers limped to a fourth-place finish.

Tailback Johnny Clement helped Pittsburgh beat the Giants 38–28 in the final home game of 1948.
MVP Books Collection

KINGS OF NEW YORK

Steelers Crown Giants, Bulldogs, but Finish at .500

Facing the Bears at Wrigley Field on December 4, 1949, Bob Gage romped for the longest rush in NFL history—107 yards. Actually, the official distance was 97 yards, which still tied for the league's longest run from scrimmage until University of Pittsburgh legend Tony Dorsett ran for 99 in a Monday night game in 1983.

On the Gage play, the Steelers lined up in punt formation at their own 3-yard line. With nothing to lose—they trailed in the fourth quarter 30–7—they attempted a fake punt. Gage, a first-round pick that year who would eventually be a bust, enjoyed one great burst of glory. The Clemson alum took the ball seven yards deep in the end zone and ran 107 yards down the sideline.

Outside of Gage's historic run, and the cheap thrill of an 82-yard punt off the toe of Joe Geri, the 1949 season was rather uneventful. The Steelers went 4–0 against the New York Giants and New York Bulldogs and 1–5–1 versus teams outside of Gotham City. The championship-bound Eagles blew them out twice.

Again, the Steelers lacked the talent and ingenuity to muster much offense under coach John Michelosen. Jerry Nuzum, a chiseled-featured running back who according to one Steelers employee "had a face that looked like a monument," ranked fifth in the NFL with 611 rushing yards. However, the team finished second to last in aerial yards, with leading passer Geri throwing for just 554. As the team concluded its second unsuccessful decade, fans continued to mutter about the "same old Steelers."

Game-by-Game

9/25	W, 28–7,	vs. New York Giants
10/3	L, 14–27,	vs. Washington Redskins
10/8	W, 14–7,	vs. Detroit Lions
10/16	W, 21–17,	at New York Giants
10/23	W, 24–13,	vs. New York Bulldogs
10/30	L, 7–38,	vs. Philadelphia Eagles
11/6	L, 14–27,	at Washington Redskins
11/13	T, 7–7,	vs. L.A. Rams
11/20	W, 30–7,	at Green Bay Packers
11/27	L, 17–34,	at Philadelphia Eagles
12/4	L, 21–30,	at Chicago Bears
12/11	W, 27–0,	at New York Bulldogs

Team Scoring

224 points scored
214 points allowed

Bob Gage, honored on a Bowman card, rushed 46 times for 228 yards in 1949, including 97 on one play. *MVP Books Collection*

THE 1940s RECORD BOOK

Team Leaders

(**Boldface** indicates league leader)

Scoring Leaders (Points)

1940: Armand Niccolai, 24
1941: Art Jones, 30
1942: Bill Dudley, 36
1943: Ernie Steele & Bob Thurbon, 36
1944: Bob Thurbon, 30
1945: Bill Dudley, 20
1946: Bill Dudley, 48
1947: Steve Lach, 54
1948: Joe Glamp, 56
1949: Joe Geri, 45

Passing Leaders

(Completions / Attempts / Yards)

1940: Bill Patterson, 34 / 117 / 529
1941: Boyd Brumbaugh, 13 / 41 / 260
1942: Bill Dudley, 35 / 94 / 438
1943: Roy Zimmerman, 43 / 124 / 846
1944: Johnny Grigas, 50 / 131 / 690
1945: Buist Warren, 36 / 92 / 368
1946: Bill Dudley, 32 / 90 / 452
1947: Johnny Clement, 52 / 123 / 1,004
1948: Ray Evans, 64 / 137 / 924
1949: Joe Geri, 31 / 77 / 554

Rushing Leaders

(Carries / Yards / TDs)

1940: Lou Tomasetti, 68 / 246 / 1
1941: Dick Riffle, 109 / 388 / 1
1942: Bill Dudley, **162** / **696** / 5
1943: Jack Hinkle, 116 / 571 / 4
1944: John Grigas, 185 / 610 / 3
1945: Buist Warren, 96 / 285 / 2
1946: Bill Dudley, **146** / **604** / 3
1947: Johnny Clement, 129 / 670 / 4
1948: Bob Cifers, 112 / 361 / 1
1949: Jerry Nuzum, 139 / 611 / 5

Rookie tailback Joe Geri boomed an 82-yard punt in 1949. *MVP Books Collection*

Receiving Leaders

(Receptions / Yards / TDs)

1940: George Platukis, 15 / 290 / 2
1941: Don Looney, 10 / 186 / 1
1942: Walt Kichefski, 15 / 189 / 0
1943: Tony Bova, 17 / 419 / 5
1944: Ed Rucinski, 22 / 284 / 1
1945: Tony Bova, 15 / 215 / 0
1946: Val Jansante, 10 / 136 / 1
1947: Val Jansante, 35 / 599 / 5
1948: Val Jansante, 39 / 623 / 3
1949: Val Jansante, 29 / 445 / 4

Interceptions

(Number / Yards / TDs)

1940: Tommy Thompson, 3 / 23 / 0
1941: Art Jones, **7** / 35 / 0
1942: Curt Sandig, 5 / 94 / 0
1943: Ben Kish, 5 / 114 / **1**;
      Roy Zimmerman, 5 / 19 / 0
1944: Ernie Steele, 6 / 113 / 0
1945: Roy Zimmerman, 7 / 90 / 0
1946: Bill Dudley, **10** / **242** / **1**
1947: Tony Compagno, 4 / 163 / **2**;
      Walt Slater, 4 / 38 / 0
1948: Tony Compagno, 7 / 79 / 1
1949: Howard Hartley, 6 / 63 / 0

First-Team All-Pros

1942: Bill Dudley, KR/PR/TB

Pro Bowl Selections

1940: Merl Condit, HB
1941: Chuck Cherundolo, C
1941: Joe Coomer, LT
1941: Art Jones, P/PR/WB
1941: Dick Riffle, FB
1942: Chuck Cherundolo, C
1942: Bill Dudley, KR/PR/TB
1942: Milt Simington, RG
1942: John Woudenberg, RT

1st-Round Draft Picks

1940: Kay Eakin (3), HB, Arkansas
1942: Bill Dudley (1), HB, Virginia
1945: Paul Duhart (2), Back, Florida
1946: Felix Blanchard (3), Back, Army
1947: Hub Bechtol (5), End, Texas Tech
1948: Dan Edwards (9), End, Georgia
1949: Bob Gage (6), Clemson

Fullback Tony Compagno led the Steelers defense in interceptions in 1947 and '48 while also averaging nearly four yards per rushing carry on offense. *MVP Books Collection*

THE 1950s

BUDDY, BOBBY, AND BUTLER

Parker, Layne, and Jack keep the Steelers competitive, but they are far from championship caliber.

They were the Fabulous '50s—just not for Steelers football.

Pittsburgh's smoky skies had cleared, and change was everywhere. Pittsburgh's mayor—the impatient, imperious David Lawrence—forged an unprecedented partnership with the corporate community, creating the city's first Renaissance. The Point, the confluence of the Three Rivers, now meant Gateway Center, gleaming new office towers, and quiet urban parks. The beautiful Point State Park replaced rusting railroad yards and crumbling warehouses.

Marking its 200th anniversary in 1958—two centuries since the British captured Fort Duquesne from the French, renamed it Fort Pitt for the Crown's secretary of state, and changed the language to English—Pittsburgh embraced its future. Slums were cleared, and employment was up. By and large, Pittsburghers were happy and optimistic.

Just not about the Steelers. Because in Oakland, a scant six miles from the Point, the Black and Gold continued to stumble. Fans groaned as coaching was weak and the depth chart weaker. The starters were decent enough, but injuries always cost them.

When John Michelosen's single-wing offense flamed out, fans were aghast as the Steelers marched straight into the past. Art Rooney brought back previous coaching failures Joe Bach and Walt Kiesling, and everyone knew that the team was going nowhere.

This unofficial Steelers logo was created in the 1950s. The one we know today emerged in 1962.
MVP Books Collection

Looking for a fix, the Steelers hired Buddy Parker, a retread who had led Detroit to two NFL championships. But under Parker, the Steelers played on little more than guts and horse liniment. While the hard-drinking, short-fused Parker blamed somebody, *anybody*, after every loss, he won his share of Steelers games—more than any other coach in team history up to that time. But in terms of *building* a champion, Parker was first cousin to a disaster. What had worked in the Motor City just didn't transfer to the Steel City.

Of course, there were bright spots and fan favorites. Defensive back Jack Butler starred with the Steelers from 1951 to decade's end. One of the most versatile and durable athletes in club history, Butler had great hands and even greater smarts. It added up to 52 career interceptions and a bust in Canton.

He was matched on the defensive line by Ernie Stautner. Epitomizing the killer hit, Stautner was *the* Steeler with whom fans most identified. "Winning was not a concern of ours," legendary superfan and saloon keeper Joe Chiodo commented. "Those incredible defensive hits made our week."

By 1958, fans saw a little more sunshine than smog. First, the Steelers made a part-time move to more football-friendly Pitt Stadium. It was configured for the gridiron and had a history of winning collegiate squads. Pitt magic, fans hoped, might rub off on the Steelers.

Second, the team acquired a winning quarterback, Bobby Layne. Epitomizing the hard-living, go-for-broke quarterback, Layne was an All-Pro who played like a schoolboy. Making up plays in the huddle, he'd drop to one knee and draw them in the dirt. In '58, Layne led the Steelers to a 7–4–1 record—the moral equivalent of a title.

Third, the team was finally integrated. Although the Steelers' first squad had included African American Ray Kemp, for nearly 20 years the team remained all white. In 1952, the Steelers drafted running back Jack Spinks. Lowell Perry came in 1956. After suffering a career-ending injury, he became the receivers coach—the NFL's first African-American coach. For Steelers fans, it was a harbinger of the future.

Heading into the Swinging '60s, with Dan Rooney at the helm, the fans were cautiously optimistic. The Steelers, it seemed, were finally heading in the right direction.

—A. M.

After leading the Detroit Lions to two NFL championships in the decade, coach Buddy Parker (left) and quarterback Bobby Layne (right) sought to resurrect the Steelers. *AP Images*

6–6   3rd place

Game-by-Game

10/1	**L**, 7–18, vs. New York Giants
10/7	**L**, 7–10, at Detroit Lions
10/14	**W**, 26–7, at Washington Redskins
10/21	**L**, 17–30, vs. Cleveland Browns
10/28	**W**, 17–6, at New York Giants
11/4	**L**, 10–17, vs. Philadelphia Eagles
11/11	**L**, 7–45, at Cleveland Browns
11/18	**W**, 9–7, at Philadelphia Eagles
11/25	**W**, 17–7, vs. Baltimore Colts
12/2	**W**, 28–17, at Chicago Cardinals
12/9	**L**, 7–24, vs. Washington Redskins
12/16	**W**, 28–7, vs. Chicago Cardinals

Team Scoring

180 points scored
195 points allowed

THREE BIG WEAPONS

Chandnois, Nickel, and Geri Lead the Charge

The Steelers plodded through a 6–6 season in 1950, but at least they began to make some noise. Or nois. That year, the Steelers spent their first-round pick on Lynn Chandnois, a multi-threat talent out of Michigan State. Though a capable running back and receiver, the kid was especially dynamic at returning kickoffs. In fact, his career average of 29.6 yards per kickoff return—achieved in seven NFL seasons, all with Pittsburgh—ranks second in history behind that of Gayle Sayers.

The trick to a good return, Chandnois said, as quoted in Jim Wexell's *Men of Steel*, was to "catch it on the run in full gallop." He also took advantage of Forbes Field's baseball diamond. "I'd use that pitcher's mound . . . ," he said. "I'd use that mound to get a head start, to go downhill." Chandnois, who averaged 29.3 yards per kickoff return in 1950, would lead the league in that category the following two seasons.

The '50 Steelers scored a league-low 180 points, and they started the season at 2–5 before closing strong. End Elbie Nickel, who had emerged as a big-play receiver the previous year, continued in that role, averaging 24.0 per catch on 22 grabs.

However, the biggest star of all was Joe Geri, who ranked third in the NFL in rushing yards (705) while throwing for 866 and handling all of the kicking and punting chores. He was one of only four NFL players to be unanimously selected to the 1950 All-Pro team. Geri joined fullback Jerry Shipkey and center Bill Walsh in that year's Pro Bowl, the first ever played.

Showing his athleticism on this Topps card, Lynn Chandnois averaged more than 30 yards per kickoff return for Pittsburgh from 1950 to '53 and took three of them to the house. *MVP Books Collection*

A Long Grind

Subpar Offense Results in 4–7–1 Season

When Jack Butler enrolled at St. Bonaventure's College, he wanted to become a priest. As far as Steelers fans were concerned, thank God he didn't! Butler signed with the Steelers as an undrafted free agent in 1951 and wound up picking off five passes as a defensive back that year—just a taste of great things to come.

Steelers coach John Michelosen, who had brought stability but mediocrity to the Steelers, almost cut Butler in training camp. For the last roster spot, the coach had favored a defensive back from his alma mater, the University of Pittsburgh, and Butler made the team only because that poor kid was drafted into the service.

The 1951 season turned out to be another long grind. Though the Steelers opened with a 13–13 tie at home against a strong Giants team, they dropped the next three. Consecutive shutout losses in December seemed to seal Michelosen's fate, as Pittsburgh finished 4–7–1. Ironically, a defense that featured just one Pro Bowl player, linebacker Gerry Shipkey, ranked fourth in the league in points allowed, while the offense ranked 11th out of 12 despite three Pro Bowl selections: center Bill Walsh, right guard George Hughes, and tailback/kicker/punter Joe Geri.

One wonders how Geri earned such honors. He completed just 32 percent of his passes and 50 percent of his field goals, and he averaged just 2.8 yards per carry. The totals of Pittsburgh's leading passer (Chuck Ortmann, 671 aerial yards) and top rusher (Fran Rogel, 385 yards) indicate how anemic the offense was. Michelosen, who was let go after the season, would serve as Pitt's head coach from 1955 to '65.

Game-by-Game

10/1	T, 13–13,	vs. New York Giants
10/7	L, 33–35,	at Green Bay Packers
10/14	L, 24–28,	vs. San Francisco
10/21	L, 0–17,	at Cleveland Browns
10/28	W, 28–14,	at Chicago Cardinals
11/4	L, 13–34,	vs. Philadelphia Eagles
11/11	W, 28–7,	vs. Green Bay Packers
11/18	L, 7–22,	vs. Washington Redskins
11/25	W, 17–13,	at Philadelphia Eagles
12/2	L, 0–14,	at New York Giants
12/9	L, 0–28,	vs. Cleveland Browns
12/16	W, 20–10,	at Washington Redskins

Team Scoring

183 points scored
235 points allowed

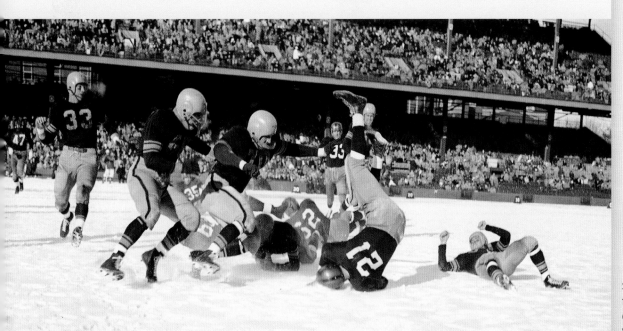

Steelers and Redskins slip and slide in the snow at Washington's Griffith Stadium on December 16, 1951. Pittsburgh won 20–10 in a game that featured 14 turnovers. *AP Images*

1952

5–7   4th place

Game-by-Game

9/28	**L,** 25–31, vs. Philadelphia Eagles
10/4	**L,** 20–21, vs. Cleveland Browns
10/12	**L,** 21–26, at Philadelphia Eagles
10/19	**L,** 24–28, vs. Washington Redskins
10/26	**W,** 34–28, at Chicago Cardinals
11/2	**W,** 24–23, at Washington Redskins
11/9	**L,** 6–31, vs. Detroit Lions
11/16	**L,** 28–29, at Cleveland Browns
11/23	**W,** 17–14, vs. Chicago Cardinals
11/30	**W,** 63–7, vs. New York Giants
12/7	**W,** 24–7, at San Francisco 49ers
12/14	**L,** 14–28, at L.A. Rams

Team Scoring

300 points scored

273 points allowed

FINKS AIRS IT OUT

Steelers Adopt T-Formation, Demolish Team Passing Record

Steelers fans had lots of reasons to pull out their hair in 1952. First, Art Rooney rehired one of his old cronies to coach the team—Joe Bach, who had led the Pirates to two mediocre finishes during the Great Depression. Nevertheless, Bach deserved credit for introducing the T-formation to the Pittsburgh offense in 1952, making the Steelers the last NFL team to come out of the Dark Ages. As the Steelers rolled to 300 points, demolishing the team record and scoring 120 more points than the year before, fans must have wondered what Bach's predecessor, John Michelosen, had been waiting for.

Jim Finks, a former 12th-round pick who averaged 186 yards passing from 1949 to '51, flourished under the new system. Finks obliterated the team's passing record by throwing for 2,307 yards, including 884 to Elbie Nickel, and his 20 touchdown tosses were an NFL high. Yet while the offense soared under Bach, the defense sagged, allowing a league-high 2,545 yards through the air and a whopping 4,289 overall.

The Steelers finished at 5–7, but at least they excited the crowds. Lynn Chandnois averaged an unheard-of 35.2 yards per kickoff return and took two kicks to the house. One of them came on November 30, when the Steelers crushed the Giants 65–7. Finks threw for four touchdowns, the defense picked off seven passes, and All-Pro defensive tackle Ernie Stautner knocked quarterback Tom Landry out of the game. The win may have been meaningless, but it didn't stop Steelers fans from tearing down the goalposts.

Pittsburgh halfback Ray Mathews hauls in a pass from quarterback Jim Finks in a 26–21 loss at Philadelphia. Finks's 20 touchdown passes in 1952 led the NFL. *AP Images*

Steel Tough

In the 1800s, Pittsburgh laborers mined massive quantities of coal and cranked out iron, tin, brass, and glass. All the while, their byproducts choked the city. "The smoke permeated and penetrated everything," wrote Andrew Carnegie. "If you washed your face and hands they were as dirty as ever in an hour. The soot gathered in the hair and irritated the skin."

Nevertheless, jobs were plentiful, and immigrants from Germany, Poland, Ireland, Hungary, and Italy toiled hard to support their families. Carnegie's steel helped forge the Industrial Revolution, build America's skyscrapers, and defeat Hitler and Hirohito. Smoke was so thick that streetlights sometimes shone during the day. After the war, civic leaders enforced Smoke Control and began urban renewal projects, yet air inversions led to coughing, choking, and many deaths.

The 1950s were the heyday of Big Steel, and many of the fans who filled (or half-filled) Forbes Field were steelworkers looking to blow off steam. Though they came to expect losing, fans reveled in the violent collisions down on the field. "Winning was not a concern of ours," said fan Joe Chiodo. "It was how hard they played. Jack Butler, Ernie Stautner . . . ."

From the 1970s on up, the Steelers have been known for their smashmouth defense and extremely loyal fan base—ranked the best in the NFL by ESPN.com. Despite brutal weather conditions at times, every Steelers ticket at Three Rivers Stadium and Heinz Field has been sold since 1972. Some fans arrive in yellow or black hard hats—emblematic of the toughness of the city, team, and fans.

The Steelers themselves left it all out on the field. In 2008, it was reported that 17 former Steelers—all under the age of 60—had died since 2000, eight of them due to heart failure.

After a long week of hard labor, steelworkers expected their team to put forth a similar effort on the gridiron. *Library of Congress Prints and Photographs Division*

Game-by-Game

9/27	**L, 21–38,**	at Detroit Lions
10/3	**W, 24–14,**	vs. New York Giants
10/11	**W, 31–28,**	vs. Chicago Cardinals
10/17	**L, 7–23,**	at Philadelphia Eagles
10/24	**W, 31–14,**	vs. Green Bay Packers
11/1	**L, 7–35,**	vs. Philadelphia Eagles
11/8	**L, 16–34,**	at Cleveland Browns
11/15	**W, 14–10,**	at New York Giants
11/22	**L, 16–20,**	vs. Cleveland Browns
11/29	**L, 9–17,**	vs. Washington Redskins
12/6	**W, 21–17,**	at Chicago Cardinals
12/13	**W, 14–13,**	at Washington Redskins

Team Scoring

211 points scored

263 points allowed

BACH TO BACH

Coach Joe Bach Leads Team to Another Mediocre Record

On Halloween, 1953, the Steelers could have dressed up as pretenders. They had the city abuzz with a 3–2 start, yet each of their victories was over a league doormat—the Giants, Cardinals, and Packers, all at Forbes Field. On November 1, fans came down from their sugar high when the Eagles put the Steelers in their place, winning 35–7. Pittsburgh would finish at 6–6.

Quarterback Jim Finks lost his magic in 1952, as his aerial yards dropped to 1,484 and he threw just eight touchdown passes against 14 interceptions. Elbie Nickel continued as his favorite target, ranking second in the league with 62 catches.

The Steelers actually had a fair share of talent. Defensive back Jack Butler picked off nine passes. Middle guard Dale Dodrill earned All-Pro recognition, as did defensive tackle Ernie Stautner and defensive end Bill McPeak. Pat Brady led the NFL with a punting average of 46.9 yards (although unfortunately he also led the league in punts). And fullback Fran Rogel, who would earn Pro Bowl honors in '56, paced the team in rushing with 527 yards. "Hey diddle diddle, Rogel up the middle," would become a popular chant among Steelers fans.

The Steelers' Achilles' heel throughout the 1950s was depth, according to Dan Rooney. "When they got hurt—and you get hurt in this game—it would be a disastrous blow," Rooney said.

Pittsburgh closed the season with tight wins over the Cardinals and Redskins, but the triumphs weren't enough to save the season. Coach Joe Bach would never return to the Pittsburgh sidelines . . . although another of Art Rooney's cronies would.

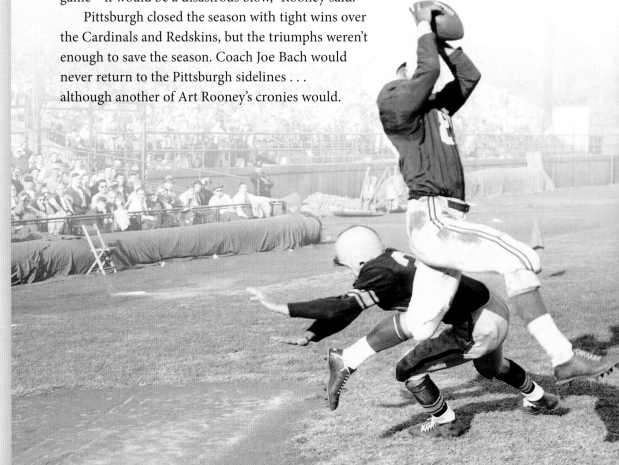

Don Stonesifer of the Chicago Cardinals burns Pittsburgh's Art DeCarlo for a touchdown during a game at Wrigley Field on October 11, although the Steelers won the contest 31–28. *AP Images*

INCHES SHORT

Close Call, Bad Finish Mar a Once-Promising Season

The Steelers might have started the 1954 season at 5–0 if it weren't for an excruciatingly close call. Under new/old head coach Walt Kiesling, the team's bench boss from 1939 to '44, Pittsburgh opened the '54 campaign at 2–0 and was on the verge of an upset win at Philadelphia. With the Steelers up 22–17 late in the game, rookie running back Johnny Lattner got the ball on fourth and a foot. "I swear to God I made the foot," Lattner told *Men of Steel* author Jack Wexell a half century later. "I swear to God."

But the officials didn't give it to him, and the Eagles took over on downs and marched to the winning touchdown. The Steelers won their next two games to improve to 4–1, but they dropped the following affair to the lowly Chicago Cardinals 17–14 as Ollie Matson burned them for a 91-yard kickoff return. "That was our demise," Lattner said. They finished the season at 5–7.

They also lost Lattner for good, which was a shame considering his promise. The Heisman Trophy winner with Notre Dame in 1953, Lattner went in the first round to the Steelers the following year. The 6-foot-1, 190-pounder earned All-Pro honors in '54 after ranking eighth in the league with 1,028 all-purpose yards—achieved mostly on kickoff and punt returns. But Lattner had been ROTC at Notre Dame, and that required him to join the service after his one season of pro ball. While in the Air Force, he suffered a knee injury on the gridiron that would end his football career. The Steelers would feel his loss in '55.

5–7   4th place

Game-by-Game

9/26	W, 21–20, at Green Bay Packers
10/2	W, 37–7, vs. Washington Redskins
10/9	L, 22–24, at Philadelphia Eagles
10/17	W, 55–27, vs. Cleveland Browns
10/23	W, 17–7, vs. Philadelphia Eagles
10/31	L, 14–17, at Chicago Cardinals
11/7	L, 6–31, vs. New York Giants
11/14	L, 14–17, at Washington Redskins
11/20	L, 3–31, vs. San Francisco 49ers
11/28	W, 20–17, vs. Chicago Cardinals
12/5	L, 3–24, at New York Giants
12/12	L, 7–42, at Cleveland Browns

Team Scoring

219 points scored
263 points allowed

The '54 Steelers got off to a strong 4–1 start to the season, but then stumbled to a 5–7 finish. *MVP Books Collection*

4–8   6th place

Game-by-Game

9/26	W, 14–7, vs. Chicago Cardinals
10/2	L, 26–27, at L.A. Rams
10/9	W, 30–23, vs. New York Giants
10/15	W, 13–7, vs. Philadelphia Eagles
10/23	W, 19–17, at New York Giants
10/30	L, 0–24, at Philadelphia Eagles
11/5	L, 13–27, at Chicago Cardinals
11/13	L, 28–31, vs. Detroit Lions
11/20	L, 14–41, at Cleveland Browns
11/27	L, 14–23, vs. Washington Redskins
12/4	L, 7–30, vs. Cleveland Browns
12/11	L, 17–28, at Washington Redskins

Team Scoring

195 points scored
285 points allowed

PASSING ON JOHNNY U

Kiesling Cuts "Dumb" Quarterback Johnny Unitas

The last thing the Steelers needed in the 1955 draft, or so it seemed at the time, was a quarterback. Starter Jim Finks had been fairly productive, Vic Eaton was a versatile backup, and young Ted Marchibroda had the talent to start in the NFL. Yet on draft day, Dan Rooney was pleading with Ray Byrne, the team's college personnel director, to select Louisville quarterback and Pittsburgh native Johnny Unitas.

Unitas was a gangly, awkward-looking kid, "but I knew he had great talent," Dan Rooney wrote in *My 75 Years With the Pittsburgh Steelers and the NFL*. "With his wiry strength and those big hands he could fire a football like a bullet and knock down any receiver who wasn't ready for the power of his passes."

The Steelers took Unitas in the ninth round, but stubborn, ol' coach Walt Kiesling opposed the move. According to Dan Rooney, Unitas was "too dumb to play," and he cut him at training camp. After hooking up with the Baltimore Colts, Johnny U led the team to two NFL championships and a Super Bowl and became the first quarterback to throw for 40,000 yards. While the Steelers floundered from the late '50s to early '70s with a string of subpar quarterbacks, Unitas acquired the reputation as the greatest QB who had ever lived.

In 1955, Kiesling's man, Finks, led Pittsburgh to a 4–8 record while throwing an alarming 26 interceptions to go along with his league-high 2,270 yards. Even though his team had the worst point differential in the NFL (minus-90) and lost their last seven games, Kiesling would return to coach the Steelers.

A ninth-round pick out of Louisville, Johnny Unitas would never get the chance to lead his hometown team on the gridiron. The Pittsburgh native was cut at training camp in 1955, seen here. *AP Images*

Heart of the Defense:
Ernie Stautner

Ernie Stautner was the classic overachiever—an undersized defensive tackle who was as tough as a two-dollar steak. Though the Steelers never made the playoffs during Stautner's 14 years with the team (1950–63), fans knew that at least Ernie had left it all on the field. And they loved him for it.

Born in Germany, Stautner moved with his family to Albany, New York, when he was three years old. He served in the Marines, played at Boston College, and was drafted by the Steelers in the third round in 1950. At 6-foot-1, 230 pounds, Ernie was small for a defensive tackle, yet he was stronger than most.

"He was one of those Germans—know what I mean?—a tough dude," teammate Jack Butler told the *Pittsburgh Post-Gazette*. "Quick off the ball, he'd explode off the ball, make great contact, and pound the hell out of offensive tackles. And he could chase."

Extremely mobile for his position, Stautner once sacked the Giants quarterback "three times in a row," according to Dan Rooney. Ernie scored three safeties and recovered 23 fumbles—tied for the most in NFL history by a defensive tackle. Lautner earned All-NFL honors four times and won the league's Best Lineman Award in 1957.

The Pro Football Hall of Fame lauds Stautner for his "competitive nature, team spirit, grim determination, and the will to win." He missed only six NFL games in his career despite suffering two broken shoulders, multiple cracked ribs, and a nose broken more times than he could remember.

After his playing days, Stautner coached for the Dallas Cowboys for 23 years, serving as defensive coordinator during a glory-filled era (1973–88). But in Pittsburgh, Stautner will always be known as a Steeler. His No. 70 is the only number that the team has ever officially retired.

Ernie Stautner, shown here on a 1951 Bowman card, was an all-star nine times from 1952 to 1961 and won the NFL's Best Lineman Award in 1957. *MVP Books Collection*

1956

Game-by-Game

9/30	**W,** 30–13, vs. Washington Redskins
10/6	**L,** 10–14, vs. Cleveland Browns
10/14	**L,** 12–35, vs. Philadelphia Eagles
10/21	**L,** 10–38, at New York Giants
10/28	**W,** 24–16, at Cleveland Browns
11/4	**L,** 14–17, vs. New York Giants
11/11	**L,** 7–14, at Philadelphia Eagles
11/18	**W,** 14–7, vs. Chicago Cardinals
11/25	**L,** 27–38, at Chicago Cardinals
12/2	**W,** 30–13, vs. Los Angeles Rams
12/9	**L,** 7–45, at Detroit Lions
12/16	**W,** 23–0, at Washington Redskins

Team Scoring

217 points scored
250 points allowed

Stubborn Ol' Coach

Rooney Frustrated with Kiesling's Play Calling

It's hard to differentiate between the Steelers' 1954, '55, and '56 seasons, as coach Walt Kiesling led the team to losing records while running the same old plays. Art Rooney was an extremely loyal, patient man, but even he got fed up watching Kiesling run fullback Fran Rogel up the middle on first down.

"Look, Kies, I want you to throw on first down," Rooney told his old-school coach in 1956, according to Dan Rooney's autobiography.

"No," Kiesling responded, "you don't throw the ball on first down!"

Kiesling believed in establishing dominance at the line of scrimmage. The Steelers' "dominance" resulted in 3.5 yards per rush in 1954 and—after everyone knew what was coming—NFL lows of 3.1 in '55 and 3.3 in '56.

Anyway, in a 1956 game, Kiesling finally threw on first down, an act so stunning that receiver Goose McClaren turned the pass into an 80-yard touchdown. The play was called back because a Steelers player had jumped offsides—*deliberately*, as ordered by Kiesling. On the next play, Rogel ran up the middle for one yard.

The Steelers finished 5–7 in 1956. While quarterback Ted Marchibroda performed decently in his sole season as a starter (1,585 passing yards, 12 touchdowns), Pittsburgh finished last in rushing yards with just 1,350. Halfback Sid Watson finished second behind workhorse Rogel with 298 yards, at a 2.7 clip.

On December 9, the Detroit Lions humiliated the Steelers 45–7. Though coach Buddy Parker's team continuously stuffed the run that afternoon, Kiesling kept running it—33 times for 25 yards! Though Kiesling's teams were known as tough and hard-hitting, it was clear that he couldn't lead them to glory. After the season, he was gone.

LIONS GRIDIRON NEWS
25 CENTS

Detroit Lions vs Pittsburgh Steelers

December 9, 1956
KICKOFF 1:30 P.M.
BRIGGS STADIUM

LOW AND MIGHTY *Newest Buick Yet*

SEE YOUR BUICK DEALER—NOW

The Lions succeeded in their attempt to scald the Steelers on December 9, 1956, winning 45–7 in a game in which coach Walt Kiesling was criticized for his play-calling. *MVP Books Collection*

THE PARKER GAMBLE

Lions' Loss Is Steelers' Gain—They Hope

As coach of the Lions in August 1957, Buddy Parker "lost it" while speaking to 600 fans at an annual team banquet. "I can't handle this team anymore," he told the startled gathering. "It is the worst team I have ever seen in training camp . . . just a completely dead team."

Parker resigned on August 12. But despite giving up on his players, the coach attracted the attention of Art Rooney. After all, Parker had gone 47–23–2 in his six years with Detroit, winning two NFL championships and going 9–3 the previous year—including that 45–7 embarrassment of the Steelers.

The tempestuous Parker had a drinking problem, and he also cut players on a whim—including Steelers star Lynn Chandnois before the 1957 season began. The coach then regretted the decision after watching Chandnois outrun opponents in game film. "If I'd known that," Parker said, "I'd never would have let him go."

Parker also didn't like using young players, believing that veterans were much more trustworthy. Ironically, the three young quarterbacks that he was "stuck" with in 1957 happened to be Earl Morrall (the 23-year-old starter), Jack Kemp (22), and Len Dawson (22). All would leave the Steelers before the decade was over, and each would earn All-Pro honors with other teams.

While the 1957 Steelers finished second in the NFL in fewest points allowed (thanks in part to Jack Butler's 10 interceptions), they were dead last in scoring. While halfback Billy Wells led the team with 532 yards, the Steelers averaged a league-worst 3.0 yards per carry. They finished at 6–6, prompting Rooney to set his eyes on Detroit yet again.

New Steelers coach Buddy Parker kept players on edge due to his penchant for cutting guys on a whim. *AP Images*

Game-by-Game

9/29	**W**, 28–7, vs. Washington Redskins
10/5	**L**, 12–23, vs. Cleveland Browns
10/13	**W**, 29–20, vs. Chicago Cardinals
10/20	**L**, 0–35, at New York Giants
10/27	**W**, 6–0, vs. Philadelphia Eagles
11/3	**W**, 19–13, at Baltimore Colts
11/10	**L**, 0–24, at Cleveland Browns
11/24	**L**, 10–27, vs. Green Bay Packers
12/1	**L**, 6–7, at Philadelphia Eagles
12/7	**W**, 21–10, vs. New York Giants
12/15	**L**, 3–10, at Washington Redskins
12/22	**W**, 27–2, at Chicago Cardinals

Team Scoring

161 points scored
178 points allowed

Ball Thief:
Jack Butler

The Steelers have two Bradshaws in the Pro Football Hall of Fame. But while Terry Bradshaw was the first overall pick in the 1970 NFL Draft, Jack Bradshaw Butler wasn't drafted at all.

Butler rose to NFL stardom due to divine intervention—only in reverse. A native of Whitehall, Pennsylvania, Jack enrolled at St. Bonaventure with the desire to become a priest. His three roommates, all football players, encouraged him to join the team. Though the equipment manager turned him away, a Father Silas—who just happened to be Art Rooney's brother!—helped Butler land a roster spot.

Though a record-breaking receiver with the Bonnies, Butler was passed over in the 1951 draft and was the last man to make the squad—as an undersized defensive end. After he moved to cornerback early in the season, he didn't miss a snap for the next eight years.

Butler was the scourge of NFL quarterbacks, picking off five passes as a rookie and seven a year later. In 1953, he intercepted nine balls, including an NFL record-tying four in one game against the Redskins. He returned two picks for touchdowns in 1954, and in '57 and '58 he logged 10 and nine interceptions, respectively. In each of the last three years of the decade, he was named First Team All-Pro.

Butler excelled due to his athleticism, smarts, and work ethic. He also knew how to manipulate the rules. "You could bump 'em and push 'em and do things," Butler said, as quoted by the Associated Press. "You could grab onto his jersey so he doesn't get far from you. You could hold on a little bit."

Going undrafted in 1950 wasn't Butler's only snub. Through 2011, he was one of only two members of the NFL's 1950s All-Decade Team (out of 23) not to earn enshrinement in the Hall of Fame. When he was finally inducted in 2012, he was in poor health—but at least he was able to travel to Canton. He died less than a year later.

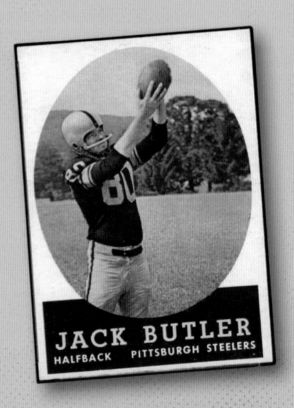

Jack Butler's career-ending injury nearly killed him in 1959 when a staph infection set in. This is his 1958 card, a season in which he was named All-Pro for the second straight time. *MVP Books Collection*

LAYNE TO THE RESCUE

Charismatic QB Brings Winning Ways to Pittsburgh

7–4–1   3rd place

Art Rooney was playing with fire. A year after signing the tyrannical Buddy Parker in 1957, he went after Bobby Layne—the hard-living quarterback who had led Parker's Lions to two NFL championships. Like Parker, Layne loved the bottle. And while Bobby could drink all night and be ready to go the next day, his drinking buddies on the Steelers couldn't, and that eventually would be a problem. Yet Parker and Layne were brilliant at their craft, and in 1958 it looked like they could lead the Steelers to the promised land.

In 1958, a quarterback controversy brewed in Detroit, and the Lions were ready to part with Layne. Since Parker had an affection for his old field general, and didn't care for young players, the Steelers traded 23-year-old quarterback Earl Morrall and two draft picks for Layne following the second game of the 1958 season.

When Dan Rooney picked him up from the airport, Layne peppered him with questions about the coaches, players, and city. Soon, the swashbuckling quarterback brought the team together, on and off the field. Though the Steelers lost the first two games, they went 7–2–1 after Layne arrived, including a 6–0–1 finish. Layne ranked second in the league with 2,510 passing yards (with 404 in one game), and rookie speedster Jimmy Orr ranked third with 910 receiving yards. His 27.6 yards per catch that season remains an NFL record.

While the Lions finished 4–7–1 without Layne, the Steelers finished 7–4–1 with him. Unfortunately, the playoffs at the time consisted of only the NFL Championship Game, and Pittsburgh finished third in the East Division.

Bobby Layne was capable of taking teams on incredible hot streaks, such as Pittsburgh's 6–0–1 stretch to end the 1958 season. *Robert Riger/Getty Images*

Game-by-Game

9/28	L, 20–23,	at San Francisco 49ers
10/5	L, 12–45,	vs. Cleveland Browns
10/12	W, 24–3,	vs. Philadelphia Eagles
10/19	L, 10–27,	at Cleveland Browns
10/26	L, 6–17,	at New York Giants
11/2	W, 24–16,	vs. Washington Redskins
11/9	W, 31–24,	at Philadelphia Eagles
11/16	W, 31–10,	vs. New York Giants
11/23	W, 27–20,	at Chicago Cardinals
11/30	W, 24–10,	vs. Chicago Bears
12/7	T, 14–14,	at Washington Redskins
12/13	W, 38–21,	vs. Chicago Cardinals

Team Scoring

261 points scored
230 points allowed

Texan Gunslinger:
Bobby Layne

End Jimmy Orr was drafted in the 25th round in 1957, yet as a rookie a year later, he finished third in the NFL with 910 receiving yards. How did he do it? Simple. He went out drinking with Bobby Layne. "If you went out with him at night," Orr said in *Men of Steel*, "he threw to you during the day."

The Mickey Mantle of the NFL, Layne was a play-hard, drink-hard trailblazer who led his teams to glory. His legend began at Highland Park High School in Dallas, where he teamed with future Heisman Trophy winner Doak Walker. "[He] was a general on the field and off the field in every way," Walker said, as quoted in the *Los Angeles Times*. "He was the greatest two-minute quarterback I have ever seen."

After smashing passing records at the University of Texas, Layne led the Detroit Lions to the NFL championship in 1952, '53, and '57. Statistically, he was unimpressive; as of 2013, he ranked 193rd in league history in passer rating. But no one denied his leadership ability. "He'd call you right out of the huddle," Lions offensive tackle Lou Creekmur told the Associated Press. "He would stand there, raving at you and shaking a finger in your face and you wanted to punch him. . . . But off the field, there's nothing he wouldn't do for us."

According to Dan Rooney, Layne took charge of the Steelers offense the first day he stepped on the practice field in 1958. "We never had anybody like Bobby Layne," cornerback Jack Butler said. "He played one way—all out."

The trade to Pittsburgh also resulted in what many call the "Curse of Bobby Layne" in Detroit. After he led the Lions to an NFL championship in 1957, Detroit won just one playoff game over the next 56 years, with no regular-season wins in Pittsburgh.

In five seasons with Pittsburgh, Layne posted a 27–22–2 record. Some worried that his drinking would be the demise of his career and those of his drinking-buddy teammates. But even in his 15th and final year in the league, 1962, Layne led the Steelers to a 9–5 mark. The booze did eventually get him, as he died at age 59 after suffering from a chronic liver ailment.

Despite his self-destructive off-field habits, Bobby Layne set records on the field. When he retired in 1962, he held the top NFL career marks in pass attempts, completions, yardage, and touchdowns. *MVP Books Collection*

Top-Tier Team

6–5–1 Record Doesn't Reflect the Steelers' Talent

With his growing potbelly and a helmet without a facemask—he was the last NFL player to play without one—Bobby Layne stood out on the football field. In 1959, his last Pro Bowl season, Layne added kicking to his list of duties. Though he had kicked for a couple seasons with Detroit, this was the first time that Buddy Parker let him boot it with Pittsburgh. The results: 11-of-17 on field goals and 32-of-32 on extra points.

Like the year before, the Steelers were an upper-echelon team in 1959. Layne ranked fifth in the NFL with 1,986 passing yards, with Jimmy Orr (604 yards) and rookie Buddy Dial (26.8 per catch) his primary targets. Halfback Tom "The Bomb" Tracy, an All-Pro halfback the year prior, rushed for a career-high 794 yards—fourth best in the league. Paving the way for Tracy was right tackle Frank Varrichione, a four-time Pro Bowl selection whom opponent Gino Marchetti included as "among the best I ever faced" and "the most persistent."

Defensively, cornerback Jack Butler earned All-Pro honors despite a career-ending knee injury. Ernie Stautner was still stuffing the run on the defensive line, and defensive back Dean Derby earned Pro Bowl honors after picking off seven passes.

The Steelers finished at 6–5–1 in what Layne must have considered a failure of his season, as Pittsburgh lost four games by less than a touchdown. Still, Layne led the team to fourth-quarter comeback wins over the Giants and Browns as well as a comeback tie against Detroit.

The worst loss of all was that of NFL Commissioner and former Eagles owner (and Steelers co-owner) Bert Bell. With two minutes to go in a tight Eagles-Steelers game on October 11 in Philadelphia, Bell suffered a fatal heart attack.

1959

6–5–1   4th place

Game-by-Game

9/26	W, 17–7, vs. Cleveland Browns
10/4	L, 17–23, vs. Washington Redskins
10/11	L, 24–28, at Philadelphia Eagles
10/18	W, 27–6, at Washington Redskins
10/25	L, 16–21, vs. New York Giants
11/1	L, 24–45, at Chicago Cardinals
11/8	T, 10–10, vs. Detroit Lions
11/15	W, 14–9, at New York Giants
11/22	W, 21–20, at Cleveland Browns
11/29	W, 31–0, vs. Philadelphia Eagles
12/6	L, 21–27, at Chicago Bears
12/13	W, 35–20, vs. Chicago Cardinals

Team Scoring

257 points scored
216 points allowed

Steelers linebacker Dick Campbell (66) and defensive back Don Sutherin (20) zero in on Giants halfback Frank Gifford on November 15. That day, Pittsburgh handed New York one of its two losses of the season. *Diamond Images/ Getty Images*

Team Leaders

(**Boldface** indicates league leader)

Scoring Leaders (Points)

1950: Joe Geri, 64
1951: Joe Geri, 67
1952: Elbie Nickel, 54
1953: Nick Bolkovac, 45
1954: Ray Mathews, 48
1955: Ray Mathews, 42
1956: Sid Watson, 37
1957: Earl Girard, 29
1958: Tom Miner, 73
1959: Bobby Layne, 77

Passing Leaders

(Completions / Attempts / Yards)

1950: Joe Geri, 41 / 113 / 866
1951: Chuck Ortmann, 56 / 139 / 671
1952: Jim Finks, 158 / 336 / 2,307
1953: Jim Finks, 131 / 292 / 1,484
1954: Jim Finks, 164 / 306 / 2,003
1955: Jim Finks, **165 / 344 / 2,270**
1956: Ted Marchibroda, 124 / 275 / 1,585
1957: Earl Morrall, 139 / 289 / 1,900
1958: Bobby Layne, 133 / 268 / 2,339
1959: Bobby Layne, 142 / 297 / 1,986

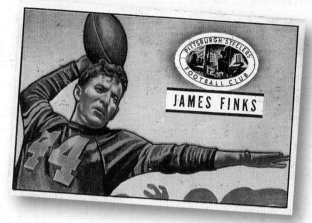

Jim Finks was the first quarterback to throw for more than 2,000 career yards with the Steelers, and he reached the milestone in just one season, in 1952. *MVP Books Collection*

Rushing Leaders

(Carries / Yards / TDs)

1950: Joe Geri, **188** / 705 / 2
1951: Fran Rogel, 109 / 385 / 3
1952: Ray Mathews, 66 / 315 / 0
1953: Fran Rogel, 137 / 527 / 2
1954: Fran Rogel, 111 / 415 / 1
1955: Fran Rogel, 168 / 588 / 2
1956: Fran Rogel, 131 / 476 / 2
1957: Billy Wells, 154 / 532 / 0
1958: Tom Tracy, 169 / 714 / 5
1959: Tom Tracy, 199 / 794 / 3

Receiving Leaders

(Receptions / Yards / TDs)

1950: Val Jansante, 26 / 353 / 0
1951: Hank Minarik, 35 / 459 / 1
1952: Elbie Nickel, 55 / 884 / 9
1953: Elbie Nickel, 62 / 743 / 4
1954: Ray Mathews, 44 / 652 / 6
1955: Ray Mathews, 42 / 762 / 6
1956: Ray Mathews, 31 / 540 / 5
1957: Jack McClairen, 46 / 630 / 2
1958: Jimmy Orr, 33 / 910 / 7
1959: Jimmy Orr, 35 / 604 / 5

Fran Rogel, portrayed on this Topps card, was the Steelers' career rushing leader (3,271 yards) when he retired in 1957. *MVP Books Collection*

the Record Book

Interceptions

(Number / Yards / TDs)

1950: Howard Hartley 5 / 84 / 0
1951: Howard Hartley 10 / 69 / 0
1952: Jack Butler 7 / 168 / 0
1953: Jack Butler 9 / 147 / 1
1954: Paul Cameron 7 / 118 / 0
1955: Richie McCabe 3 / 29 / 0
1956: Jack Butler 6 / 113 / 0
1957: Jack Butler 10 / 85 / 0
1958: Jack Butler 9 / 81 / 0
1959: Dean Derby 7 / 127 / 0

First-Team All-Pros

1950: Joe Geri, K/P/TB
1951: Jerry Shipkey, LB
1952: Jerry Shipkey, LB
1954: Bill Walsh, C
1954: Dale Dodrill, MG
1957: Jack Butler, S
1958: Jack Butler, S
1958: Ernie Stautner, DE
1959: Jack Butler, S

Pro Bowl Selections

1950: Joe Geri, K/P/TB
1950: Jerry Shipkey, FB/LB
1950: Bill Walsh, C
1951: Joe Geri, K/P/TB
1951: George Hughes, G
1951: Jerry Shipkey, LB
1951: Bill Walsh, C
1952: Lynn Chandnois, KR/HB
1952: Jim Finks, QB
1952: Ray Mathews, HB/PR
1952: Bill McPeak, DE
1952: Elbie Nickel, End
1952: Jerry Shipkey, LB
1952: Ernie Stautner, DT
1953: Lynn Chandnois, KR/PR/HB
1953: Dale Dodrill, MG
1953: George Hughes, OT
1953: Marv Matuszak, LB
1953: Bill McPeak, DE

1953: Elbie Nickel, End
1953: Ernie Stautner, DT
1954: Dale Dodrill, MG
1954: Johnny Lattner, KR/PR/RH
1955: Jack Butler, DB
1955: Dale Dodrill, MG
1955: Ray Mathews, HB
1955: Ernie Stautner, DG
1955: Frank Varrichione, OT
1956: Jack Butler, S
1956: Bill McPeak, DE
1956: Elbie Nickel, HB
1956: Fran Rogel, FB
1956: Ernie Stautner, DT
1957: Jack Butler, S
1957: Dale Dodrill, LB
1957: Jack McLairen, LB
1957: Earl Morrall, QB
1957: Ernie Stautner, DT
1957: Frank Varrichione, OT
1958: Jack Butler, S
1958: Ernie Stautner, DE
1958: Tom Tracy, HB
1958: Frank Varrichione, OT
1959: Dean Derby, DB
1959: Bobby Layne, QB/K
1959: John Nisby, G
1959: Jimmy Orr, WR
1959: John Reger, LB
1959: Ernie Stautner, DE

1st-Round Draft Picks

1950: Lynn Chadnois (8), HB, Michigan St.
1951: Butch Avinger (9), FB, Alabama
1952: Ed Modzelewski (6), FB, Maryland
1953: Ted Marchibroda (5), QB, Detroit
1954: Johnny Lattner (7), HB, Notre Dame
1955: Frank Varrichione (6), T, Notre Dame
1956: Gary Glick (1), DB, Colorado St.
1957: Len Dawson (5), QB, Purdue

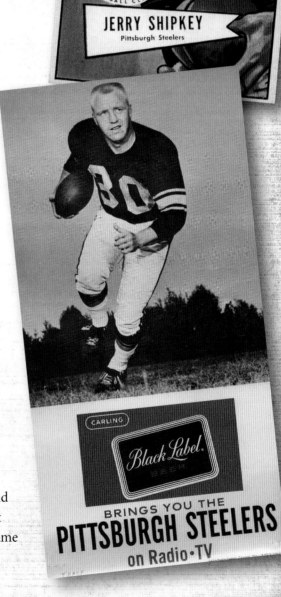

Bowman captures the game face of Jerry Shipkey, who rushed for eight touchdowns as a fullback in 1948 and later was a two-time All-Pro at linebacker. *MVP Books Collection*

JERRY SHIPKEY
Pittsburgh Steelers

CARLING
Black Label BEER

BRINGS YOU THE
PITTSBURGH STEELERS
on Radio·TV

Tom Tracy was "the Bomb"—that was the nickname of this halfback who played for the Steelers from 1958 to '63. A two-time all-star, he appeared in an ad for Steeler sponsor Black Label beer. *MVP Books Collection*

THE 1960s

BIG DADDY, JOHN HENRY, AND PITT STADIUM

The times are a-changing for the Steelers, with exciting
African American stars and—at decade's end—a
forward-thinking head coach.

This image of a happy a steelworker
kicking could be misinterpreted as a
bumbling steelworker about to fall on
his keister. *MVP Books Collection*

As the 1960s swung, as the Beatles and the Rolling Stones—and the NHL's just-born
Penguins—played Pittsburgh's new Civic Arena, the Steelers skulked into 40-year-
old Pitt Stadium, 70,000 unsheltered bleacher seats and all.

Not surprisingly, nothing near that kind of attendance ever showed up. Because
the Steelers experience of the 1960s was more of the same—sometimes slightly better,
sometimes a whole lot worse.

With a revolving door full of coaches, and a stadium full of worn, wooden benches,
sitting through Steelers games required calm, patience, and a sturdy seat cushion. With
Pitt Stadium entirely open to the elements, everyone froze and got drenched whenever it
was cold and rainy. There were also outdated rest facilities, hardly any concession stands,
and the real promise of picking splinters out of bell-bottoms and double knits. With no
parking, and "Cardiac Hill" to climb, fans stayed away in droves.

The diehards agreed with Dan Rooney, that Buddy Parker and his pursuit of aged
veterans had to go. At first, Parker's philosophy made sense—bring in guys who could
play pro ball instead of drafting untested college kids. But by the time teams were willing
to trade away players, they had lost the juice that had made them great. Sure, they were
good. Just not good enough.

Fans loved Eugene "Big Daddy" Lipscomb, who started the '60s just right. A powerful
defensive lineman who presaged the '70s "Steel Curtain," Big Daddy beat up offensive

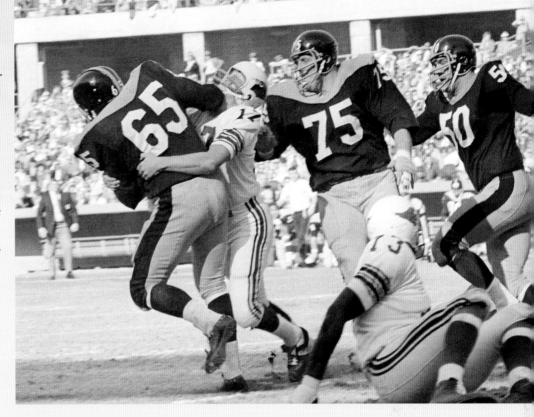

linemen and punished running backs. But after two seasons, he died of a heroin overdose.

His counterpart on offense was John Henry Johnson. A classic power back, Johnson set the standard for the next half century—Franco Harris through Barry Foster through Jerome Bettis. Hitting as hard as he ran, John Henry was the first Steeler to rush for 1,000 yards, and he did it twice. The fans loved it.

They hardly failed to notice that both Big Daddy and John Henry were black—in a league that was still predominantly white. Dan Rooney saw that, too, and he realized there was an enormous talent pool that traditional scouting missed. So in 1967, Rooney hired *Pittsburgh Courier* sports editor Bill Nunn as a scout.

A man who traveled extensively to small black colleges, Nunn covered talent-rich places generally overlooked—or outright ignored—by established scouting systems. It didn't take long for fans to discover that Nunn's finds included future Super Bowl champions.

In the 1960s, change was everywhere, nowhere more than in fans' knotty-pine rec rooms. Televised football brought unprecedented visibility and a new generation of fans to the game. The days of wearing work boots and taking trolleys to games were over. Now fans wore sport jackets and drove the family station wagon. They lived in the suburbs, worked white-collar jobs, wanted clean and comfortable seats, and hungered for more substantial fare than Iron City beer and hot dogs.

Pitt Stadium would no longer do. That was fine, because on the North Side, across the Allegheny River from downtown, steel was rising for the new, multipurpose Three Rivers Stadium.

Still, the Steelers needed someone to lead. Fans knew that Buddy Parker, Jock Sutherland acolyte Mike Nixon, and Vince Lombardi assistant Bill Austin didn't have the right stuff. When Dan Rooney got wind of a canny Colts assistant named Chuck Noll, who thought the way he did—about systems, scouting, building though the draft—he took a chance.

Fans groaned at the 1–13 decade closer, and they shook their heads over Noll's No. 1 draft choice, a tall, powerful Texan by the name of Joe Greene.

They didn't really know either man.

Very soon they would.

—A. M.

St. Louis quarterback Jim Hart tries in vain to bring down Pittsburgh's 256-pound lineman Lloyd Voss (65) as he runs back an interception during this 1967 contest. Despite the new uniform designs, the Steelers couldn't avoid another one of what would be six straight losing seasons to close out the decade. *Fred Waters/AP Images*

1960

5–6–1   5th place

Game-by-Game

9/24	W, 35–28, at DallasCowboys
10/2	L, 20–28, at Cleveland Browns
10/9	L, 17–19, vs. New York Giants
10/16	W, 27–14, vs. St. Louis Cardinals
10/23	T, 27–27, at Washington Redskins
10/30	L, 13–19, vs. Green Bay Packers
11/6	L, 7–34, at Philadelphia Eagles
11/13	L, 24–27, at New York Giants
11/20	W, 14–10, vs. Cleveland Browns
11/27	W, 22–10, vs. Washington Redskins
12/11	W, 27–21, vs. Philadelphia Eagles
12/18	L, 7–38, at St. Louis Cardinals

Team Scoring

240 points scored

275 points allowed

DRAFT DAY BLUES

Once Again, Steelers Have No Picks Through Round Seven

As the steel and construction workers of Pittsburgh could tell you, every structure needs a strong foundation. But as the Steelers rolled into the 1960s, fans began to realize that the team's foundation was turning to putty. Due to coach Buddy Parker's win-now approach, the Steelers had been dealing away their draft picks like Topps trading cards. Incredibly, Pittsburgh's first pick in the 1959 NFL Draft didn't come until the *eighth* round. The same was true the following year.

In 1960, the Steelers began to sag. A year after recording a plus-41 point differential, they dropped to minus-35. After beating a horrible Dallas team by just a touchdown in the season opener (the Cowboys would go winless in this their inaugural season), the Steelers endured a dismal 1–5–1 stretch. They then won three in a row, including upsets of the powerful Browns and Eagles, the league's winningest teams. They closed the season with a blowout loss to the Cardinals, who had moved from Chicago to St. Louis.

To their credit, the Steelers had acquired two dynamic offensive players. Split end Buddy Dial became Bobby Layne's new go-to guy, amassing 972 receiving yards in 1960 with a league-high 24.3 average. "He catches every damn thing that comes to him," said opposing defensive back Jimmy Hill. In addition, 31-year-old fullback John Henry Johnson found new life in his first year with Pittsburgh in '60, rushing for 621 yards on a 5.3-yard average. Amazingly, his four best seasons lay ahead.

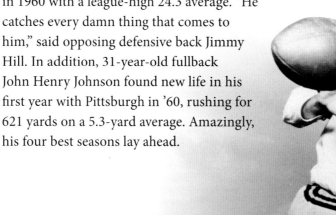

Buddy Dial, who led the NFL with 24.3 yards per reception in 1960, ranks fifth on the league career list with 20.8 yards per grab. *AP Images*

A Not-So-Great 6–8

Steelers Play More Games, but It's More of the Same

The NFL became a bigger business in 1961, as the schedule was expanded to 14 games and young commissioner Pete Rozelle signed the NFL's first league-wide television deal. In Pittsburgh, though, it was more of the same. A 27–24 season-opening loss to Dallas—the Cowboys' first-ever victory—triggered a 0–4 start, and Buddy Parker led them to a 6–8 finish.

Bobby Layne, 35, split duties with journeyman quarterback Rudy Bukich. It was hard to tell who was better. Each threw 11 touchdown passes. Each threw 16 interceptions. Surprisingly, it was Bukich who came through in the clutch, going 4–3 in his starts compared to Layne's 2–5. John Henry Johnson led the ground-gainers with 787 yards, while Buddy Dial became the first Steeler ever to top 1,000 receiving yards.

Though Pittsburgh had only three picks in the first seven rounds of the 1961 draft, they made the most of them. Middle linebacker Myron Pottios would earn All-Pro honors in each of his first three seasons. Then there was the selection of Dick Hoak, who was not related to star third baseman Don Hoak of the reigning world champion Pirates. Despite being routinely criticized for his small stature and lack of speed, Dick Hoak would rush for 3,965 yards and lay down heavy blocks in his 10 years with the Steelers.

In 1961, the Steelers also welcomed former All-Pro defensive lineman Eugene "Big Daddy" Lipscomb. "Once Big D puts his clamps on you," he once told a runner after tackling him, "you're dead." Lipscomb, a pro wrestler in the off-season, was known for his huge appetites. He died of a heroin overdose in 1963.

1961

6–8   5th place

Game-by-Game

9/17	L, 24–27, at Dallas Cowboys
9/24	L, 14–17, vs. New York Giants
10/1	L, 14–24, at L.A. Rams
10/8	L, 16–21, at Philadelphia Eagles
10/15	W, 20–0, vs. Washington Redskins
10/22	L, 28–30, vs. Cleveland Browns
10/29	W, 20–10, vs. San Francisco 49ers
11/5	W, 17–13, at Cleveland Browns
11/12	W, 37–7, vs. Dallas Cowboys
11/19	L, 21–42, at New York Giants
11/26	W, 30–27, vs. St. Louis Cardinals
12/3	L, 24–35, vs. Philadelphia Eagles
12/10	W, 30–14, at Washington Redskins
12/17	L, 0–20, at St. Louis Cardinals

Team Scoring

295 points scored
287 points allowed

The massive, 6-foot-6 Gene "Big Daddy" Lipscomb forces his way through a Cowboys offensive lineman in pursuit of quarterback Eddie LeBaron. Lipscomb spent eight seasons with the Rams and Colts before coming to Pittsburgh, where he played two year before dying of a heroin overdose. *Robert Riger/Getty Images*

59

1962

9–5 2nd place

Game-by-Game

9/16	**L,** 7–45, at Detroit Lions
9/23	**W,** 30–28, at Dallas Cowboys
9/30	**L,** 27–31, vs. New York Giants
10/6	**W,** 13–7, vs. Philadelphia Eagles
10/14	**W,** 20–17, at New York Giants
10/21	**L,** 27–42, vs. Dallas Cowboys
10/28	**L,** 14–41, vs. Cleveland Browns
11/4	**W,** 39–31, vs. Minnesota Vikings
11/11	**W,** 26–17, at St. Louis Cardinals
11/18	**W,** 23–21, vs. Washington Redskins
11/25	**L,** 14–35, at Cleveland Browns
12/2	**W,** 19–7, vs. St. Louis Cardinals
12/9	**W,** 26–17, at Philadelphia Eagles
12/16	**W,** 27–24, at Washington Redskins

Team Scoring

312 points scored
363 points allowed

BOUND FOR MIAMI

Steelers Finish 9–5, Play in Runner-Up Bowl

If only Art Rooney had thought of it 30 years earlier. In 1962, the Steelers added their famous Steelmark logo to one side of their formerly plain gold helmets. The logo seemed to magically transform the long-dormant team into a world-beater, as the Steelers finished 9–5 and earned a spot in the Bert Bell Benefit Bowl. Although the postseason game was merely a battle of division runner-ups, with the winner bestowed the honor of finishing third in the NFL, at least the players got to go to Miami.

With the New York Giants en route to a 12–2 season, Steelers fans had no illusions about winning the East Division. Yet the season was a lot of fun. Though the defense gave up 26 points per game, Bobby Layne distributed the ball in expert fashion on offense. Buddy Dial caught 50 passes for 981 yards, and tight end Preston Carpenter earned All-Pro accolades after pulling in 36 passes.

John Henry Johnson, age 33, became the first back in team history to rush for more than 1,000 yards, as his 1,141 ranked second in the league. Though Johnson had the speed to rip off big gains, his Steeler-tough attitude set him apart. "You've got to scare your opponent," Johnson once said. "I can run away from a lot of guys after I get them afraid of a collision with me. . . . I always dish out more than I take."

A soft second-half schedule helped the Steelers prevail in six of their last seven en route to their first-ever nine-win season. Then it was off to the Bert Bell Benefit Bowl, also called the Playoff Bowl, even though it wasn't really a playoff. Layne and Steelers coach Buddy Parker lost to their old team, the Lions, 17–10 at the Orange Bowl in front of 36,284 fans. Six Lions sacks doomed the Steelers.

The lasting memory of the trip may have been a card game that preceded the bowl game by several days. Dick Hoak remembered leaving the table at 5:30 a.m. while Bobby Layne was still dealing cards. At 9:00 a.m., everyone arrived for a team meeting—including a fresh-faced Layne. "He looked like he had 10 hours of sleep," Hoak recalled in disbelief.

After the season, the Steelers changed the color of their helmets to black while leaving the Steelmark logo. Equipment manager Jack Hart asked Dan Rooney if he wanted the logo on both sides of the helmet. "We got here with the logo only on the right side," Rooney responded, "so let's keep it that way." To this day, the Steelers are the only team in the NFL with a one-sided logo.

Head coach Buddy Parker and quarterback Bobby Layne discuss strategy on the sidelines during a 35–14 loss to the Cleveland Browns on November 25. *Tony Tomsic/Getty Images*

The STEELERETTES

While there was a whole lotta shakin' going on in American society in the late 1950s and early '60s, none of it happened on the sidelines of the Pittsburgh Steelers—not with old-school Catholic Art Rooney running the show. With attendance lagging, The Chief agreed to allow cheerleaders at Forbes Field and Pitt Stadium beginning in 1961. But cheers were all the fans would get. The Steelerettes wore long sleeves and full, pleated skirts!

All of the Steelerettes came from Robert Morris Junior College, and applicants were evaluated based on coordination, gymnastics, personality, and appearance. A 2.00 GPA was required, and each woman had to pass a basic football test so that she'd know when to cheer.

As the cultural and sexual revolutions flourished during the decade, the Steelerettes continued to dress like young Nancy Reagans. When people suggested to Rooney that male fans wanted to see more skin, The Chief replied, "Let 'em go to burlesque." The Steelerettes disbanded after the 1969 season, the same year that the modern-era Dallas Cowboys Cheerleaders began.

The Steelerettes, 1960s. *MVP Books Collection*

Smashmouth RB:
John Henry Johnson

Running back John Henry Johnson was elusive enough to run around defenders, but sometimes he preferred to plow right over them. "All the defensive guys said, 'Watch him!'" said Detroit Lions linebacker Wayne Walker. "Because if you didn't keep your eye on him, next thing you know you'd have your jaw wired."

Walker was not dabbling in hyperbole. In a 1955 preseason game, Johnson hit Chicago Cardinals star Charley Trippi so hard that he fractured Trippi's face in multiple places.

"Football was like a combat zone," Johnson explained. "I was always told that you carry the impact to the opponent. If you wait for it, the impact will be on you."

Born in Waterproof, Louisiana, Johnson starred at Saint Mary's College of California and Arizona State before being drafted by the Steelers in 1953. But he didn't sign with Pittsburgh, instead going to Calgary of the Canadian Football League for a year before playing three seasons each with San Francisco and Detroit. With the 49ers, Johnson was part of the "Million Dollar Backfield," which included fellow future Hall of Famers Hugh McElhenny, Y. A. Tittle, and Joe Perry.

Johnson played for coach Buddy Parker in both Detroit and Pittsburgh. In his five-plus seasons with the Steelers (1960–66), Johnson ran for a team-record 4,381 yards. After becoming the team's first 1,000-yard rusher in 1962 (1,141), he turned the trick again as a 35-year-old in '64 (1,048). Johnson's career highlights with the Steelers included a 182-yard game against Philadelphia in 1960 (which included an 87-yard romp to the house) and a 30-carry, 200-yard afternoon versus Cleveland in 1964.

Tragically, but not surprisingly, the bashing that Johnson doled out came back to haunt him, as he was suspected of suffering from chronic traumatic encephalopathy, a disorder linked to repeated brain trauma. Johnson, who was inducted into the Pro Football Hall of Fame in 1987, died in 2011 at the age of 81.

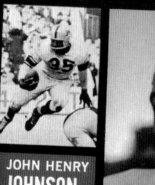

John Henry Johnson's Topps card from 1962, the year he became the Steelers' first 1,000-yard rusher. *MVP Books Collection*

SHOCK AND TRAGEDY

Season Marred by Deaths of Lipscomb and JFK—and Nearly Reger

The Steelers went 7–4–3 in 1963, but their season is remembered more for who was lost. While stunned and saddened by the death of Eugene "Big Daddy" Lipscomb, the team was shaken by the forced retirement of Bobby Layne, who was shown the door by his longtime coach, Buddy Parker.

Then, in the season opener at Philadelphia, Steelers linebacker John Reger nearly died on the field. After colliding head-on with an Eagles ball-carrier, Reger swallowed his tongue. As he turned blue, Steelers personnel yanked out two of his teeth with scissors before finally dislodging his tongue. "I was dead on the field!" Reger recalled. "At first I could hear people yelling, 'Get a doctor! Get an ambulance!'" Reger passed out and didn't awake until after he reached the hospital.

As if paralyzed by the experience, the Steelers finished that game in a 17–17 tie. On November 22, five days after Pittsburgh beat the Redskins in Washington, President John F. Kennedy was assassinated. Two days later, the still-numb Steelers tied the Bears 17–17. The next week, they tied the Eagles again, 20–20. Then it was off to a game in Dallas, where JFK had been killed.

Despite the circumstances, quarterback Ed Brown, who had been on the decline with the Bears since his mid-'50s heyday, performed admirably. He compiled 2,982 passing yards and averaged a league-best 17.8 yards per completion, and in an October matchup with Dallas, he threw for 377 yards and four touchdowns. His favorite target, Buddy Dial, ranked second in the NFL with 1,295 receiving yards. After a loss to the 11–2, first-place Giants in the season finale, the Steelers finished fourth in the East Division.

7-4-3   4th place

Game-by-Game

9/15	T, 21–21,	at Philadelphia Eagles
9/22	W, 31–0,	vs. New York Giants
9/29	W, 23–10,	vs. St. Louis Cardinals
10/5	L, 23–35,	at Cleveland Browns
10/13	L, 23–24,	at St. Louis Cardinals
10/20	W, 38–27,	vs. Washington Redskins
10/27	W, 27–21,	vs. Dallas Cowboys
11/3	L, 14–33,	at Green Bay Packers
11/10	W, 9–7,	vs. Cleveland Browns
11/17	W, 34–28,	at Washington Redskins
11/24	T, 17–17,	vs. Chicago Bears
12/1	T, 20–20,	vs. Philadelphia Eagles
12/8	W, 24–19,	at Dallas Cowboys
12/15	L, 17–33,	at New York Giants

Team Scoring

321 points scored
295 points allowed

John Henry Johnson finds a big hole to run through against the Giants in the 1963 season finale. Although Johnson gained 104 yards that day, the Steelers lost the game 33–17. *Robert Reger/Getty Images*

5–9   6th place

Game-by-Game

9/13	**L**, 14–26,	vs. L.A. Rams
9/20	**W**, 27–24,	vs. New York Giants
9/27	**W**, 23–17,	vs. Dallas Cowboys
10/4	**L**, 7–21,	at Philadelphia Eagles
10/10	**W**, 23–7,	at Cleveland Browns
10/18	**L**, 10–30,	at Minnesota Vikings
10/25	**L**, 10–34,	vs. Philadelphia Eagles
11/1	**L**, 17–30,	vs. Cleveland Browns
11/8	**L**, 30–34,	at St. Louis Cardinals
11/15	**L**, 0–30,	vs. Washington Redskins
11/22	**W**, 44–17,	at New York Giants
11/29	**L**, 20–21,	vs. St. Louis Cardinals
12/6	**W**, 14–7,	at Washington Redskins
12/13	**L**, 14–17,	at Dallas Cowboys

Team Scoring

253 points scored
315 points allowed

Pittsburgh defensive end John Baker delivers a crushing blow to Giants quarterback Y. A. Tittle during an early season win over New York at Pitt Stadium. *Dozier Mobley/AP Images*

So Long, Buddy

Dan Rooney Runs Out of Patience with Coach Parker

By 1964, Dan Rooney—who had assumed more control of the team from his father—was losing his patience with Buddy Parker. Sure, the coach had brought winning football to Pittsburgh. But, Rooney wrote in his autobiography, Parker "fought authority," including the Rooneys, and "refused to play rookies because they made mistakes. His players both respected and feared him. Parker could not earn their loyalty because he traded them at the drop of a hat."

At the annual Draft Day, the Steelers should have been too embarrassed to show up. In 1962 and '63, they had only one selection before round eight. That was Bob Ferguson, the great Ohio State fullback, who was take No. 2 overall in '62. But Ferguson rushed for barely 200 yards with the Steelers before being forced to retire due to injury.

The Steelers opened the 1964 season at 3–2 (despite eight turnovers in a season-opening loss) before the normally stout defense let them down. Pittsburgh lost five straight contests, surrendering at least 30 points in every game. Quarterback Ed Brown threw one less interception in 1964 than the previous year, but his passing yards dropped by 992. If it weren't for the age-defying performance of John Henry Johnson—whose 1,048 rushing yards included a 200-yard game in a win over Cleveland—the season would have been a total disaster. As it was, the Steelers finished at 5–9.

The following summer, Parker tried to test Dan Rooney's authority by telling him he would trade defensive end Ben McGee. When the two began to argue, Parker said he would resign. Fine, Rooney said. He accepted the resignation the next day.

Black, Gold, and Steel

Pittsburgh is the only city in America in which all the pro sports teams wear the same colors. The first of the Pittsburgh clubs to don black and gold was the Pirates. No, not the baseball Pirates. Not even Art Rooney's 1930s NFL Pirates. We're talking about the NHL's Pittsburgh Pirates, who wore black and gold (or mustard yellow) sweaters during their five years of existence from 1925 to 1930. The Pirates baseball team went black and gold beginning in 1948, and the NHL Penguins copped the color scheme in 1980.

The colors black and gold date back to the coat of arms of Sir William Pitt, for whom the city is named. In the 1800s, city leaders began using those colors as emblems of Pittsburgh. Black represented coal and iron, and gold symbolized the money that they made. A man of great civic pride, Art Rooney incorporated these city colors into the team's uniforms in 1933, and for that initial season he even included the coat of arms on the front of the jerseys.

The style of the Steelers' uniforms has changed several times over the years, but the colors have remained the same. Even their "Batman" jerseys of 1966–67 were black and gold. The V-shaped gold neckline contrasted sharply with the rest of the jersey, giving the appearance that the players were wearing black capes, like Batman and Robin.

The famous Steelers logo, which was first slapped on the team's helmets in 1962, was developed by U.S. Steel in 1958. The three asteroids in a circle were meant to represent the lightness, smartness, and versatility of steel. By the 1970s, the logo simply came to represent the Pittsburgh Steelers.

The Steelers' classic black and gold color scheme took an interesting twist for the 1967 uniforms, as depicted on this program cover artwork. *MVP Books Collection*

1965

2–12 7th place

Game-by-Game

9/19 **L, 9–41,**
vs. Green Bay Packers

9/26 **L, 17–27,**
at San Francisco

10/3 **L, 13–23,**
vs. New York Giants

10/9 **L, 19–24,**
at Cleveland Browns

10/17 **L, 7–20,**
vs. St. Louis Cardinals

10/24 **W, 20–14,**
at Philadelphia Eagles

10/31 **W, 22–13,**
vs. Dallas Cowboys

11/7 **L, 17–21,**
at St. Louis Cardinals

11/4 **L, 17–24,**
at Dallas Cowboys

11/21 **L, 3–31,**
vs. Washington Redskins

11/28 **L, 21–42,**
vs. Cleveland Browns

12/5 **L, 10–35,**
at New York Giants

12/12 **L, 13–47,**
vs. Philadelphia Eagles

12/19 **L, 14–35,**
at Washington Redskins

Team Scoring

202 points scored
397 points allowed

Despite this excellent tackle by Ben McGee, Ken Willard and the San Francisco 49ers handed the Steelers their second of five consecutive losses on September 26th, 1965, at Kezar Stadium in San Francisco. *Focus on Sport/Getty Images*

ONE AND DONE FOR NIXON

New Head Coach Is Canned After 2–12 Season

Buddy Parker had picked a fine time to force his power play on the Steelers. The man who had resigned from the Lions in August of 1957 waited until early September to stiff the Steelers in 1965. With no time to find a legitimate head coach, the Rooneys promoted assistant Mike Nixon to the head position.

A University of Pittsburgh alum, who had played and coached under Jock Sutherland, Nixon went 4–18–2 as Washington's head coach in 1959–60. He clearly was not up for the challenge with the Steelers, who finished 12th in the 14-team league in points allowed, last in scoring, and last in overall record (2–14).

Dick Hoak led Pittsburgh in rushing with a paltry 426 yards. Bill Nelson, a 10th-round pick in 1963 out of USC, earned the starting nod, but with knee problems and a porous offensive line, he threw for just eight touchdowns against 17 interceptions. Flanker Gary Ballman, who caught 40 passes for 859 yards, earned his second straight Pro Bowl nod.

While few fans noticed, center Ray Mansfield was forging a 13-year career with the Steelers. Including one year with Philadelphia, the 250-pounder played in 182 consecutive games. "My attitude always was, 'Never say die. Never be defeated. Go down fighting on the beach,'" Mansfield said.

Too bad the Pittsburgh defense didn't have that fighting spirit. The Steelers D played dead the last four games, allowing 23 touchdowns. The Rooneys knew that Mike Nixon wasn't the answer, and after the season they aggressively pursued a new head coach.

Fan Favorite:
Andy Russell

Pittsburgh's blue-collar fans appreciated Andy Russell's service—to the Steelers and to his country. After toiling at linebacker as a Pittsburgh rookie in 1963, Andy fulfilled his ROTC commitment by serving two years in Europe as an Army lieutenant. In 1968, he traveled to Vietnam during the Tet Offensive, where "I visited a hospital full of our badly wounded soldiers," he wrote in *Pittsburgh Steelers: Yesterday & Today*. "Trying to comfort them, I was stunned when one of the injured yelled, 'Go, Steelers!'"

Though not extraordinarily athletic, Russell excelled by putting in the extra work—such as bringing home game films. He was an integral part of Pittsburgh's dynasty teams of the 1970s, earning Pro Bowl invitations each year from 1970 to '75. Yet like center Ray Mansfield, Andy's ties to the organization dug much deeper, since he had endured the hardships of the pre-Chuck Noll era and also played with the legends of the '50s. His mentors included nail-spitting lineman Ernie Stautner and safety/receiver Clendon Thomas, the latter of whom "taught me that the greatest badge of honor in the NFL was to 'play hurt.'"

Russell also had the privilege of playing alongside two of the greatest linebackers of the 1970s: Jack Ham and Jack Lambert. Together, they formed a second impenetrable wall should opponents somehow get through the "Steel Curtain."

Russell's finest moment occurred on December 27, 1975, in a playoff game at Three Rivers Stadium. The Steelers led 21–10 with less than 12 minutes left, but Baltimore was on Pittsburgh's 3-yard line. That's when Ham nailed quarterback Bert Jones, jarring the ball loose. Russell scooped it up and ran 93 yards for a touchdown—despite the grizzled veteran's less-than-blinding speed.

"That play has been a source of embarrassment for me for years," Russell said. "There have been so many jokes. Ray Mansfield was the one that said NBC cut to a commercial during the return and came back to catch me score the touchdown."

Russell remains active in the Pittsburgh area, still contributing to charitable causes.

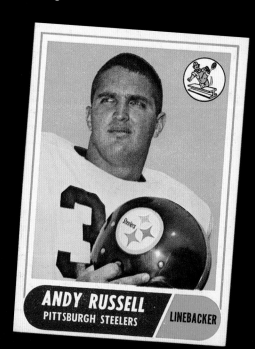

Andy Russell said that he was amazed by the Steelers' fan support in the late 1960s, when the team was an NFL doormat. This Topps card is from 1968. *MVP Books Collection*

1966

5–8–1   6th place

Game-by-Game

9/11	**T, 34–34,**	vs. New York Giants
9/18	**W, 17–3,**	vs. Detroit Lions
9/25	**L, 27–33,**	vs. Washington Redskins
10/2	**L, 10–24,**	at Washington Redskins
10/8	**L, 10–41,**	at Cleveland Browns
10/16	**L, 14–31,**	vs. Philadelphia Eagles
10/30	**L, 21–52,**	at Dallas Cowboys
11/6	**W, 16–6,**	vs. Cleveland Browns
11/13	**W, 30–9,**	vs. St. Louis Cardinals
11/20	**L, 7–20,**	vs. Dallas Cowboys
11/27	**L, 3–6,**	at St. Louis Cardinals
12/4	**L, 23–27,**	at Philadelphia Eagles
12/11	**W, 47–28,**	at New York Giants
12/18	**W, 57–33,**	at Atlanta Falcons

Team Scoring

316 points scored
347 points allowed

HE'S NO LOMBARDI

Packers Assistant Austin Is Wrong Guy for Steelers

As Dan Rooney tried to lead the Steelers into the modern era, he was dragged down by old-school thinking. For the first time since 1946, the Rooneys could take their time in hiring a head coach in 1966. Dan was prepared to interview many coaches and carefully scrutinize each candidate. His old man, though, insisted on hiring the first guy they interviewed. Bill Austin had been an assistant coach with the great Green Bay Packers, and Vince Lombardi gave him a glowing recommendation. "If Vince says he's okay, let's take him!" Art Rooney told his son.

Dan didn't agree, but Austin got the job. It was a huge mistake. Austin had been effective at implementing Lombardi's orders in Green Bay, but he was no leader. Berating players and delivering canned pep talks was his idea of leadership. He didn't believe in weight training and conditioning, opting instead for hard, intense practices—which resulted in numerous injuries to his out-of-shape players.

The Steelers featured a lot of new faces at key positions in 1966, but they mustered only five wins. The offense finished last in the NFL, worse than that of the expansion Atlanta Falcons. Rookie fullback Willie Asbury led the team with 544 yards while averaging just 3.2 yards per carry. The next two top runners, Dick Hoak and Cannonball Butler, mustered only 2.6 and 2.5 per lug, respectively. Six-foot-5 quarterback Ron C. Smith, a 10th-round pick of the L.A. Rams a year earlier, compiled a dismal 54.3 passer rating in nine games. The subpar, no-name defense allowed 52 points to Dallas on October 30.

Despite the big coaching change in '66, these were still the same old Steelers.

Steelers coach Bill Austin lacked the development skills of his mentor, Vince Lombardi, and his successor, Chuck Noll. *The Washington Post/Getty Images*

Family Man:
Dan Rooney

Considering that the Steelers have been around for more than 80 years, it is astounding that one man has been with them since the very beginning. When Art Rooney's team took their first steps on the playing field in 1933, his son Dan—born the previous July—was learning to walk. Dan Rooney grew up with the team and turned the Steelers into the most respected organization in the NFL.

As with The Chief, Dan has been a man of loyalty and respect. "The biggest thing my father passed on to me, and I hope we've continued it, is to treat people right," he said prior to Super Bowl XL. "We treat our players as family, not workers. We're concerned for them away from the field and whatever problems they might have. My father always had a relationship with the players, and I've tried to do the same."

Dan Rooney embraced the game from the very beginning. He shined as quarterback for North Catholic High School, and after graduating from Duquesne University in 1955, he joined the front office. By the 1960s, the lines blurred as to who was running the team. Dan was heading daily operations, such as signing players and handling budgets. Yet he also took a stronger role in vital matters, such as hiring head coaches.

Dan personally selected Chuck Noll as head coach in 1969, and in 1975 he became the team's president, a title he would hold until 2003, when his son, Art Rooney II, took the reins. Dan has played a large role in league functions, including membership on the board of directors for the NFL Trust Fund, NFL Films, and the Scheduling Committee.

Dan Rooney's charitable nature has known no bounds. In 1976, he helped found the American Ireland Fund, which has raised more than $300 million for peace advocacy and education. In 2009, President Barack Obama tapped him to be the U.S. ambassador to Ireland, a role he fulfilled nobly for three years.

Dan Rooney (right) assumed increasing control of the team from his father (left) throughout the 1960s and '70s. Harry Cabluck/*AP Images*

4–9–1   4th place

Game-by-Game

9/17	**W, 41–13,** vs. Chicago Bears
9/24	**L, 14–28,** vs. St. Louis Cardinals
10/1	**L, 24–34,** at Philadelphia Eagles
10/7	**L, 10–21,** at Cleveland Browns
10/15	**L, 24–27,** vs. New York Giants
10/22	**L, 21–24,** vs. Dallas Cowboys
10/29	**W, 14–10,** at New Orleans Saints
11/5	**L, 14–34,** vs. Cleveland Browns
11/12	**T, 14–14,** at St. Louis Cardinals
11/19	**L, 20–28,** at New York Giants
11/26	**L, 27–41,** vs. Minnesota Vikings
12/3	**W, 24–14,** at Detroit Lions
12/10	**L, 10–15,** vs. Washington Redskins
12/17	**W, 24–17,** at Green Bay Packers

Team Scoring

281 points scored
320 points allowed

OPENING-DAY FOOLER

Steelers Maul the Bears Before Reverting to Old Ways

On a mild afternoon at Pitt Stadium in 1967, the Steelers gave their fans a taste of championship-style football. Facing a solid Bears team that featured legends Dick Butkus and Gale Sayers, the Steelers outgained them 393–95, tallied 23 first downs to Chicago's six, and prevailed 41–13. It was the kind of dominating performance that the Chuck Noll-era Steelers would achieve in the 1970s.

But these were not the '70s Steelers, and coach Bill Austin was no Chuck Noll. After the stunningly impressive opening-day win, in which Willie Asbury ran for 107 yards and two touchdowns on just 12 carries, the Steelers lost their next five games. At 4–9–1, they finished in fourth place, which happened to be last place since the league had realigned into four divisions. Now with 16 teams due to the addition of the New Orleans Saints, the NFL was divided into the Capital, Century, Coastal, and Century divisions. The Browns, Giants, and Cardinals—in that order—finished ahead of Pittsburgh in the Century.

The Steelers were fortunate that rookie quarterback Kent Nix played as well as he did. An undrafted, waiver-wire pickup, Nix took over for an injured Bill Nelson and finished ninth in the league in completions (136) despite starting just nine games. Cowboys coach Tom Landry called Nix the best rookie quarterback he had seen in 10 years—although his career record would be only 4–14.

The '67 Steelers sent two men to the Pro Bowl: cornerback Marv Woodson, who intercepted seven passes, and running back Dick Hoak, who averaged 10.1 rushing yards per game and 2.7 per carry. That was the best the Steelers could offer.

Fullback Willie Asbury (30) ran for a career-best 107 yards in Pittsburgh's 41–13 win over Chicago in the 1967 opener. Asbury outgained Bears Hall of Fame back Gale Sayers by 105 yards in the blowout. *AP Images*

The Pitt Stadium Experience

Fans of old-time football are familiar with the photograph. Giants quarterback Y. A. Tittle is on his knees in an end zone, head bowed, shell-shocked, looking double his 37 years, blood etched on his temple and brow. The photograph so captures the agony of defeat that it became one of three pictures to hang in the lobby of the National Press Photographers Association headquarters, alongside the flag-raising at Iwo Jima and the explosion of the Hindenburg.

Adding to the humanity of the Tittle photograph is the background: a smattering of fans sitting on card chairs at field level and a few half-interested folks sitting on mostly empty bleachers near the end zone. This famous photograph was taken at Pitt Stadium, where the Steelers played some of their games from 1958 to '63 and all of their contests from 1964 to '69—before moving to Three Rivers Stadium.

Located on the University of Pittsburgh campus in the Oakland section of Pittsburgh, Pitt Stadium hosted the school's football games for 75 years, beginning in 1925. While Forbes Field offered fans wooden chairs—good for resting a steelworker's tired back—it seated less than 40,000. Pitt Stadium sat nearly 70,000, bleacher style.

On every football Sunday, Pitt Stadium was largely empty. From 1964 to '69, the Steelers usually drew in the 30,000s or 40,000s. Only occasionally would attendance sneak past 50,000. Late-season games, when it was cold and the Steelers were out if it, normally drew in the 20,000s. At least the players had the benefit of playing on grass—not the rock-hard infield dirt at Forbes Field (home of the Pirates) or the fake turf that carpeted Three Rivers Stadium for 31 years.

When Pitt Stadium was demolished in 1999–2000, it troubled Pitt Panthers fans. "They're tearing down memories," said student Dana Mazzarini. It didn't bother Steelers fans nearly as much. For them, good memories were hard to recollect.

A dazed Y. A. Tittle suffers alone in a Pitt Stadium end zone, as Steelers fans look on. *Dozier Mobley/AP Images*

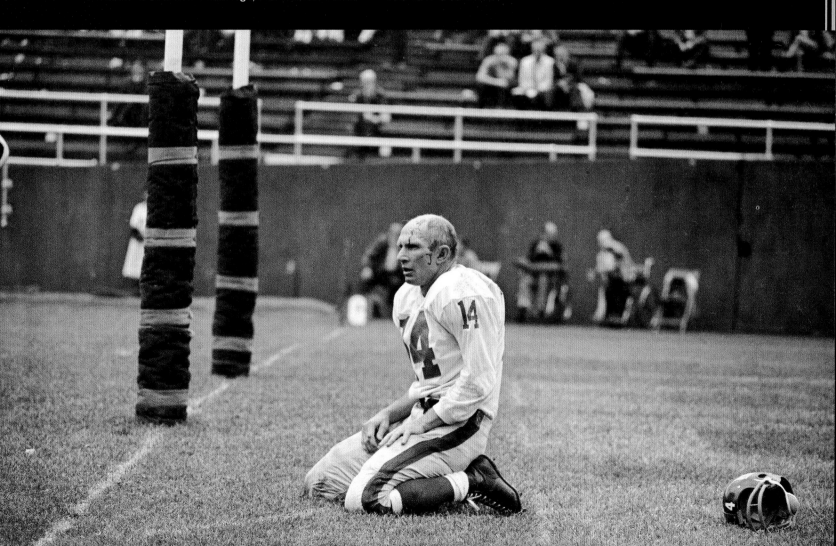

1968

2–11–1   4th place

Game-by-Game

9/15	L, 20–34,	vs. New York Giants
9/22	L, 10–45,	at L.A. Rams
9/29	L, 7–41,	vs. Baltimore Colts
10/5	L, 24–31,	at Cleveland Browns
10/13	L, 13–16,	at Washington Redskins
10/20	L, 12–16,	vs. New Orleans Saints
10/27	W, 6–3,	vs. Philadelphia Eagles
11/3	W, 41–21,	at Atlanta Falcons
11/10	T, 28–28,	at St. Louis Cardinals
11/17	L, 24–45,	vs. Cleveland Browns
11/24	L, 28–45,	vs. San Francisco 49ers
12/1	L, 10–20,	vs. St. Louis Cardinals
12/8	L, 7–28,	at Dallas Cowboys
12/15	L, 14–24,	at New Orleans Saints

Team Scoring

244 points scored
397 points allowed

Despite an NFL-leading 1,074 yards on the ground during 1968, all-star running back Roy Jefferson could do little as the Steelers suffered loss after loss under Bill Austin. *Getty Images*

AUSTIN LOSES THE TEAM

Steelers Drink Too Much, Train Too Little

Long before starring in the 1976 blaxploitation feature film *Brotherhood of Death* ("When these brothers stick it to you . . . it's fatal"), Roy Jefferson was an All-Pro wideout for the Steelers. "He was tough," said quarterback Dick Shiner, "a running back at wide receiver." In 1968, Jefferson led the NFL with 1,074 receiving yards, highlighted by a 199-yard, four-touchdown performance against Atlanta. It's easy for Steelers fans to recall that November afternoon; it was the only highlight of the season. Unless you count their 6–3 snoozer of a win over Philadelphia. Other than that, the team went 0–11–1.

By 1968, the Steelers were the joke of the NFL, lacking both conditioning and discipline. Linebacker Bill Saul became legendary for his drinking ability, in both quantity and technique. "He could take a whole glass of beer, put it in his mouth, tilt it, and swallow the beer in one gulp without taking a breath," teammate Ken Kortas told the *Pittsburgh Sports Daily Bulletin*. Added center Ray Mansfield: "Drinking was a big part of that team. "I don't remember ever running a wind sprint."

Coach Bill Austin, a former offensive lineman, did a nice job improving the O-line with Pittsburgh in 1968. Dick Hoak ran for a career-high 858 yards, and Dick Shiner—another castoff quarterback (formerly of Washington and Cleveland)—ranked seventh in the league with 18 touchdown passes. The defense, however, was abysmal, allowing a league-high 397 points and surrendering more than 40 points four times.

"Austin had lost the team, and I knew I had to make a change," Dan Rooney wrote in his autobiography. "By the end of the 1968 season, I had already begun the search for a new coach."

Joe Greene (75) and Jim Shorter (left) converge on Eagles fullback Tom Woodeshick in Week 2 of the '69 season. After jumping out to a 13–0 lead, the Steelers lost 41–27, kicking off a 13-game losing streak. *Bill Ingraham/AP Images*

1–13 4th place

Game-by-Game

9/21	W, 16–13, vs. Detroit Lions
9/28	L, 27–41, at Philadelphia Eagles
10/5	L, 14–27, vs. St. Louis Cardinals
10/12	L, 7–10, at New York Giants
10/18	L, 31–42, at Cleveland Browns
10/26	L, 7–14, vs. Washington Redskins
11/2	L, 34–38, vs. Green Bay Packers
11/9	L, 7–38, at Chicago Bears
11/16	L, 3–24, vs. Cleveland Browns
11/23	L, 14–52, at Minnesota Vikings
11/30	L, 10–47, at St. Louis Cardinals
12/7	L, 7–10, vs. Dallas Cowboys
12/14	L, 17–21, vs. New York Giants
12/21	L, 24–27, at New Orleans Saints

Team Scoring

218 points scored
404 points allowed

ROONEYS PICK A WINNER

Noll Is the Right Man for Pittsburgh, Despite 1–13 Start

In his first interview with Dan Rooney, on January 13, 1969, Chuck Noll—who had won NFL championships with the Browns (player) and Colts (assistant coach)—explained how he would turn the Steelers into champions. "[H]e's telling me details about our offense and defense I would have thought only our coaches would know," Rooney wrote in his autobiography. "He pointed out that the Steelers had traded away their future. He thought the way to build a championship team was through the draft. Get young, raw talent, then teach the fundamentals of the game. Above all, he counseled patience."

Rooney was impressed, to say the least, as was his father during the second interview. Since fellow A-list candidate Joe Paterno was committed to Penn State, the Rooneys went with Noll, making the announcement on January 27. Two days later, the Steelers drafted 275-pound defensive tackle Joe Greene out of North Texas State with the fourth pick of the first round. The Steelers' scouting corps had planned to draft Notre Dame All-American quarterback Terry Hanratty with that pick, but Noll convinced them otherwise. They wound up drafting Hanratty in the second round.

Outside of All-Pro receiver Roy Jefferson (1,079 receiving yards) and ferocious rookie "Mean" Joe Greene, Pittsburgh was woefully short on talent in 1969. After beating Detroit on opening day, the Steelers lost their remaining 13 games, including back-to-back 52–14 and 47–10 blowouts. Noll was undeterred. He knew that through his system, smart drafting, proper teaching, and strict discipline, the Steelers would eventually climb the NFL ladder. The Rooneys believed in Noll, and, more importantly, so did the players.

Quiet Mastermind:
Chuck Noll

Four decades after Chuck Noll won four Super Bowls, there hadn't been a single biography written about him. He wasn't interested in talking about himself, and besides, who would be interested in stories about the NFL's Bob Newhart (sans the humor)?

Chuck Noll didn't give rah-rah speeches like Vince Lombardi or effuse colorful verbiage like John Madden. He didn't believe in berating his players in order to light a fire under them. Noll, like future coaching great Bill Belichick, was calm, cool, and cerebral. He focused on drafting and

acquiring the right players, teaching them proper technique, constructing a long-term plan, and being thoroughly prepared. His players viewed him as emotionally detached, but they respected him nonetheless.

"People think motivation is yelling at somebody," Noll said. "It's not. It's [teaching players] *how* to do something. Because if you know how to do something, you *want* to do it because you're successful at it. . . . You prepare hard, and you expect to be successful."

An all-state high school player in Cleveland in the 1940s, Noll played college ball at the University of Dayton. His hometown Browns drafted him in 1953, and for seven years he served as a messenger guard and linebacker under legendary coach Paul Brown, winning two NFL championships. Such tutelage served him well, as did his three years as an assistant coach to the brilliant Don Shula in Baltimore, where he won another NFL title. By the time he became the head coach of the Steelers in 1969, Noll knew exactly how to build a Super Bowl contender.

Noll knew what kind of players the Steelers should draft: self-starters who were determined to learn, improve, and succeed. In '69, Noll inherited a train wreck of a football team, and he didn't panic when the club went 1–13 that year. He was focused on the big picture. For the first half hour of every practice, he worked on the fundamentals—proper stance, tackling, blocking.

In *The Last Headbangers*, author Kevin Cook offered this perspective on Noll and Madden: "They were space-age coaches who saw their jobs as similar to that of the lead engineer on a NASA mission: Manage your personnel, draw up a game plan, anticipate surprises, and create multiple responses to possible setbacks, including last-ditch options. When the game starts, let your men execute the mission."

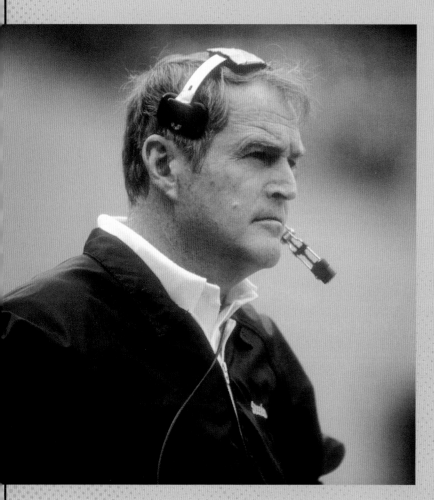

Chuck Noll always exhibited a focused and calm intensity on the sidelines as the Steelers head coach. *Focus on Sport/Getty Images*

In his 23 seasons as an NFL head coach, all with Pittsburgh, Noll compiled a record of 193–148–1, won 11 division titles, and went 4–0 in Super Bowls. His win total ranks seventh in NFL history, and as of 2013 no coach had matched his four Super Bowl victories.

At Noll's first Super Bowl in January 1975, the national media didn't take kindly to his short-answer responses at the initial press conference. "'Condescending' was the adjective they hung on him," wrote Myron Cope in *Double Yoi!* "Rarely, I think, did Noll enjoy discussing football with anyone other than players, coaches, or scouts. Did Einstein enjoy discussing his theory of relatively with the editor of Princeton's campus newspaper?"

Noll, who had one child with his wife, Marianne, actually had many interests outside of football. "He was an unusual guy," Ed Kiely, a longtime Steelers employee, told Elizabeth Merrill of ESPN.com. "One week he'd be taking lessons for golf, and the next week he'd be learning how to buy a boat and take it down South. He was a man for all seasons."

Merrill told the story of how Lynn Swann and some teammates summoned the courage to go caroling at the Noll house on a December night in the late 1970s. Chuck invited them in, showed them some photographs he had taken, and then actually played his ukulele for them. "I thought we were breaking the ice," Swann said. "We're getting to the core of this man—this is great. Wonderful. A breakthrough. The next morning, we walk in there, and I thought we were going to have a new relationship. He looked at us and nodded his head. It was like we were never in his home for a second. He never acknowledged it. But that was Chuck."

Coach Noll was always prepared on game days. *MVP Books Collection*

For Noll, it all came down to fundamentals. "Champions do ordinary things better than everyone else," he said. *Harry Cabluck/AP Images*

THE 1960s RECORD BOOK

Team Leaders

(**Boldface** indicates league leader)

Scoring Leaders (Points)

1960: Tom Tracy, 63
1961: Buddy Dial, 72;
    Lou Michaels, 72
1962: Lou Michaels, 110
1963: Lou Michaels, 95
1964: Mike Clark, 67
1965: Mike Clark, 52
1966: Mike Clark, 97
1967: Mike Clark, 71
1968: Roy Jefferson, 72
1969: Gene Mingo, 62

Passing Leaders

(Completions / Attempts / Yards)

1960: Bobby Layne, 103 / 209 / 1,814
1961: Rudy Bukich, 89 / 156 / 1,253
1962: Bobby Layne, 116 / 233 / 1,686
1963: Ed Brown, 168 / 362 / 2,982
1964: Ed Brown, 121 / 272 / 1,990
1965: Bill Nelsen, 121 / 270 / 1,917
1966: Ron Smith, 79 / 181 / 1,249
1967: Kent Nix, 136 / 268 / 1,587
1968: Dick Shiner, 148 / 304 / 1,856
1969: Dick Shiner, 97 / 209 / 1,422

Rushing Leaders

(Carries / Yards / TDs)

1960: Tom Tracy, 192 / 680 / 5
1961: John Henry Johnson, 213 / 787 / 6
1962: John Henry Johnson, 251 / 1,141 / 7
1963: John Henry Johnson, 186 / 773 / 4
1964: John Henry Johnson, 235 / 1,048 / 7
1965: Dick Hoak, 131 / 426 / 5
1966: Bill Asbury, 169 / 544 / 7
1967: Don Shy, 99 / 341 / 4
1968: Dick Hoak, 175 / 858 / 3
1969: Dick Hoak, 151 / 531 / 2

Topps highlights wide receiver Roy Jefferson, one of the few bright spots on the 1969 Steelers. *MVP Books Collection*

Receiving Leaders

(Receptions / Yards / TDs)

1960: Buddy Dial, 40 / 972 / 9
1961: Buddy Dial, 53 / 1,047 / 12
1962: Buddy Dial, 50 / 981 / 6
1963: Buddy Dial, 60 / 1,295 / 9
1964: Gary Ballman, 47 / 935 / 7
1965: Gary Ballman, 40 / 859 / 5
1966: John Hilton, 46 / 603 / 4
1967: J. R. Wilburn, 51 / 767 / 5
1968: Roy Jefferson, 58 / **1,074** / 11
1969: Roy Jefferson, 67 / 1,079 / 9

Interceptions

(Number / Yards / TDs)

1960: Dick Moegle, 6 / 49 / 0
1961: John Sample, 8 / 141 / 1
1962: Clendon Thomas, 7 / 48 / 0
1963: Clendon Thomas, 8 / 122 / 0
1964: Brady Keys, 2 / 11 / 0;
    Dick Haley, 2 / 11 / 0;
    Willie Daniel, 2 / 4 / 0
1965: Jim Bradshaw, 5 / 117 / 1
1966: Jim Bradshaw, 4 / 82 / 1;
    Marv Woodson, 4 / 91 / 1;
    Brady Keys, 4 / 0 / 0

the Record Book

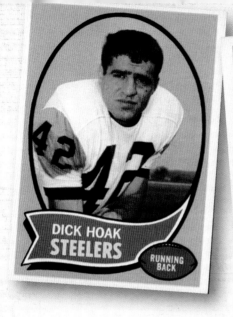

Dick Hoak, pictured on a Topps card, ranked fourth in the NFL with 858 rushing yards in 1968. *MVP Books Collection*

Linebacker Myron Pottios was a three-time Pro Bowl selection in his four seasons with the Steelers. *MVP Books Collection*

1967: Marv Woodson, 7 / 49 / 0
1968: Paul Martha, 3 / 43 / 0;
    Ray May, 3 / 31 / 1;
    Marv Woodson, 3 / 23 / 0;
    Clendon Thomas, 3 / 0 / 0
1969: Bob Hohn, 5 / 64 / 0;
    Paul Martha, 5 / 37 / 0

First-Team All-Pros

1969: Joe Greene, DT
1969: Roy Jefferson, WR

Pro Bowl Selections

1960: John Reger, LB
1960: Mike Sandusky, G
1960: Ernie Stautner, DT
1960: Tom Tracy, HB
1960: Frank Varrichione, OT
1961: Buddy Dial, WR
1961: John Nisby, G
1961: Myron Pottios, LB
1961: John Reger, LB
1961: Ernie Stautner, DE
1962: Preston Carpenter, PR/TE
1962: John Henry Johnson, FB
1962: Gene Lipscomb, DT
1962: Lou Michaels, K/DE
1962: Buzz Nutter, C
1963: Charlie Bradshaw, OT
1963: Buddy Dial, WR

1963: John Henry Johnson, FB
1963: Joe Krupa, DT
1963: Lou Michaels, K/DE
1963: Myron Pottios, LB
1963: Clendon Thomas, S
1964: Gary Ballman, WR/KR
1964: Charlie Bradshaw, OT
1964: John Henry Johnson, FB
1964: Myron Pottios, LB
1965: Gary Ballman, WR
1966: Mike Clark, K
1966: Brady Keys, CB
1966: Ben McGee, DE
1967: Dick Hoak, HB
1967: Marv Woodson, CB
1968: Roy Jefferson, PR/WR
1968: Ben McGee, DE
1968: Andy Russell, LB
1969: Joe Greene, DT
1969: Roy Jefferson, WR
1969: Bobby Walden, P

1st-Round Draft Picks

1960: Jack Spikes (6), FB, Texas Christian
1962: Bob Ferguson (5), FB, Ohio St.
1964: Paul Martha (10), DB, Pittsburgh
1966: Dick Leftridge (3), FB, West Virginia
1968: Mike Taylor (10), OT, Southern California
1969: Joe Greene (4), DT, North Texas

MVP Books Collection

THE 1970s

CHUCK NOLL, JOE GREENE, AND THREE RIVERS

Noll's brilliant leadership and an endless parade of Hall of Fame-bound draft picks result in four Super Bowl titles and the emergence of Steelers Nation.

It was the most sudden and spectacular transformation of a franchise in the history of American sports, and the most dramatic change in Pittsburgh's self-image in more than a century. The 1970s forever changed the Steelers—and the city itself. The loose amalgam of fans grew into Steelers Nation and morphed into the identity of Pittsburgh.

On the field, the 1970s began in confusion and ended in championships—an unprecedented grouping of Super Bowl victories, one that has yet to be repeated. Although the fans groaned *Joe who?* at Chuck Noll's first draft pick, in 1969, the freshman coach had promised he would build a champion through the draft. In a series of stellar moves, the Steelers from 1970 to '74 drafted future Hall of Famers Terry Bradshaw, Mel Blount, Jack Ham, Franco Harris, Jack Lambert, Mike Webster, and Lynn Swann.

In 1972, the Steelers won their first division title in 40 years and their first-ever playoff game, making history with the "Immaculate Reception." Franco Harris's miracle catch marked them as a team of destiny, something mythic in the fans' eyes.

Then, in almost blinding succession, came ultimate victories:

Super Bowl IX: miraculous.

Super Bowl X: astonishing.

Super Bowl XIII: triumphant.

Super Bowl XIV: lordly.

Four Lombardi Trophies in six years: 1974–79. Dizzying. Unbelievable.

This pin highlights the four Super Bowl victories for the Steelers teams of the 1970s. *MVP Books Collection*

In their adulation, the fans didn't know where to turn. The Rooneys credited Noll and his canny, patient, brilliant way of creating a system and putting it into effect.

Noll credited the 1970 move to Three Rivers Stadium. For the first time in its history, the Steelers had modern locker rooms and practice facilities, amenities necessary for football.

Joe Greene, Noll's first draft choice, set the tone by taking play to a higher level—and refusing to lose.

Greene credited Franco Harris, an extraordinarily nimble power back who could read plays at lightning speed and adapt. From the time Harris arrived, in 1972, through his departure a dozen years later, the Steelers never had a losing season.

The offense credited the defense, that incredibly effective "Steel Curtain." In a town full of weird topography and oddball characters, it didn't hurt that the Curtain (itself a nickname) had great nicknames—"Hollywood Bags," "Mean Joe," "Fats," and "Mad Dog."

Behind them came linebackers Andy Russell, Jack Ham, and Jack Lambert. All undersized and brilliant, they won by anticipating and never making mistakes.

If Joe Greene put the Steelers in the Pittsburgh mindset, Jack Lambert forever put the team in the fans' hearts. In Super Bowl X, when Cowboys safety Cliff Harris taunted kicker Roy Gerela by patting him on the helmet, the enraged Lambert picked up Harris and dumped him.

Steelers Nation was born that moment.

From that time, what happened off the field defined the Steelers Experience. With Three Rivers ringed by a sea of space, Steelers Nation showed up hours before kickoff for *another* new thing: tailgating. Eating barbecue and drinking Iron City, fans began to create their own subgroups: "Franco's Italian Army," "Gerela's Gorillas," and so on.

Coming in the "Me" decade, costumes were mandatory—helmets for the Italian Army, gorilla suits for Gerela. Inside Three Rivers, homemade banners hung everywhere. Fans eschewed civvies and came in jerseys and waved "Terrible Towels."

Suddenly, fans defined the Steelers Experience in ways that franchise leaders could not have predicted, created, or controlled. Suddenly, it belonged to *us*.

—A. M.

John Stallworth starts his pass rout against the Miami Dolphins. Stallworth was a key contributor to Pittsburgh's triumphs in Super Bowls X, XIII and XIV. *Focus on Sport/ Getty Images*

1970

5–9 3rd place

Game-by-Game

9/20	L, 7–19,	vs. Houston Oilers
9/27	L, 13–16,	at Denver Broncos
10/3	L, 7–15,	at Cleveland Browns
10/11	W, 23–10,	vs. Buffalo Bills
10/18	W, 7–3,	at Houston Oilers
10/25	L, 14–31,	at Oakland Raiders
11/2	W, 21–10,	vs. Cincinnati Bengals
11/8	W, 21–17,	vs. New York Jets
11/15	L, 14–31,	vs. Kansas City Chiefs
11/22	L, 7–34,	at Cincinnati Bengals
11/29	W, 28–9,	vs. Cleveland Browns
12/6	L, 12–20,	vs. Green Bay Packers
12/13	L, 16–27,	at Atlanta Falcons
12/20	L, 20–30,	at Philadelphia Eagles

Team Scoring

210 points scored
272 points allowed

A NEW ERA DAWNS

Steelers Forge Ahead with New Conference, Stadium, QB

If Steelers history were the Bible, 1970 would mark the first book of the New Testament. That was the year that Art Rooney's franchise was reborn. The Steelers entered a new decade, a new stadium (Three Rivers), a new conference (American Football Conference, since the NFL had merged with the American Football League), and a new division. The AFC Central included Pittsburgh, the Houston Oilers, Cincinnati Bengals, and Cleveland Browns.

In January 1970 the savior arrived, as the Steelers drafted quarterback Terry Bradshaw with the first overall pick. Though claiming he "hadn't learned any football" while starring at Louisiana Tech, the country boy possessed a golden arm, one that had flung a javelin 245 feet to set a national record. Bradshaw excelled at the deep pass—his 17.0 yards per completion in 1970 would be the best of his career—but was very much a work in progress. He completed just 38.1 percent of his passes and threw six touchdowns against an NFL-high 24 interceptions. In six starts at quarterback, Terry Hanratty offered more stability but far less potential.

If it weren't for their 48 turnovers, the Steelers might have done better than their 5–9 performance. Fullback John "Frenchy" Fuqua (whose platform shoes included mini aquariums) rushed for 691 yards on 5.0 per carry. And the defense began to come together, finishing seventh out of 26 NFL teams against the run. "Mean" Joe Greene and veteran Andy Russell were selected for the Pro Bowl, and rookie Mel Blount began his Hall of Fame career at cornerback. For the first time in ages, excitement was in the air.

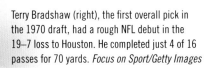

Terry Bradshaw (right), the first overall pick in the 1970 draft, had a rough NFL debut in the 19–7 loss to Houston. He completed just 4 of 16 passes for 70 yards. *Focus on Sport/Getty Images*

DRAFT DAY BONANZA

Top Picks Include Ham, White, Holmes, and Wagner

Like Art Rooney at Saratoga, the Steelers were on a roll at the 1971 NFL Draft—although they wouldn't know it until their pickings bore fruit in upcoming years. Though their first-round selection, receiver Frank Lewis out of Grambling, would be a bit of a bust (128 career receptions with Pittsburgh), the rest of the draft was bountiful.

In the second round, the Steelers took linebacker and future Hall of Famer Jack Ham, whom Rooney would soon mistake for a bellhop when he met him at a hotel. In Rounds 4 and 8, respectively, Pittsburgh landed soon-to-be "Steel Curtain" linemen Dwight White and Ernie Holmes. Fourth-rounder Gerry "Moon" Mullins would start the rest of the decade on the offensive line, and tight end Larry Brown—taken in the following round—would become a Pro Bowl tackle for Pittsburgh. Strong safety Mike Wagner, an 11th-round choice, would lead the NFL in interceptions two years later.

The young but definitely up-and-coming Steelers started the season at 5–5, which put them in a tie with Cleveland atop the AFC Central. However, while the Browns won out, Pittsburgh finished at 6–8. Terry Bradshaw improved dramatically, transforming from a long-ball chucker to a game manager who completed 54.4 percent of his passes and improved his touchdown/interception ratio to 13/22.

Offensively, Pittsburgh still lacked big-play performers. Leading rushers John Fuqua (625 yards) and Preston Pearson (605) teamed with leading receivers Dave L. Smith (663) and Ron Shanklin (652). Pro Bowlers Joe Greene and Andy Russell led a still-developing defense that allowed just 3.4 yards per rush—third best in the league.

John "Frenchy" Fuqua led the team in rushing in 1971. *James Flores/Getty Images*

6–8 2nd place

Game-by-Game

9/19	L, 15–17, at Chicago Bears
9/26	W, 21–10, vs. Cincinnati Bengals
10/3	W, 21–17, vs. San Diego Chargers
10/10	L, 17–27, at Cleveland Browns
10/18	L, 16–38, at Kansas City Chiefs
10/24	W, 23–16, vs. Houston Oilers
10/31	L, 21–34, at Baltimore Colts
11/7	W, 26–9, vs. Cleveland Browns
11/14	L, 21–24, at Miami Dolphins
11/21	W, 17–13, vs. New York Giants
11/28	L, 10–22, vs. Denver Broncos
12/5	L, 3–29, at Houston Oilers
12/12	W, 21–13, at Cincinnati Bengals
12/19	L, 14–23, vs. L.A. Rams

Team Scoring

246 points scored
292 points allowed

Ferocious and Mean:
Joe Greene

There's a reason why Joe Greene's 1979 Coca-Cola commercial became an all-time classic. It wasn't just because "Mean" Joe cracked a smile and showed a soft side by throwing his jersey to an adoring kid. It was because of the man's commanding aura.

"I remember walking into the locker room with Joe for the Pro Bowl one year," Steelers defensive coordinator George Perles said in *Super Steelers: The Making of a Dynasty*. "Here we had superstars from all over the league, and they all seemed humbled by his presence. This may sound incredible, but Joe commanded respect without having to utter a single word."

Even the Steelers themselves were awed by Greene, who lined up at left defensive tackle for Pittsburgh from 1969 to '81. In one game, Greene kicked fellow Steel Curtain linemate Ernie Holmes off the field for freelancing. A dumbfounded Perles ordered the massive Holmes to get back out there. "Not until Joe says I can," Holmes responded.

Immediately upon accepting the Steelers' head-coaching job in January 1969, Chuck Noll insisted upon taking Greene with the fourth overall pick in that year's draft—if he were still available. Though Greene had toiled in relative obscurity at North Texas State, he was an immensely talented, 275-pound All-American. The Philadelphia Eagles, who chose Purdue running back Leroy Keyes (369 career rushing yards in the NFL) with the third pick, apparently didn't recognize the fire that burned within Joe Greene. Chuck Noll did.

In his book *Looking Deep*, Terry Bradshaw recalled the first day he saw Joe walking down the hill to practice: "socks down around his ankles, huge thighs, big Afro, jersey hanging

out, looking like he had been up all night. What a sight!"

Greene psyched himself up to the point where he played angry, in a controlled—or in his early days, sometimes out-of-control—rage. "He took cheap shots at quarterbacks," Bradshaw continued, "driving them out of bounds and into the bench if he could. He was ferocious. He couldn't be blocked because he was so overpowering."

In 1969, the Associated Press tabbed Greene as the NFL Defensive Rookie of the Year. In 1972 and '74, the AP named him the NFL Defensive Player of the Year. He was invited to 10 Pro Bowls and earned First Team All-Pro honors five times.

But, Perles said in *Super Steelers*, "personal commendations mean nothing to Joe Greene unless he wins." Perles praised Mean Joe for his relentless study of game film and scouting reports, ability to map out strategies for upcoming opponents, and eagerness to help his teammates. In addition, his physical talent was off the charts. "Physically, he's a guy who can take all the strength and quickness, collect it, and fit it together like a spring, and then explode," Perles said.

Greene was frequently double-teamed, which meant opposing offenses were going 9-on-10 against one of the best defenses in football. Injuries reduced Greene's effectiveness in 1976 and '77, and some cynics were saying that he was washed up. That just made Joe angry, and he came back with a vengeance in '78, leading all Steelers linemen in tackles while logging five fumble recoveries (a career high) and four sacks. Roused by their spiritual leader, the Steelers allowed a league-low 195 points that year and won their third Super

Bowl. Greene won his fourth ring and went to his final Pro Bowl a year later. Unofficially, he was credited with 78.5 career sacks.

Teammate Andy Russell said that Mean Joe was "unquestionably" the "Player of the Decade" in the NFL during the 1970s. "There was no player more valuable to his team," he said. Greene served as the Steelers' defensive line coach under Noll from 1987 to '91. He later worked in the team's personnel department, evaluating pro and college players, until his retirement in 2013.

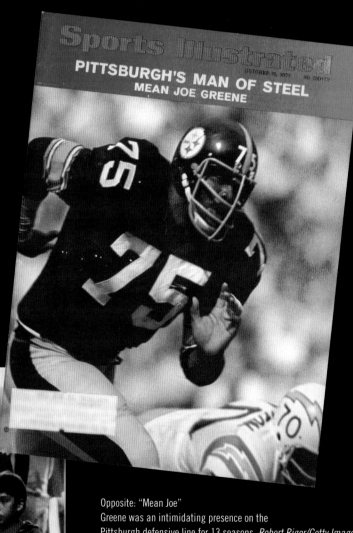

Opposite: "Mean Joe"
Greene was an intimidating presence on the
Pittsburgh defensive line for 13 seasons. *Robert Riger/Getty Images*

Above: In 1971, Greene became the first Steelers player to grace the cover of *Sports Illustrated*. *MVP Books Collection*

Left: In 1980, Greene won an award for his acting—a CLIO for best male performance in a television ad with his now-legendary Coke commercial. *MVP Books Collection*

1972

11–3 1st place

Game-by-Game

9/17	W, 34–28, vs. Oakland Raiders
9/24	L, 10–15, at Cincinnati Bengals
10/1	W, 25–19, at St. Louis Cardinals
10/8	L, 13–17, at Dallas Cowboys
10/15	W, 24–7, vs. Houston Oilers
10/22	W, 33–3, vs. New England Patriots
10/29	W, 38–21, at Buffalo Bills
11/5	W, 40–17, vs. Cincinnati Bengals
11/12	W, 16–7, vs. Kansas City Chiefs
11/19	L, 24–26, at Cleveland Browns
11/26	W, 23–10, vs. Minnesota Vikings
12/3	W, 30–0, vs. Cleveland Browns
12/10	W, 9–3, at Houston Oilers
12/17	W, 24–2, at San Diego Chargers

Playoffs

| 12/23 | W, 13–7, vs. Oakland Raiders |
| 12/31 | L, 17–21, vs. Miami Dolphins |

Team Scoring

343 points scored

175 points allowed

Linebacker Jack Ham runs back an interception during the 24–2 trouncing of the Chargers in the season finale. It was one of four picks by the Steelers defense in the game. *James Flores / Getty Images*

BREAKTHROUGH!

Steelers Win First Division Title, First Playoff Game

With all the tremendous talent Pittsburgh had drafted in recent years, coupled with the astute tutelage of Chuck Noll and his staff, the Steelers entered 1972 on the verge of greatness. All they needed was a big-time halfback, and they got him with the 13th pick in the first round. Franco Harris, a hard-driving, 230-pound back out of Penn State, would rush for 1,055 yards as a rookie while averaging a spectacular 5.6 yards per carry, helping the Steelers finish second in the NFL in rushing.

With Terry Bradshaw coming into his own as a field general and a defense that now ranked among the league's finest, the Steelers were ready to roll. The opening game was a statement win over the hard-hitting, bad-boy Oakland Raiders. Pittsburgh's Henry Davis returned a blocked punt for a touchdown, and Bradshaw ran for two scores in a 34–28 triumph.

Though they opened at 2–2, the Steelers won their next five games before falling to Cleveland. The next week, they defeated the visiting Minnesota Vikings, a perennial power, 23–10. "The weather never seems to change much here this time of year," wrote Dave Anderson in the *New York Times*. "It's usually cloudy and gloomy. . . . Art Rooney never seems to change much, either. . . . But his Pittsburgh Steelers have changed."

On December 10, an injury-wracked, flu-ridden Steelers team went to Houston and gutted out a 9–3 victory. Joe Greene played Superman with five sacks, a forced fumble, a fumble recovery, and a blocked field goal. With a 24–2 victory at San Diego a week later, the Steelers finished with their best record ever at the time (11–3) and, incredibly enough, captured their first division title in their 40-year history. The Steelers opened the playoffs in Oakland against the menacing Raiders, who featured

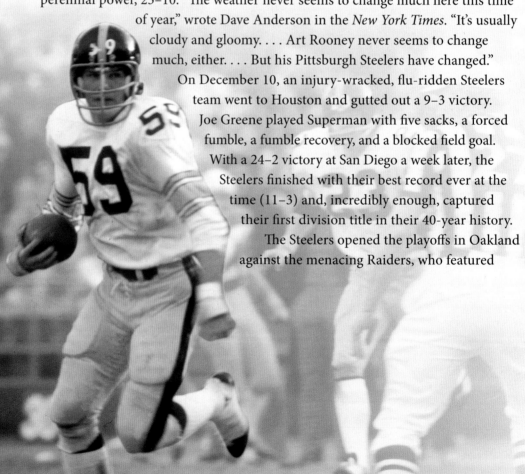

The Immaculate Reception

Franco Harris sheds a tackle attempt by Oakland's Jimmy Ware during his immaculate run to glory. *Harry Cabluck/AP Images*

With the Steelers facing fourth down with 22 seconds to go against Oakland, Art Rooney prepared for his seemingly destined lot in life: giving his team his condolences. The Chief took the elevator down to field level, thus missing the greatest play in Steelers history.

Franco Harris's "Immaculate Reception" could have easily been overturned. A rule stated that if an offensive player caught a ball that had caromed off a teammate, it was not a completion. Terry Bradshaw's pass had reached Pittsburgh's John Fuqua and Oakland's Jack Tatum at the same time, and it was unclear whom it hit first. The Raiders claimed that the ball had hit Fuqua, but the officials thought differently. So, Harris's heads-up play stood.

The play unfolded when Bradshaw, after scrambling for his life, threw the ball to the Raiders' 35-yard line. The ball hit Tatum or Fuqua (as Tatum hit Fuqua) and bounced backward, and Harris—running forward—caught the ricochet inches from the ground and continued down the left sideline.

As Harris scored with five seconds to go, pandemonium broke loose at Three Rivers. Fans jumped up and down, arms flailing, like orangutans, and some jumped over the high wall and mobbed Harris in the end zone. "You talk about Christmas miracles," Curt Gowdy blared on the NBC telecast. "Here's the miracle of all miracles."

In Pittsburgh, the luster of the Immaculate Reception has never diminished. In fact, Harris said, the "play just gets bigger every year."

such bruisers as Art Shell, Gene Upshaw, and Jack "The Assassin" Tatum. In an epic defensive battle, the Steelers led 6–0 until Oakland quarterback Ken Stabler romped 30 yards for a touchdown with 1:13 left. Down 7–6, Bradshaw threw three incomplete passes, leaving Pittsburgh in a desperate situation: fourth down at its own 40 with 22 seconds remaining.

Every Steelers fan knows what happened next: the "Immaculate Reception," in which Bradshaw's pass ricocheted off running back John Fuqua and/or Tatum and was snatched by Harris, who turned it into a 60-yard touchdown reception. The Steelers' first-ever playoff win, 13–7, came on perhaps the most famous play in football history.

Unfortunately for the Steelers, they faced the only perfect team in football history in the AFC Championship Game. Though the Miami Dolphins had gone 14–0, the conference title game was played at Three Rivers due to a rotation formula; best record was irrelevant. Gerry Mullins gave Pittsburgh a 7–0 advantage with a fumble recovery in the end zone, but Miami methodically built a 21–10 lead. Bradshaw's 12-yard touchdown pass to Al Young in the fourth quarter was too little too late, as the Dolphins prevailed 21–17. They would cap their fabled season with a 14–7 win over Washington in the Super Bowl.

Golden Arm:
Terry Bradshaw

When the Cowboys' Thomas "Hollywood" Henderson said that Terry Bradshaw "couldn't spell *cat* if you spotted him the *c* and the *t*," there was a grain of truth to his putdown. As a student in Shreveport, Louisiana, Terry "believed I just wasn't as smart as the other kids," he wrote in his autobiography, *It's Only a Game*. "It was a horrible feeling. Awful." Terry felt so defeated in geometry one semester that he never opened the textbook, and he flunked every test.

Bradshaw's mother said that her son was a squirmer and a fireball. "Terry really likes to hang from the ceiling," he recalled her saying. Looking back, Bradshaw was certain that he suffered from attention-deficit disorder (ADD), but such a concept didn't exist in the 1960s. Terry was simply known as a hyper kid who could throw objects a country mile.

In a high school state track meet, Bradshaw chucked a javelin a quarter-inch shy of 245 feet. It was a national record, and about 35 feet farther than what he normally threw. Apparently, he excelled on the big stage.

At Louisiana Tech, Bradshaw started out as the backup quarterback to Phil Robertson, who would invent the Duck Commander duck call and become a regular on the smash-hit reality TV show *Duck Dynasty*. Because Robertson was, even at the time, more into hunting than football, Bradshaw won the starting QB job and rewrote the Louisiana Tech record book. Due to his golden arm, the Steelers took him with the first overall pick in the 1970 draft.

If it weren't for the mentoring of Chuck Noll and his staff, Bradshaw might have become a colossal bust. His first-season numbers were atrocious: 38.1 percent completion rate (although his completions were for large gains), six touchdowns, and an NFL-high 24 interceptions. His quarterback rating was an alarmingly low 30.4. From there, he steadily got better. Both Bradshaw and Dan Rooney credited Noll for the improvement, but they remembered the situation differently.

Bradshaw: "Chuck recognized my strengths—strong arm, impatient, hated short passes, loved to challenge safeties and corners as opposed to linebackers—and put this offense in for me."

Rooney: "Chuck handled Bradshaw perfectly. He'd give him sympathy. He'd be tough. He'd talk to him and tell him what to do. He let Bradshaw call the play. Chuck really did the job."

After riding the bench for the first six games of 1974, behind immensely talented pass-happy Joe Gilliam, Bradshaw got the nod on Monday, October 28 and never looked back. Ironically, Bradshaw had re-won the quarterback job due to his game-managing ability—proof that he was indeed a good student. Under his steady leadership, Pittsburgh went 6–2 over the rest of the regular season and romped to the Super Bowl title.

Bradshaw earned his first Pro Bowl invitation in 1975, when he went 12–2 and threw for 18 touchdowns versus nine interceptions. He peaked in 1978, earning NFL Player of the Year honors after leading the league with 28 touchdown passes. Bradshaw was named MVP of that year's Super Bowl (318 yards, four touchdowns) as well as the next (14-of-21, 309 yards). His 3,724 passing yards in 1979 were a career high, and in '80 he led the NFL with four game-winning drives.

In 14 years with the Steelers, Bradshaw threw for 27,989 yards. While critics point to his 210 interceptions and 70.9 career passer rating—which isn't even among the top 150 of all time—Bradshaw can simply point to his fingers. Entering 2013, he and Joe Montana were the only quarterbacks to win four Super Bowl rings.

The outgoing, hammy Bradshaw recorded several country & western and gospel records, and he enjoyed a successful second career as a fun-loving, knee-slapping football analyst. He was inducted into the Pro Football Hall of Fame in 1989.

Opposite: The rifle-armed Bradshaw saw both his completion percentage and his yards-per-completion rate steadily rise as his career progressed. *Scott Cunningham/Getty Images*

10–4   2nd place

Game-by-Game

9/16	**W, 24–10,** vs. Detroit Lions
9/23	**W, 33–6,** vs. Cleveland Browns
9/30	**W, 36–7,** at Houston Oilers
10/7	**W, 38–21,** vs. San Diego Chargers
10/14	**L, 7–19,** at Cincinnati Bengals
10/21	**W, 26–14,** vs. New York Jets
10/28	**W, 20–13,** vs. Cincinnati Bengals
11/5	**W, 21–16,** vs. Washington Redskins
11/11	**W, 17–9,** at Oakland Raiders
11/18	**L, 13–23,** vs. Denver Broncos
11/25	**L, 16–21,** at Cleveland Browns
12/3	**L, 26–30,** at Miami Dolphins
12/9	**W, 33–7,** vs. Houston Oilers
12/15	**W, 37–14,** at San Francisco 49ers

Playoffs

12/22	**L, 14–33,** at Oakland Raiders

Team Scoring

347 points scored
210 points allowed

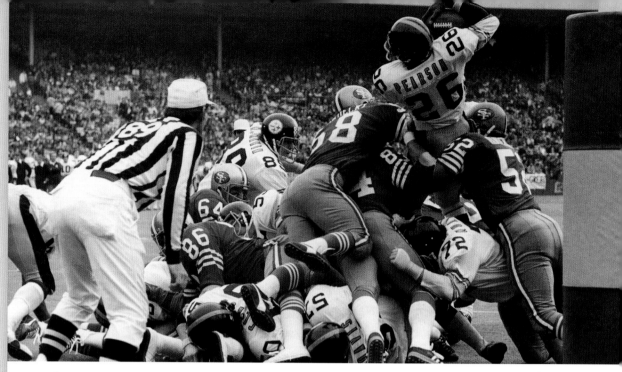

Preston Pearson leaps into the end zone to put Pittsburgh ahead early in the season-ending game at San Francisco. The Steelers went on to defeat the 49ers 37–14 to ensure a playoff spot. *Michael Zagaris/Getty Images*

STEELER OBSESSION

Fans Can't Get Enough of Emerging Powerhouse

After the Immaculate Reception, interest in the Steelers reached the obsessive level that we know today. Fans gobbled up season tickets, beginning a sellout streak that hasn't ended. *Sports Illustrated* editors became so interested in this burgeoning club that they assigned Roy Blount, Jr., to virtually live with and report on the team. And throughout the 1973 season, Pittsburghers engaged in endless conversations about who should be the team's quarterback.

Terry Bradshaw missed four games with a shoulder injury and averaged just 118 yards per game in his 10 contests—although he won nine of his 10 starts. Terry Hanratty, who had seemed to lose focus while riding the bench for two seasons, won two of four starts while throwing eight touchdowns versus just five interceptions. "Jefferson Street" Joe Gilliam, one of the NFL's first African American quarterbacks, completed just 20 of 60 passes on the season.

A solid running game, a big-threat receiver in All-Pro Ron Shanklin, and, most importantly, a crushing defense helped the Steelers start 8–1 and finish at 10–4. Three members of the "Steel Curtain" defensive line made the Pro Bowl— Joe Greene, of course, as well as Dwight White and L. C. Greenwood—as did linebackers Jack Ham and Andy Russell.

As the AFC's wildcard team, the Steelers opened the playoffs in Oakland, where they got smoked 33–14. Four field goals by 46-year-old George Blanda, and a pick-six off the arm of Bradshaw, were notable scores. The real news, though, was that Oakland outrushed Pittsburgh 232–65. The Steelers needed more firepower, and they would get it in the 1974 draft.

SUPER BOWL BOUND

Steelers Stifle O. J., Raiders En Route to AFC Title

The Steelers were at a disadvantage entering the 1974 NFL Draft. They wouldn't have a pick until the 21st selection, and they didn't have a third-round pick. As such, Art Rooney, Jr., wrote in his book *Ruanaidh*, the team would be "looking for 'exceptions'—players deficient in size and/or speed but with qualities not easy to assess, qualities like intelligence, tenacity, an instinct for the game."

While looking for players with intangibles, the Steelers ended up selecting four future Hall of Famers, making it the greatest draft day by any team in NFL history. Wide receiver Lynn Swann (Round 1) was only 5-foot-11, but his training in ballet would lead to legendary acrobatic catches. Jack Lambert (Round 2), a 220-pounder, would become a master at pass coverage and an eight-time All-Pro. Steelers super scout Bill Nunn found a gem of a receiver, John Stallworth (Round 4), at tiny Alabama A&M. Undersized center Mike Webster (Round 5), a seven-time All-Pro, rounded out the Canton-bound quartet.

An NFL players strike delayed training camp for the veterans, and the Steelers' season opened with a surprise starter at quarterback. Rifle-armed Joe Gilliam led the team to a 4–1–1 record to open the season, with the tie coming in the NFL's first-ever regular-season overtime game, a 35–35 scuffle at Denver. Gilliam, though, was horrible in a 17–0 loss to Oakland, going 8-for-31 with two interceptions while Terry Bradshaw fidgeted on the sidelines. In late October, tired of Gilliam's reliance on the pass, coach Chuck Noll made a permanent switch at quarterback. "We've got to have more balance in the offense," Noll said.

Bradshaw proved to be a slightly more stable field general, though statistically he and Gilliam finished with nearly identical numbers—completion rates of 45.3

Running back Franco Harris scampers into the endzone during a 32-14 rout of the Buffalo Bills during the AFC divisional playoffs on December 22, 1974 at Three Rivers Stadium. *Focus on Sport / Getty Images*

Game-by-Game

9/15	**W,** 30–0,	vs. Baltimore Colts
9/22	**T,** 35–35 (OT),	at Denver Broncos
9/29	**L,** 0–17,	vs. Oakland Raiders
10/6	**W,** 13–7,	at Houston Oilers
10/13	**W,** 34–24,	at Kansas City Chiefs
10/20	**W,** 20–16,	vs. Cleveland Browns
10/28	**W,** 24–17,	vs. Atlanta Falcons
11/3	**W,** 27–0,	vs. Philadelphia Eagles
11/10	**L,** 10–17,	at Cincinnati Bengals
11/17	**W,** 26–16,	at Cleveland Browns
11/25	**W,** 28–7,	at New Orleans Saints
12/1	**L,** 10–13,	vs. Houston Oilers
12/8	**W,** 21–17,	at New England Patriots
12/14	**W,** 27–3,	vs. Cincinnati Bengals

Playoffs

12/22	**W,** 32–14,	vs. Buffalo Bills
12/29	**W,** 24–13,	at Oakland Raiders
1/12	**Super Bowl:** W, 16–6,	vs. Minnesota Vikings

Team Scoring

305 points scored
189 points allowed

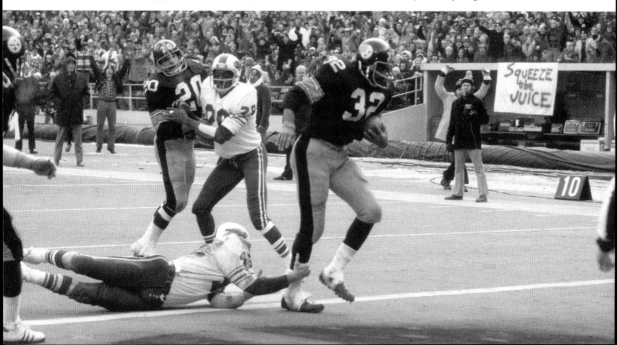

and passer ratings of 55.2 and 55.4, respectively. But while Bradshaw would go on to win four Super Bowls, Gilliam would be like Pete Best of the Beatles; he would play only four more games in his NFL career.

Pittsburgh went 6–2 under Bradshaw to finish at 10–3–1, winning the division by a mile over the 7–7 Oilers and Bengals. Bradshaw had his own mulligan in a home game against Houston on December 1. Despite decent weather, he went 6-for-25 for 60 yards and three picks, as Pittsburgh managed just 84 yards of offense in a 13–10 loss. Nevertheless, the Steelers finished the season eighth in the NFL in offensive yardage, second in rushing (behind Franco Harris's 1,006 yards), first in defensive yardage, and first in takeaways.

Girded by the "Steel Curtain" defensive line and a linebacker corpse that featured Jack Ham, Jack Lambert, and Andy Russell, the Steelers' defense entered the playoffs in peak form. In the opening game against Buffalo at Three Rivers, they held the great O. J. Simpson—who a year earlier had set the NFL season rushing record with 2,003 yards—to 49 yards on 15 carries. "Their defense is the best," Simpson said afterward. Meanwhile, the Steelers erupted for four touchdowns in the second quarter, including three by Harris, and breezed to a 32–14 victory.

That same weekend, Oakland defeated Miami in what Raiders coach John Madden referred to as "the best" playing "the best." That remarked irked Noll, who told his troops on Tuesday, as recalled by Russell, "Well, they're not the best. And neither one of them's going to the Super Bowl."

"Man, did he fire us up," Russell said. "Joe Greene leaped up and started talking it up. We were ready for them."

The host Raiders took a 10–3 lead into the fourth quarter of the AFC Championship Game. While Pittsburgh dominated the line—outrushing Oakland 224–29 in the game—Ken Stabler threw for 271 yards. But in the fourth quarter, it was all Steelers, as Harris ran for two touchdowns and Swann caught a TD pass. With their 24–13 victory, the Steelers were headed to their first-ever Super Bowl.

"We put it right here," Noll said after the game, pointing to his heart. Added the veteran Russell: "The personal satisfaction that I get from this is beyond belief."

Wide receiver Lynn Swann of the Pittsburgh Steelers finds open ground against the Cincinnati Bengals at Three Rivers Stadium. *Tony Tomsic / Getty Images*

Super Bowl IX: Steelers Reign at Tulane

As the Steelers prepared for Super Bowl IX in New Orleans, starting Steelers defensive end Dwight White lay in a hospital bed. Sick with pneumonia, he had lost 20 pounds. As 80,997 fans poured into dilapidated Tulane Stadium, on a chilly, windy afternoon, no one expected to see White on the sidelines. But there he was, in uniform, ready to take on the Minnesota Vikings. "It was too big a game to miss," he explained.

Steelers defensive coordinator George Perles expected to play White for only one series, yet "Mad Dog" wound up playing the entire game. In fact, in the first half, he accounted for all the points. As Vikings quarterback Fran Tarkenton retreated into his own end zone to retrieve a fumble, White jumped on him for a safety.

While controlling the line of scrimmage, the Steelers took a 2–0 lead into the locker room. "Chuck told us at halftime to keep doing what we're doing and we'd win," center Ray Mansfield said, and they did.

The Steelers moved ahead 9–0 in the third quarter on a nine-yard rushing touchdown by Franco Harris. After Minnesota's Terry Brown recovered a blocked Bobby Walden punt for a touchdown in the fourth period, Larry Brown answered with a 30-yard reception on third down and, later in the drive, a four-yard touchdown catch thrown by Bradshaw. Pittsburgh prevailed 16–6.

While the Steelers amassed 333 yards against Minnesota's "Purple People Eaters" defense, the Vikings mustered just 119 yards, including 17 rushing yards on 21 carries. Franco Harris rumbled for 158 yards to earn the Super Bowl MVP Award.

Afterward, 42 years' worth of tears were shed as Art Rooney, Sr., accepted the Lombardi Trophy from Commissioner Pete Rozelle. Always humble, Rooney deflected the attention. "I didn't want to accept the trophy," he said. "Dan Rooney and Chuck Noll deserved it. I guess they just wanted me to be a big shot for a day."

Terry Bradshaw looks downfield at Tulane Stadium in New Orleans as the Steelers thwarted Minnesota's "Purple People Eater" defense in a 16-6 victory during Super Bowl IX. *Sylvia Allen / Getty Images*

The Steel Curtain

When Dwight White first met Ernie Holmes at a reception for Steelers rookies in 1971, he walked up to shake his hand. But Holmes was not about to make friends. "Yeah, fat boy," he told White, as reported in *The Ones Who Hit the Hardest*, "you know you're going to have to leave here. There's not room for more than one of us here."

Holmes was half right, as he didn't make the team in 1971. However, Ernie returned in '72 and found a home, along with White, on the defensive line. Together with 1969 draftees Joe Greene and L. C. Greenwood, they formed the "Steel Curtain," a barrier that opponents found impenetrable in the 1970s. Defensive ends "Mad Dog" White and L. C. "Hollywood Bags" Greenwood anchored the line. Tackles "Mean" Joe Greene and "Fats" Holmes clogged the middle.

"The four of us together had a great time," Greenwood said. "We didn't care who we played against. The better they were, the better we reacted against them. We were in sync. We had goals and objectives. We knew what we wanted to do—and what we had to do."

From 1973 to '79, Pittsburgh's defense ranked among the NFL's top four in yards against six times, leading in that category in 1974 and '76. In four seasons, they gave up no more than six rushing touchdowns. And in 1976, they allowed only one rushing TD all season.

The Steel Curtain was greater than the sum of its parts, but the parts were extraordinary on their own. Holmes, the right defensive tackle, arrived in 1971 with a crazed desire to succeed. He already had two kids he needed to support, and, as he once told *Time* magazine, "there's something pounding in the back of my head." "He had a look that was really scary," teammate Mike Wagner said in *The Ones Who Hit the Hardest*. "I think he wanted to beat people to death—within the rules of the game." Holmes was named second-team all-conference in 1975.

Greenwood, the oldest of nine children from severely segregated Canton, Mississippi, lined up at left defensive end. "L. C.," he told author Roy Blount, stood for "Lover Cool," but he later said that the initials didn't stand for anything.

First-team All-Pro in 1974 and '75 and a six-time Pro Bowler, Greenwood had flair for the dramatic. Known for his gold hightops, he unofficially recorded 73 ½ sacks. He deflected three Fran Tarkenton passes in Super Bowl IX and sacked Roger Staubach three times in the following year's Super Bowl.

White earned his nickname because of his intensity, and he often said that playing on the defensive line was like having "a dog's life." He recorded 33 ½ regular-season and playoff sacks from 1972 to '75, including three in Super Bowl X. "He always seemed to rise to the occasion when it counted most and added an element of toughness that was synonymous with our teams of the 1970s," said Art Rooney II.

Considering his interior position, and that he was often double-teamed, Greene didn't put up the gaudiest defensive statistics. "The kind of role I play is like an offensive lineman; doing a good job but not being noticed," he said. "I feel sorry for myself sometimes. But as long as the end result is there, I can dig it." Greene had plenty of accolades. He was named to 11 straight Pro Bowls, and he is the only Steel Curtain member in the Pro Football Hall of Fame.

Except for Greene, the Steel Curtain stars have left us. Holmes died in a car accident in 2008, and White passed away later that year after complications from back surgery. Greenwood died in 2013 from kidney failure.

Dwight White's words could serve as their epitaph. "You come to Pittsburgh, don't even try it," he once said. "You're going to lose the game, and we're going to dominate it. It was almost arrogance, but as Dizzy Dean said, 'It ain't braggin' if you can do it.' And we did it."

The *Time* article on the Steel Curtain opens with an anecdote about Ernie Holmes killing a calf to use the meat for his birthday party. Holmes said he knocked the animal into a fence and then shot him with a rifle. *MVP Books Collection*

Above: The vaunted Steel Curtain converges on the New England offensive line during a 30-27 Steelers victory over the Patriots. *Tony Tomsic / Getty Images*

Below: Still today fans pay tribute to their Steel Curtain heroes (left to right): Dwight White, Ernie Holmes, Joe Greene, and L. C. Greenwood. *George Gojkovich/Getty Images*

1,000-Yard Man: Franco Harris

When he toiled for Penn State, Franco Harris wasn't the best player in the backfield; he was largely a blocking back for All-American Lydell Mitchell. Nor was he the best college player in his own family; his brother Pete would become an All-American safety at PSU. Yet when Franco Harris retired after the 1984 season, he was the most prolific running back in NFL history. His 13,676 rushing yards, including the postseason, were 44 more than Walter Payton's combined total.

The Steelers took Harris with the 13th overall pick in the 1972 draft on the recommendation of Penn State coach Joe Paterno. "Not many people are aware of it," Paterno said, "but Harris can run the 40 in 4.5 seconds. That's terrific speed for a big man." So the Steelers chose Franco, but not without

criticism. Many would have preferred Mitchell, especially after Harris's mediocre preseason and awful start to his rookie year.

Harris was so lousy after his first two games that "I felt like chucking the whole thing," he said in *Super Steelers*. In the next two and a half games, he carried only three times. But in the second half of that fifth game, against Houston, Franco found redemption. "I kept telling myself, 'Give it everything you've got on every play, no matter what,'" he said in *Super Steelers*. In 13 carries that half, Franco rushed for 115 yards and scored the first of his 100 career regular-season touchdowns. "Boy, was I happy," he said.

Harris strung together six 100-yard rushing games in 1972 and became the fourth NFL rookie ever to rush for 1,000 yards.

Franco Harris powers past Colts defenders late in his career with the Pittsburgh Steelers. *Getty Images*

A Pro Bowl selection in each of his first nine seasons, Franco became the first NFL runner with eight 1,000-yard rushing campaigns. His season bests included 5.6 yards per carry in '72, 1,246 rushing yards in '75, and 14 rushing TDs in '76.

Besides his 4.5 speed and quick feet, Harris was a huge running back for his time—6-foot-2, 230 pounds. Like so many other players on the Steelers, Franco was that much smarter than his opponents. "I had vision, anticipation," he said. "My strong suit was reading. I could read certain situations quickly. I could see a guy flinch and know what was going to develop."

Though criticized for preferring to run out of bounds rather than lowering his shoulder for more yards, Franco responded that he was more valuable if he were healthy. He was healthy enough to compete in 19 playoff games, setting NFL postseason records with 17 touchdowns and 1,556 yards, including 158 in an MVP performance in Super Bowl IX.

Harris left Pittsburgh in a contract dispute following the 1983 season, and he retired after a year with Seattle. Joe Greene remembered Franco as "the single most important guy, who got us that rough first down, who kept the ball when we needed it, the guy the team rallied around."

Franco's Italian Army

As late as 1967, when Franco Harris attended high school in New Jersey, racially mixed marriage was outlawed in 16 states. Yet the vast majority of Steelers fans could not have cared less that Franco was half Italian, half African American. In fact, a group of fans embraced his Italian heritage, calling themselves Franco's Italian Army.

Franco's mother, Gina, had come directly from Italy. She had met Cadillac "Cad" Harris, a U.S. Army medic, during World War II. Franco's Italian Army, a group of about 20 fans who sat together at Three Rivers Stadium, embraced Harris's Italian heritage. Led by burly "five-star general" Tony Stagno, the Army wore battle helmets to the games and waved the Italian flag. Four-star general Al Vento operated a pizzeria.

Harris became buddies with the Army troops, accompanying them to hospitals and schools for children with disabilities. The highlight came when the Army and Franco met Frank Sinatra before a practice. As Myron Cope recalled in *Double Yoi!*, Stagno and Vento placed a one-star helmet on Sinatra's head and gave him a welcoming kiss. "It was like kissing God," Stagno told his wife.

Enlistees in Franco's army. *Heinz Kluetmeier/Sports Illustrated/Getty Images*

Game-by-Game

9/21   **W,** 37–0,
at San Diego Chargers

9/28   **L,** 21–30,
vs. Buffalo Bills

10/5   **W,** 42–6,
at Cleveland Browns

10/12   **W,** 20–9,
vs. Denver Broncos

10/19   **W,** 34–3,
vs. Chicago Bears

10/26   **W,** 16–13,
at Green Bay Packers

11/2   **W,** 30–24,
at Cincinnati Bengals

11/9   **W,** 24–17,
vs. Houston Oilers

11/16   **W,** 28–3,
vs. Kansas City Chiefs

11/24   **W,** 32–9,
at Houston Oilers

11/30   **W,** 20–7,
at New York Jets

12/7   **W,** 31–17,
vs. Cleveland Browns

12/13   **W,** 35–14,
vs. Cincinnati Bengals

12/20   **L,** 3–10,
at L.A. Rams

Playoffs

12/27   **W,** 28–10,
vs. Baltimore Colts

1/4   **W,** 16–10,
vs. Oakland Raiders

1/18   **Super Bowl:** W, 21–17,
vs. Dallas Cowboys

Team Scoring

373 points scored

162 points allowed

PITTSBURGH POWERHOUSE

Steelers Dominate on Both Sides of the Ball

While Steelers fans were still riding the high of Pittsburgh's Super Bowl IX victory, a secular passion play unfolded in the offseason. Officials of the World Football League, which had debuted in 1974, made tempting offers to members of the Steel Curtain defensive line. Joe Greene rejected their blood money, proclaiming, "I'm not going anywhere. I'm a Steeler." L. C. Greenwood gave into temptation and signed a contract, but he eventually succumbed to remorse and begged out of the deal.

While the WFL folded in the middle of the 1975 season, Pittsburgh remained steel tough. Franco Harris set a Steelers record, and finished second in the NFL, with 1,246 rushing yards. Then there was Rocky Bleier, an enormous fan favorite. The undersized Notre Dame alum had been chosen in the 16th round in 1968 as a sentimental pick of Art Rooney; both were Irish and had grown up above a saloon. Despite taking a bullet in his left leg and shrapnel in his right foot in Vietnam, Bleier returned to the Steelers in 1971 and became an outstanding blocking back. In '75, he rushed for 528 yards.

The 1975 season saw the emergence of receivers Lynn Swann (49 catches) and John Stallworth (21.2 yards per catch). Their presence helped Terry Bradshaw finish fourth in the NFL in passer rating (88.0), his first appearance in the top 10. For the first time in team history, the Steelers were the complete package on offense. In an interview with NBC's *Sports Machine*, Bradshaw remembered "the thrill of taking that snap with those two great receivers that I had, and those two great running backs, and big hogs up front of me, and knowing that those boys over there

[defenders] were scared to death. Heh heh heh! God, I loved that!"

Opposing offenses were even more panicky. The 1975 Steelers sent *eight* defensive players to the Pro Bowl, including linemen Greene and Greenwood, linebackers Jack Ham, Jack Lambert, and Andy Russell, and three members of the increasingly respected secondary: Mike Wagner, Glen Edwards, and Mel Blount, who led the NFL with 11 interceptions.

Despite a Week 2 loss to Buffalo, Pittsburgh dominated in its first four wins, prevailing by a combined score of 133–18. From October 5 to December 13, the Steelers didn't lose, capping their 11-game winning streak with a 35–14 rout of a Bengals team that at the time was 10–2. Pittsburgh finished at 12–2 with the best point differential (plus-211) in the league.

On December 27, the Steelers gave their city a belated Christmas present with 28–10 playoff thumping of Baltimore. The Colts averaged 2.0 yards per rush, and their quarterbacks completed just eight passes while throwing two interceptions and being sacked five times. Their 100 yards through the air was nearly matched by Andy Russell's 93-yard fumble return for a fourth-quarter touchdown, which drove the home crowd into a frenzy.

A week later, the Steelers hosted the rival Raiders in what was dubbed the "Ice Bowl." During a sleet storm the night before, the grounds crew covered the field with a tarp and blew hot air under it so that the field wouldn't freeze. However, strong winds split the tarp and snow melted on the AstroTurf, creating a sheet of ice by game time—which the Raiders erroneously accused the Steelers of creating on purpose.

Despite the slick surface, a wind-chill factor below zero, and two great defenses, the two teams combined for 653 yards. The field apparently wasn't as slippery as the ball; the teams combined for 12 turnovers, with the ever-alert Lambert grabbing three fumbles. The Steelers led 3–0 entering the fourth quarter when Harris raced 25 yards for a score. After Oakland responded with a touchdown, Bradshaw connected with Stallworth for a 20-yard touchdown pass. Pittsburgh prevailed 16–10.

Despite the victory, the lasting image of the game was George Atkinson's vicious hit on Swann, which knocked him unconscious. As the receiver lay motionless, Joe Greene picked him up and carried him off the field. Doctors wouldn't allow Greene to do that today. Nor would Swann, who suffered a serious concussion, be allowed to play two weeks later in the Super Bowl. But he did.

Opposite: Franco Harris scorched the Colts with 153 yards rushing and one touchdown in Pittsburgh's 28–10 win over Baltimore in the opening round of the 1975 playoffs. *AP Images*

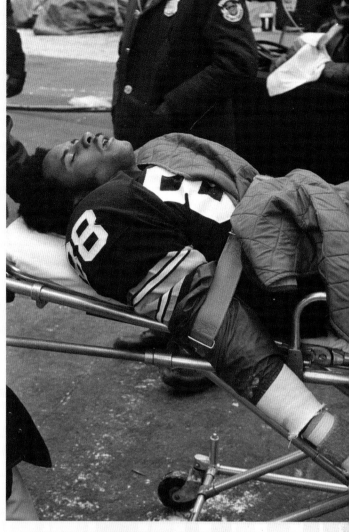

After Joe Greene carried him to the sideline in the AFC Championship Game, an unconscious Lynn Swann lay on a stretcher before being carted off the field. *George Gojkovich/Getty Images*

Below: The local Iron City Beer honored the 1975 championship team with special cans. *MVP Books Collection*

The Steelers, 1975 Super Bowl Champs

Super Bowl X: Swann Song

Super Bowl X in Miami was a dream matchup. The Dallas Cowboys were billed as "America's Team," led by revered coach Tom Landry, clean-cut quarterback Roger Staubach, and a sophisticated "flex" defense. The Steelers were working-class heroes. Or as John Stallworth described it in *Steel Dynasty*, "We were very much a punch-you-in-the-mouth football team, and they were finesse."

Wearing bicentennial patches on their sleeves, the NFL's two most popular teams squared off on a cool afternoon in the Orange Bowl. Dallas scored first on a 29-yard pass from Staubach to Drew Pearson, but Terry Bradshaw responded with a seven-yard TD toss to tight end Randy Grossman. "Early in the game, we had run on that play to give them a look at it," Grossman said afterward. "Then we threw the pass."

Dallas went up 10–7 before Lynn Swann made one of the most memorable catches in Super Bowl history. Playing two weeks after being knocked unconscious, Swann skied for a long bomb thrown by Bradshaw. While draped by cornerback Mark Washington, Swann tipped the ball in the air and then caught it as he fell—an extraordinary display of concentration and body control from the ballet-trained receiver.

The play led to a 36-yard field goal attempt by Roy Gerela, who muffed it. When Dallas safety Cliff Harris gave Gerela a taunting pat on the helmet, an enraged Jack Lambert picked up Harris and dumped him. "Lambert was the guy who sparked us," Joe Greene said.

The second half belonged to Pittsburgh. Reggie Harrison blocked a punt for a safety, cutting the deficit to 10–9. Gerela booted two short field goals, and Swann caught a howitzer of a pass from Bradshaw for a 64-yard touchdown. Staubach, aka "Captain Comeback," threw a late touchdown pass to pull Dallas within four, 21–10. His "Hail Mary" toss on the final play was batted away by Mike Wagner.

Swann, who should not have played in the game, finished with four catches for 161 yards. He was named the Super Bowl MVP.

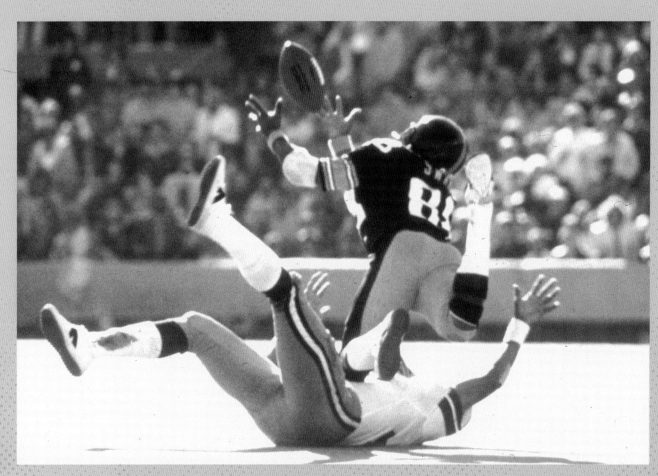

Lynn Swann makes his legendary balletic catch while tumbling over Cowboys cornerback Mark Washington. *AP Images*

Profile in Courage:
Rocky Bleier

Rocky Bleier played halfback for Notre Dame, and in 1968 he made the Steelers as a 16th-round pick. Yet such status didn't earn him a deferment from the military draft. On August 20, 1969, Bleier and fellow soldiers were ambushed in a rice paddy in Vietnam. He was shot in his left thigh, then wounded and knocked unconscious by a grenade. More than a hundred pieces of shrapnel were embedded in his skin. He recovered, but doctors said he would never play football again.

While recovering in a Tokyo hospital, Bleier received a postcard. "Rock—the team's not doing well. We need you. Art Rooney."

This real-life Rocky pushed himself to get back on the field, lifting weights and running two, three times a day. In 1971, he returned to training camp, where he was undersized and plagued by shrapnel in his foot. Recalled Jack Ham: "I said to myself, 'Geez, this guy'll never play.'"

Coach Chuck Noll was ready to cut Bleier, but the Rooneys—inspired by Bleier's efforts—paid for medical care to get him healthy. Rocky did the rest, muscling up and actually improving his 40-yard dash time from his rookie year. From there, Bleier became a poster boy for courage and a hero across the land.

The Rock performed on special teams until 1974, when he served as an outstanding blocking back and a smart, effective runner. In 1976, in the season finale against Houston, Bleier rushed for 107 yards to eclipse 1,000 for the season. He retired with four Super Bowl rings and 3,865 rushing yards—at the time, the fourth most in Pittsburgh history. His book, *Fighting Back: The Rocky Bleier Story*, was made into a television movie in 1980, his final year with the Steelers.

Rocky Bleier was a hard-nosed running back on the field from 1968 to 1980, despite missing two and half seasons to military service during the Vietnam War. *MVP Books Collection*

Game-by-Game

9/12	**L**, 28–31,	at Oakland Raiders
9/19	**W**, 31–14,	vs. Cleveland Browns
9/26	**L**, 27–30,	vs. New England Patriots
10/4	**L**, 6–17,	at Minnesota Vikings
10/10	**L**, 16–18,	at Cleveland Browns
10/17	**W**, 23–6,	vs. Cincinnati Bengals
10/24	**W**, 27–0,	at New York Giants
10/31	**W**, 23–0,	vs. San Diego Chargers
11/7	**W**, 45–0,	at Kansas City Chiefs
11/14	**W**, 14–3,	vs. Miami Dolphins
11/21	**W**, 32–16,	vs. Houston Oilers
11/28	**W**, 7–3,	at Cincinnati Bengals
12/5	**W**, 42–0,	vs. Tampa Bay Buccaneers
12/11	**W**, 21–0,	at Houston Oilers

Playoffs

12/19	**W**, 40–14,	at Baltimore Colts
12/26	**L**, 7–24,	at Oakland Raiders

Team Scoring

342 points scored
138 points allowed

CHEAP SHOTS

Swann, Bradshaw Are Victims, but Steelers D Rises Up

In 1976, teams finally found a way to beat the Steelers: play dirty.

Eight months after Oakland's George Atkinson knocked Lynn Swann unconscious in the AFC Championship Game, the Steelers opened the new season in Oakland. Incredibly, as Franco Harris ran with the ball down the left sideline, Atkinson—far away from the play—slammed his forearm against the back of Swann's head, again knocking him unconscious. With their star receiver out for the entire second half, the Steelers lost 31–28.

After the game, Chuck Noll told reporters, "You have a criminal element in all aspects of society. Apparently we have it in the NFL, too." NFL Commissioner Pete Rozelle would fine Atkinson $1,500—and Noll $1,000 for his comment.

The Atkinson blow wasn't the only cheap shot against the Steelers. In Week 5, Cleveland's Joe "Turkey" Jones—after the whistle—flipped Terry Bradshaw and spiked his head into the turf. The Browns rallied to win 18–16, dropping Pittsburgh to 1–4, and Bradshaw would miss the next six games. Left with a rookie quarterback in Mike Kruczek, the coaching staff, running game, and defense would have to step up big-time for the Steelers to make the playoffs. Boy, did they ever!

Not only did Harris top 1,000 yards rushing, but so did underdog hero Rocky Bleier. Meanwhile, the defense enjoyed, arguably, the greatest nine-game stretch in the history of the league. Stunningly, they allowed only 28 points overall during the streak (all victories) while shutting out the Giants, Chargers, and Chiefs in succession. They then closed the season by blanking Tampa Bay and Houston. The Buccaneers tallied just 11 net passing yards, and the Oilers amassed more punts than first downs. On the year, Pittsburgh led the NFL in fewest points (138), yards (3,323), and rushing yards (1,457) allowed.

The Steelers finished at 10–4, tied atop the AFC Central with Cincinnati, but they won the division due to their two victories over the Bengals. In the playoff opener at Baltimore, the Steelers beat the Colts so badly (40–14) that they wound up saving lives. Late in the game, with fans having already left the blowout at Memorial Stadium, a small plane crashed into the stands. No one was hurt, not even the pilot.

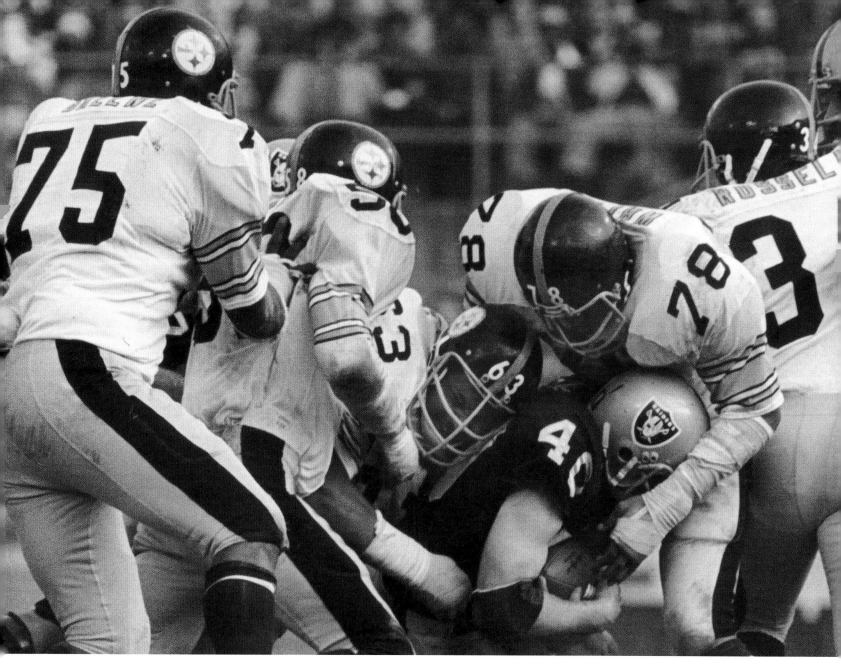

Two people who were injured during the game were Harris and Bleier, who wouldn't play in the AFC Championship Game the next week—at Oakland. Left only with backup running backs Frenchy Fuqua (who played hurt) and Reggie Harrison, Noll restructured his offense into a one-back set. Though the Steelers outgained Oakland 237 yards to 220, the "Black Menace" prevailed 24–7.

The Raiders went on to defeat Minnesota in the Super Bowl to finish at 16–1, but apparently that wasn't enough to satisfy them. Because of the "criminal" quote that Noll had made in Week 1, Atkinson sued Noll for $2 million for slander and defamation of character—a lawsuit that Dan Rooney believed was bankrolled by Raiders owner Al Davis. The suit went to trial in the summer of 1977, just in time to disrupt Noll's training camp. After two weeks of courtroom banter, a jury found the coach not liable. "I'm pleased," Noll said. "It has been the most depressing experience of my life, but I'm happy."

Pittsburgh fans couldn't wait until September 25, when the Steelers would face the Raiders again—this time in Pittsburgh.

Above: Oakland fullback Pete Banaszak is engulfed by Pittsburgh's defensive during Oakland's 24–7 victory in the 1976 AFC Championship Game.
Arthur Anderson/Getty Images

Opposite: Linebacker Jack Lambert looks on from the sidelines in a year of dirty plays, slander, and rising tempers. Lambert was named 1976 Associated Press Defensive Player of the Year.
Getty Images

9–5 1st place

Game-by-Game

9/19	**W, 27–0,**	vs. San Francisco 49ers
9/25	**L, 7–16,**	vs. Oakland Raiders
10/2	**W, 28–14,**	at Cleveland Browns
10/9	**L, 10–27,**	at Houston Oilers
10/17	**W, 20–14,**	vs. Cincinnati Bengals
10/23	**W, 27–10,**	vs. Houston Oilers
10/30	**L, 21–31,**	at Baltimore Colts
11/6	**L, 7–21,**	at Denver Broncos
11/13	**W, 35–31,**	vs. Cleveland Browns
11/20	**W, 28–13,**	vs. Dallas Cowboys
11/27	**W, 23–20,**	at New York Jets
12/4	**W, 30–20,**	vs. Seattle Seahawks
12/10	**L, 10–17,**	at Cincinnati Bengals
12/18	**W, 10–9,**	at San Diego Chargers

Playoffs

12/24	**L, 21–34,**	at Denver Broncos

Team Scoring

283 points scored
243 points allowed

Slip-Sliding Away

Distractions, Discontent, Turnovers Mar Season

The Steelers, it seemed, were coming unglued. Those who had envisioned a Steelers dynasty were disheartened by the 1977 training camp holdout of All-Pro Jack Lambert. The Atkinson lawsuit "certainly didn't help" matters either, according to Dan Rooney. Mel Blount, who was cast in a bad light by Noll's legal team during the trial, threatened to quit the Steelers and sue Noll. Lambert didn't report to the Steelers until September 1, and Blount was AWOL for eight weeks.

Pittsburgh opened the season with a 27–0 rout of San Francisco on *Monday Night Football*. Despite their hunger for vengeance against Oakland, the Steelers lost 16–7 to their archrival the following week, as they turned it over five times. Terry Bradshaw broke his wrist on October 2 against Houston, and though he didn't miss a start, he played with a cast. That likely contributed to the team's preponderance of turnovers—24 over a four-game stretch in October and 49 during the season (second most in the NFL).

Franco Harris finished fourth in the league in rushing (1,162 yards), and Bradshaw set a career high with 2,523 passing yards—as new NFL rules were put in place that favored the passing game. Due to all the discontent and upheaval on the Steelers' defense—including brief midseason walkouts by safeties Glen Edwards and Jimmy Allen—as well as the massive amount of turnovers, Pittsburgh allowed 243 points on the season. Sixteen teams did better.

The Steelers did win the AFC Central with a 9–5 record, but they got trounced 34–21 by a 12–2 Denver team in their opening playoff game on Christmas Eve. Four more turnovers, including three Bradshaw interceptions, contributed to the loss.

As if the slander lawsuit wasn't enough, Chuck Noll broke his elbow in 1977. Nevertheless, he was still able to lead the Steelers to the playoffs. *AP Images*

SAME OLD (WINNING) STEELERS

Pittsburgh Goes 14–2, Breezes to Super Bowl

In Week 4 of the 1978 season, with the Steelers and Browns tied at 9–9 in overtime, Chuck Noll took a walk on the wild side. Pittsburgh had the ball at Cleveland's 37 when Terry Bradshaw announced the next play: Fake 84 Reverse Gadget Pass. Bradshaw handed off to Rocky Bleier, who handed off to Lynn Swann. Figuring that was about as tricky as Noll would get, the Browns zeroed in on Swann. But then Lynn pitched the ball back to Bradshaw, who fired a walk-off touchdown pass to tight end Bennie Cunningham.

As he entered a room full of reporters after the game, Noll was grinning ear to ear. "It was getting so dull around here," the coach explained, "we figured we had to give somebody something to write about except up the middle."

After their tension-filled, disappointing 1977 campaign, the Steelers were their old selves again in '78. Harmony returned, Bradshaw had the offense clicking on all cylinders (356 points), and the defense once again rose to prominence, leading the NFL in fewest points allowed (195). In the first year of the 16-game schedule, Pittsburgh won 14 games.

The Steelers started the season at 7–0, winning all but the Browns game by at least 11 points. Though they dropped the next battle to Houston on a Monday night, they would avenge the loss to the Oilers not once but twice. Pittsburgh's other defeat came in L.A. against the Rams, but the Steel Curtain defense followed with 7–6, 24–7, and 13–3 performances.

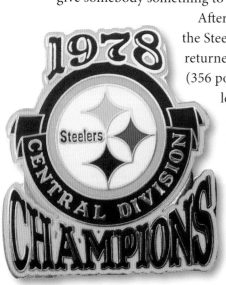

Pittsburgh captured its seventh consecutive Central Division title with a then-franchise-record 14 wins in 1978. *MVP Books Collection*

In the season finale, Pittsburgh led at Denver 21–0 before quarterback Norris Weese led a ferocious comeback. The Broncos pulled to within 21–17 when their final drive stalled near the Steelers' goal line. "We had 'em all the way, huh, coach?" Bradshaw joked.

The fun-loving QB had the best year of his career, earning first-team All-Pro honors for the first and only time and garnering NFL MVP kudos from the Associated Press. Swann and John Stallworth were a dynamic receiving duo, combining for 102 receptions and 20 touchdown catches. Franco Harris grinded out his sixth 1,000-yard rushing season.

If every team had sent as many players to the Pro Bowl as the Steelers did in January 1979, it would have been a 140-on-140 battle. Pittsburgh's 10 representatives that year included Bradshaw, Swann, Harris, center Mike Webster,

Game-by-Game

9/3	**W, 28–17,** at Buffalo Bills	
9/10	**W, 21–10,** vs. Seattle Seahawks	
9/17	**W, 28–3,** at Cincinnati Bengals	
9/24	**W, 15–9 (OT),** vs. Cleveland Browns	
10/1	**W, 28–17,** at New York Jets	
10/8	**W, 31–7,** vs. Atlanta Falcons	
10/15	**W, 34–14,** at Cleveland Browns	
10/23	**L, 17–24,** vs. Houston Oilers	
10/29	**W, 27–24,** vs. Kansas City Chiefs	
11/5	**W, 20–14,** vs. New Orleans Saints	
11/12	**L, 7–10,** at L.A. Rams	
11/19	**W, 7–6,** vs. Cincinnati Bengals	
11/27	**W, 24–7,** at San Francisco 49ers	
12/3	**W, 13–3,** at Houston Oilers	
12/9	**W, 35–13,** vs. Baltimore Colts	
12/16	**W, 21–17,** at Denver Broncos	

Playoffs

12/30	**W, 33–10,** vs. Denver Broncos
1/7	**W, 34–5,** vs. Houston Oilers
1/21	**Super Bowl:** W, 35–31, vs. Dallas Cowboys

Team Scoring

356 points scored
195 points allowed

and, on defense, Joe Greene, L. C. Greenwood, Jack Lambert, Jack Ham, Mel Blount, and emerging strong safety Donnie Shell.

Despite their season-ending loss to Pittsburgh, the Broncos won the AFC West with a 10–6 record and faced the Steelers in a divisional playoff game. Their strategy of double-teaming Swann backfired, as Stallworth burned cornerback Steve Foley to the tune of 10 catches for 156 yards. Pittsburgh rolled up a 19–10 halftime lead and cruised to a 33–10 victory. "I wasn't going to beat my head against the wall trying to force it to Swann," Bradshaw said afterward.

The next week, the Steelers hosted Houston in cold, rainy, icy weather. Used to warm temperatures and the comforts of the Astrodome, the Oilers handled the wintry conditions as badly as Texan drivers on snowy roads. They fumbled the ball four times, and quarterback Dan Pastorini fired five interceptions. The Steelers turned it over five times themselves, but otherwise it was a typical day at the office, with Swann, Stallworth, Harris, and Bleier scoring touchdowns. Pittsburgh prevailed 34–5. "They had to be frustrated," Lambert said about the Oilers afterward, "but I really don't feel too bad for them."

Both teams had a chance to warm up and dry out. The Oilers were headed back to Houston, and the Steelers were off to Miami for their third Super Bowl in four years.

Defensive lineman Dwight White of the Pittsburgh Steelers takes a breather after sacking quarterback Dan Pastorini of the Houston Oilers during a Monday Night Football game at Three Rivers Stadium on November 23, 1978, in Pittsburgh, Pennsylvania. *George Gojkovich / Getty Images*

Super Bowl XIII:
Bradshaw's Revenge

Early in his career, as in childhood, mean-spirited people liked poking fun at Terry Bradshaw's intelligence. Two Super Bowl victories seemed to have ended the criticism, but Dallas linebacker Thomas "Hollywood" Henderson decided to be cute at the quarterback's expense prior to Super Bowl XIII. Henderson announced that Bradshaw couldn't spell *cat* if you spotted him the *c* and the *t*.

In the first half against the Cowboys, Bradshaw responded to Henderson's verbal cheap shot by throwing three touchdown passes, including 28- and 75-yard heaves to John Stallworth. By halftime, he had broken Bart Starr's Super Bowl game record of 250 passing yards (he'd finish with 318) while leading Pittsburgh to a 21–14 lead.

Fortune shone on the Steelers throughout the day. Perhaps the Terrible Towel had something to do with it. Center Mike Webster wore the good-luck charm during the game, allowing Bradshaw to wipe its magic on its hands. The Steelers lucked out in the third quarter, when Cowboys tight end Jackie Smith—who had come out of retirement—dropped an easy catch in the end zone, forcing Dallas to settle for a field goal.

With Pittsburgh leading 21–17 early in the fourth quarter, the football gods taught Henderson a lesson. Officials called pass interference on Cowboys cornerback Benny Barnes for falling on Swann, missing the fact that Swann had caused Barnes to tumble. Henderson followed by sacking Bradshaw after a whistle had blown the play dead—a physical cheap shot that ticked off Franco Harris. He jawed at Henderson before shutting him up for good on the next play, a 22-yard touchdown run.

"I've never seen him run so hard . . . ," Bradshaw said. "He'd run through a brick wall if the brick wall would have kept him out of the end zone."

Bradshaw's fourth touchdown pass put Pittsburgh up 35–17. Dallas quarterback Roger Staubach fired two late scoring passes to cut the deficit to 35–31—making Smith's earlier drop all that more critical. When Rocky Bleier smothered the late onside kick, the game was effectively over. All Bradshaw had to do was sit on the ball and learn how to spell S-U-P-E-R B-O-W-L M-V-P.

Terry Bradshaw led the Steelers to their third Super Bowl championship of the decade while passing for 318 yards and four touchdowns. *Focus on Sports/Getty Images*

Jacked Up at Linebacker

Jack Lambert summed up the basic difference between him and fellow All-Pro Steelers linebacker Jack Ham. "Jack Ham plays and never says a word," Lambert told *The Pittsburgh Press*. "I yell and scream a lot."

Neither Jack was especially big. Though he stood 6-foot-4, Lambert was rail-thin at 220 pounds. Steelers radio announcer Bill Hillgrove recalled when the Kent State graduate was drafted by Pittsburgh in 1974: "One of the Steelers administrative people looked at him and said, 'Who's that?' And they said, 'That's our number-two pick.' And he goes, 'Whoop, another wasted pick.'"

Both the only things "wasted" were opposing ball carriers, as Lambert wreaked havoc on NFL gridirons for 11 seasons. The middle linebacker intimidated opponents with the "Lambert look": a sauntering gait, crazed eyes, a Hulk Hogan-style blond mustache, and missing top teeth. "I turned around and I looked at the guy and I realized . . . he didn't have any teeth up front," said Eagles cornerback Herm Edwards. "I said, 'Wow! That guy's really mean!'"

While fans reveled in Lambert's gruesome gaze and bone-jarring hits, his brethren understood his true value to the team. Chuck Noll called Lambert the most focused player he had ever coached. Fellow linebacker Andy Russell said that Lambert "killed you with his precision. He was a great anticipator. Read his keys. Took angles away from blockers. Never made a mistake."

Lambert was a man who used football to get his ya-yas out. Browns coach Sam Rutigliano recalled when Lambert came to visit Cleveland quarterback Brian Sipe in the locker room after knocking him out of the game with a hard hit. "Once the game was over . . . Jack was a very private person with a tremendous sensitivity," Rutigliano wrote in *Pressure*.

Lambert, a six-time first-team All-Pro and the 1976 NFL Defensive Player of the Year, was one of the best pass-coverage linebackers of his era. So, too, was outside linebacker Jack Ham, also a six-time first-team All-Pro. Among linebackers, Ham ranks third in NFL history with 32 interceptions—four more than Lambert amassed.

Though just 6-foot-1 and 210 pounds, Ham was trained well at Penn State, aka "Linebacker U," and Pittsburgh drafted him in the second round in 1974. The Pro Football Hall of Fame states that Ham had "speed, intelligence," and an "exceptional ability to diagnose plays."

Russell would agree with that. "Jack Ham was a brilliant player," Russell said. "He didn't make any mistakes, knew the game, and anticipated well. Plus, he was an explosive talent, probably the fastest Steeler in five yards—an incredible explosion off the blocker. And he'd make it look easy. It was astounding how good he was. He was the best linebacker I ever saw."

Quarterbacks were among those who were force-fed a Ham slam-wich. Jack recorded 25 sacks (unofficial) along with 21 fumble recoveries and those 32 picks. In fact, his 53 takeaways set an NFL record for a non-defensive back.

Ham was enshrined in the Pro Football Hall of Fame in 1988, and Lambert joined him two years later. "If I could start my life all over again, I'd be a professional football player," Lambert proclaimed at his induction, "and you'd damn well better believe I'd be a Pittsburgh Steeler."

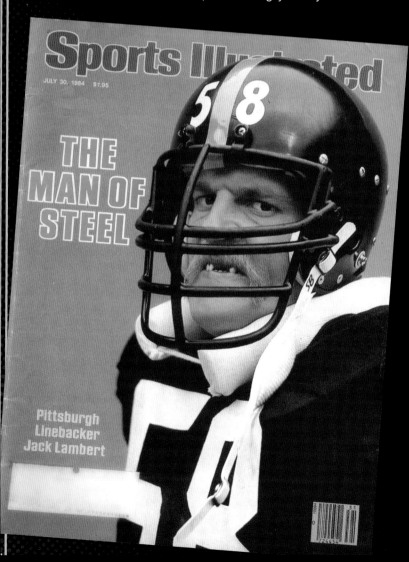

Sports Illustrated
JULY 30, 1984 $1.95
58
THE MAN OF STEEL
Pittsburgh Linebacker Jack Lambert

Despite this famous wildman look on the cover of *Sports Illustrated*, Chuck Noll called Jack Lambert the most focused player he had ever coached. *MVP Books Collection*

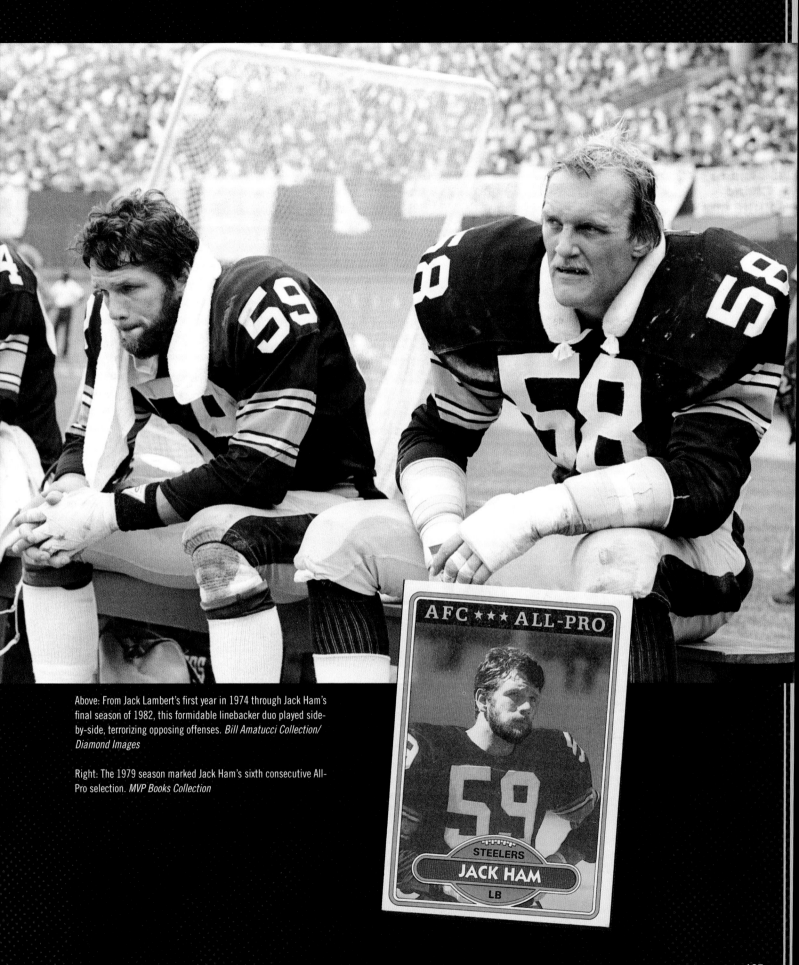

Above: From Jack Lambert's first year in 1974 through Jack Ham's final season of 1982, this formidable linebacker duo played side-by-side, terrorizing opposing offenses. *Bill Amatucci Collection/ Diamond Images*

Right: The 1979 season marked Jack Ham's sixth consecutive All-Pro selection. *MVP Books Collection*

AFC ★★★ ALL-PRO

STEELERS

JACK HAM

LB

1979

12–4   1st place

Game-by-Game

9/3	**W**, 16–13 (OT), at New England Patriots
9/9	**W**, 38–7, vs. Houston Oilers
9/16	**W**, 24–21, at St. Louis Cardinals
9/23	**W**, 17–13, vs. Baltimore Colts
9/30	**L**, 14–17, at Philadelphia Eagles
10/7	**W**, 51–35, at Cleveland Browns
10/14	**L**, 10–34, at Cincinnati Bengals
10/22	**W**, 42–7, vs. Denver Broncos
10/28	**W**, 14–3, vs. Dallas Cowboys
11/4	**W**, 38–7, vs. Washington Redskins
11/11	**W**, 30–3, at Kansas City Chiefs
11/18	**L**, 7–35, at San Diego Chargers
11/25	**W**, 33–30 (OT), vs. Cleveland Browns
12/2	**W**, 37–17, vs. Cincinnati Bengals
12/10	**L**, 17–20, at Houston Oilers
12/16	**W**, 28–0, vs. Buffalo Bills

Playoffs

12/30	**W**, 34–14, vs. Miami Dolphins
1/6	**W**, 27–13, vs. Houston Oilers
1/20	**Super Bowl:** W, 31–19, vs. L.A. Rams

Team Scoring

416 points scored
262 points allowed

GRAND OL' WARRIORS

Aging Steelers Power Their Way to AFC Title

The Steelers were exhausted. They had just battled to a 33–30 overtime victory over Cleveland on November 25, 1979, which didn't end until Matt "Radar" Bahr booted a short field goal with nine seconds left in the fifth period. In the locker room afterward, players who could barely move spoke in whispers.

"I feel like a zombie," said 35-year-old guard Sam Davis.

"I'm just so tired," said Franco Harris. "Some of us are going out to dinner, then I'm going home and go to bed."

It wasn't just the overtime game that made the Steelers more pooped than peppy. The core players of the Steelers dynasty were getting old. The stars from the legendary 1969–71 drafts—Joe Greene, L. C. Greenwood, Terry Bradshaw, Jack Ham, Dwight White, Ernie Holmes, and Mike Wagner—were in the latter stage of their careers. Harris was 29 years old, the same age that the then-NFL career rushing leader, Jim Brown, was when he retired.

Throughout the 1979 season, fans witnessed the beginning of the changing of the guard. Young backup Sidney Thornton rushed for 585 yards, approximately half of Franco's 1,186. Nevertheless, the core group still had the talent and desire to make another championship run. Jack Ham, Jack Lambert, Donnie Shell, Mike Webster, and John Stallworth all made first-team All-Pro, with Stallworth catching 70 passes for 1,183 yards. Five other Steelers made the Pro Bowl, including Terry Bradshaw, who threw for a Steelers-record 3,724 yards.

The Pittsburgh offense, in fact, was better than ever, leading the NFL with a team-record 416 points. The Steelers topped 500 yards in wins over Cleveland (51–35), Denver (42–7), and Washington (38–7), and in the OT thriller against the Browns, they amassed 606. Though just 4–4 on the road in 1979, the Steelers were a

In blustery conditions at Three Rivers Stadium, the Steelers held Houston's star running back, Earl Campbell (34), to 15 yards on 17 carries in Pittsburgh's 27–13 triumph in the AFC Championship Game. *AP Images*

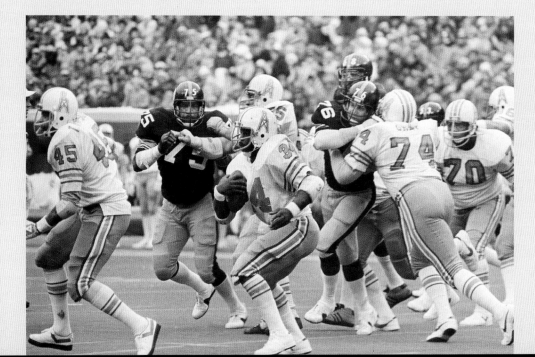

perfect 8–0 at home, and that bode well for a team that would play both of its AFC playoff games at Three Rivers.

The Pittsburgh Pirates had won the world title in 1979 while inspired by their "We Are Family" theme song. The Steelers were a tight-knit unit as well, and their Three Rivers fans were as rabid as those who had cheered the Pirates to victory over Baltimore in the World Series. In the opening playoff game, the Steelers blew the Dolphins out of the water, rolling up a 20–0 first-quarter lead and winning 34–14. Before that first period even ended, fans were already chanting, "We want Houston!"—Pittsburgh's next opponent in the AFC Championship Game.

The aging Steelers may have been exhausted, but they always rose to the occasion at this time of year. "In late December," said Dwight White, "when it's cold and people are playing hurt, you look at the guy's face in the huddle, and you see blood skeetin' out of his nose, and he's all whipped, and this guy's telling you, 'C'mon, babe, suck it up.' That's really what it's all about."

With a wind chill hovering around zero, the Steelers trounced the Oilers in the AFC title game 27–13. Bradshaw avenged an early 75-yard Vernon Perry interception return with second-quarter scoring passes to Bennie Cunningham and Stallworth. The defense held NFL rushing leader Earl Campbell to 15 yards on 17 carries. The Steelers were headed to the Super Bowl in Los Angeles, where they hoped to match the Pirates' recent feat. Said Lynn Swann, "We truly want to make Pittsburgh the 'City of Champions.'"

Steelers running back Sidney Thornton barrels into the end zone against Miami in Pittsburgh's first playoff game. The Steelers won 34–14 after holding the Dolphins to 25 rushing yards on 22 attempts. *AP Images*

Super Bowl XIV:
Lords of the Rings

Every team dreams of playing the Super Bowl in their hometown, and on January 20, 1980, the Los Angeles Rams got to do it. That afternoon, 103,985 fans—which set and remains a Super Bowl record—packed the Rose Bowl in the L.A. suburb of Pasadena.

The Rams may have had the home crowd support, but the Steelers were a better team. The Rams had snuck into the playoffs with a 9–7 record and were a 10-point underdog. Moreover, the Steelers had a special motivation. "We have an opportunity to do something that no one else has ever done," Lynn Swann said, "to win back-to-back Super Bowl titles a second time and to win the Super Bowl four times."

The first half was a back-and-forth battle that ended with a 13–10 Rams lead. One-yard touchdown runs by Cullen Bryant (L.A.) and Franco Harris were the only TDs prior to the Up With People halftime show. Both offenses opened the second half with touchdown drives. After

Bradshaw connected with Swann for a 47-yard scoring pass, Rams halfback Lawrence McCutchen completed a 24-yard touchdown toss to Ron B. Smith.

L.A. was leading 19–17 early in the fourth quarter when Bradshaw and Stallworth resurrected some Super Bowl magic. On third-and-eight, Bradshaw launched a bomb that Stallworth caught over his shoulder and turned into a 73-yard touchdown. When Rams quarterback Vince Ferragamo tried to answer, Jack Lambert picked him off at the Steelers' 32. A 45-yard pass to Stallworth followed by a 21-yard pass-interference penalty put the ball on the Rams' 1. Harris scored on third down, and Pittsburgh won 31–19.

Asked after the game if the Steelers were the greatest team in football history, Chuck Noll said, "I don't think I have to answer that. . . . I don't have to say it. The Steelers have proven themselves."

The Steelers became the first team, and to date the only one, to win four Super Bowls in a single decade.

John Stallworth burns the Rams for one of his two long fourth-quarter touchdown receptions—73 and 45 yards. *Focus on Sport/Getty Images*

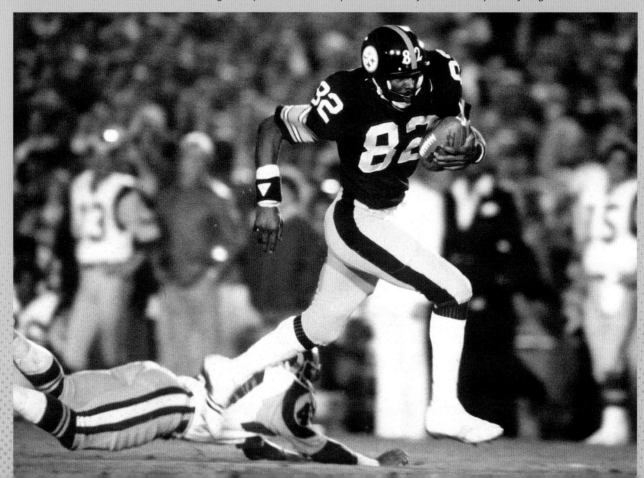

Hall of Fame Targets: Swann and Stallworth

While Lynn Swann's falling, tipped-ball catch in Super Bowl X became iconic, he made another Super Bowl grab against the Cowboys that was even more extraordinary. While racing downfield and toward the right sideline, Swann sailed high for a pass and caught the ball after it broke the out-of-bounds plane. Even though he snatched it in "foul" territory—and even though his body's momentum was headed out of bounds—Swann somehow reversed course in midair and landed with two feet inbounds.

A California state long jump champion in high school, Swann was known for his speed, hops, soft hands, and amazing grace, thanks to many years of dance classes as a youth. Though his career totals are unimpressive by modern standards (336 catches for 5,462 yards and 51 touchdowns), he frequently came up big in the postseason (48 grabs, 18.9 yards per catch). Swann was named to the NFL's All-Decade Team for the 1970s (first team) and was inducted into the Hall of Fame in 2001—in his 14th year of eligibility.

During his induction speech, Swann said he wouldn't be fully satisfied until he "could sit in that back row and John Stallworth is wearing a gold jacket making his speech."

Reared in segregated Huntsville, Alabama, Stallworth toiled in obscurity at Alabama A&M until the Steelers drafted him in 1974. Thanks in part to rules changes that opened up the passing game, Stallworth recorded three 1,000-yard seasons and set team records for receptions (537), receiving yards (8,723), and touchdown catches (74)—all of which lasted until the new millennium.

In comparing himself to Swann, Stallworth said: "Maybe I didn't do that with a lot of panache, but I got the job done. I was able to come up with the big catch when we needed the big catch."

Several of those big grabs came in Super Bowls XIII and XIV, when he made touchdown receptions of 28, 75, and 73 yards and caught another key pass for 45 yards. In 2002, he joined Swann in the Hall of Fame.

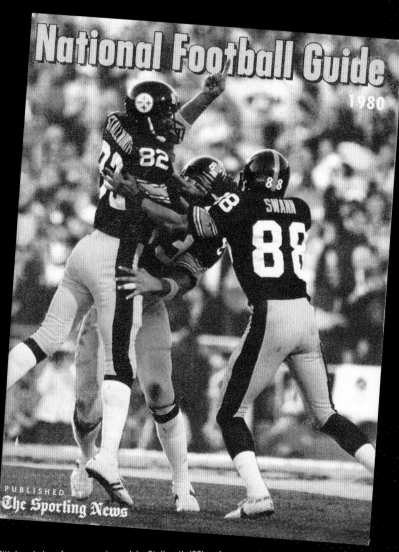

Pittsburgh duo of super receivers, John Stallworth (82) and Lynn Swann (88), appear on the cover of the *Sporting News'* 1980 season preview issue. *MVP Books Collection*

THE 1970s RECORD BOOK

Team Leaders

(**Boldface** indicates league leader)

Scoring Leaders (Points)

1970: John Fuqua, 54
1971: Roy Gerela, 78
1972: Roy Gerela, 119
1973: Roy Gerela, 123
1974: Roy Gerela, 93
1975: Roy Gerela, 95
1976: Franco Harris, 84
1977: Franco Harris, 66
1978: Roy Gerela, 80
1979: Matt Bahr, 104

Passing Leaders

(Completions / Attempts / Yards)

1970: Terry Bradshaw, 83 / 218 / 1,410
1971: Terry Bradshaw, 203 / 373 / 2,259
1972: Terry Bradshaw, 147 / 308 / 1,887
1973: Terry Bradshaw, 89 / 180 / 1,183
1974: Joe Gilliam, 96 / 212 / 1,274
1975: Terry Bradshaw, 165 / 286 / 2,055
1976: Terry Bradshaw, 92 / 192 / 1,177
1977: Terry Bradshaw, 162 / 314 / 2,523
1978: Terry Bradshaw, 207 / 368 / 2,915
1979: Terry Bradshaw, 259 / 472 / 3,724

Rushing Leaders

(Carries / Yards / TDs)

1970: John Fuqua, 138 / 691 / 7
1971: John Fuqua, 155 / 625 / 4
1972: Franco Harris, 188 / 1,055 / 10
1973: Franco Harris, 188 / 698 / 3
1974: Franco Harris, 208 / 1,006 / 5
1975: Franco Harris, 262 / 1,246 / 10
1976: Franco Harris, 289 / 1,128 / **14**
1977: Franco Harris, 300 / 1,162 / 11
1978: Franco Harris, 310 / 1,082 / 8
1979: Franco Harris, 267 / 1,186 / 11

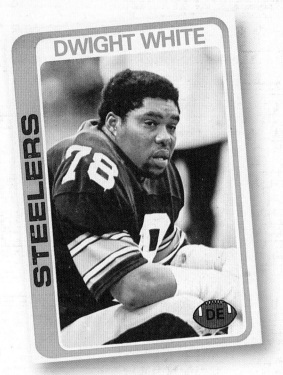

DWIGHT WHITE
STEELERS
78
DE

Receiving Leaders

(Receptions / Yards / TDs)

1970: Ron Shanklin, 30 / 691 / 4
1971: Ron Shanklin, 49 / 652 / 6;
John Fuqua, 49 / 427 / 1
1972: Ron Shanklin, 38 / 669 / 3
1973: Ron Shanklin, 30 / 711 / 10
1974: Frank Lewis, 30 / 365 / 4
1975: Lynn Swann, 49 / 781 / **11**
1976: Lynn Swann, 28 / 516 / 3
1977: Lynn Swann, 50 / 789 / 7
1978: Lynn Swann, 61 / 880 / 11
1979: John Stallworth, 70 / 1,183 / 8

Interceptions (Number / Yards / TDs)

1970: Lee Calland, 7 / 38 / 0
1971: John Rowser, 4 / 94 / 1
1972: Jack Ham, 7 / 83 / 1
1973: Mike Wagner, **8** / 134 / 0
1974: Glen Edwards, 5 / 153 / 1;
J. T. Thomas, 5 / 22 / 0;
Jack Ham, 5 / 13 / 0
1975: Mel Blount, **11** / 121 / 0

1976: Glen Edwards, 6 / 95 / 0;
Mel Blount, 6 / 75 / 0
1977: Mel Blount, 6 / 65 / 0
1978: Tony Dungy, 6 / 95 / 0
1979: Jack Lambert, 6 / 29 / 0

First-Team All-Pros

1972: Joe Greene, DT
1973: Joe Greene, DT
1974: Joe Greene, DT
1974: L. C. Greenwood, DE
1974: Jack Ham, LB
1975: Mel Blount, CB
1975: L. C. Greenwood, DE
1975: Jack Ham, LB
1976: Jack Ham, LB
1976: Jack Lambert, LB
1977: Jack Ham, LB
1977: Franco Harris, RB
1977: Joe Greene, DT
1978: Terry Bradshaw, QB
1978: Jack Ham, LB
1978: Lynn Swann, WR
1978: Mike Webster, C
1979: Jack Ham, LB
1979: Jack Lambert, LB
1979: Donnie Shell, SS
1979: John Stallworth, WR
1979: Mike Webster, C

Pro Bowl Selections

1970: Joe Greene, DT
1970: Andy Russell, LB
1971: Joe Greene, DT
1971: Andy Russell, LB
1972: Roy Gerela, K
1972: Joe Greene, DT
1972: Franco Harris, RB
1972: Andy Russell, LB
1972: Dwight White, DE
1973: Joe Greene, DT
1973: L. C. Greenwood, DE
1973: Jack Ham, LB

1973: Franco Harris, RB
1973: Andy Russell, LB
1973: Ron Shanklin, WR
1973: Bruce Van Dyke, G
1973: Dwight White, DE
1974: Roy Gerela, K
1974: Joe Greene, DT
1974: L. C. Greenwood, DE
1974: Jack Ham, LB
1974: Franco Harris, RB
1974: Andy Russell, LB
1975: Mel Blount, CB
1975: Terry Bradshaw, QB
1975: Glen Edwards, FS/PR
1975: Joe Greene, DT
1975: L. C. Greenwood, DE
1975: Jack Ham, LB
1975: Franco Harris, RB
1975: Jack Lambert, LB
1975: Andy Russell, LB
1975: Lynn Swann, WR
1975: Mike Wagner, SS
1976: Mel Blount, CB
1976: Glen Edwards, FS
1976: Joe Greene, DT
1976: L. C. Greenwood, DE
1976: Jack Ham, LB
1976: Franco Harris, RB
1976: Jack Lambert, LB
1976: J. T. Thomas, CB
1976: Mike Wagner, SS
1977: Jack Ham, LB
1977: Franco Harris, RB
1977: Jack Lambert, LB
1977: Lynn Swann, WR
1978: Mel Blount, CB
1978: Terry Bradshaw, QB
1978: Joe Greene, DT
1978: L. C. Greenwood, DE
1978: Jack Ham, LB
1978: Franco Harris, RB
1978: Jack Lambert, LB
1978: Donnie Shell, SS

1978: Lynn Swann, WR
1978: Mike Webster, C
1979: Mel Blount, CB
1979: Terry Bradshaw, QB
1979: Joe Greene, DT
1979: L. C. Greenwood, DE
1979: Jack Ham, LB
1979: Franco Harris, RB
1979: Jack Lambert, LB
1979: Donnie Shell, SS
1979: John Stallworth, WR
1979: Mike Webster, C

1st-Round Draft Picks

1970: Terry Bradshaw (1), QB, Louisiana Tech
1971: Frank Lewis (8), WR, Grambling St.
1972: Franco Harris (13), RB, Penn St.
1973: J. T. Thomas (24), DB, Florida St.
1974: Lynn Swann (21), WR, Southern California
1975: Dave Brown (26), DB, Michigan
1976: Bennie Cunningham (28), TE, Clemson
1977: Robin Cole (21), LB, New Mexico
1978: Ron Johnson (22), DB, Eastern Michigan
1979: Greg Hawthorne (28), RB, Baylor

Right: The owner of this $10.15 ticket got to witness the "Immaculate Reception."
MVP Books Collection

Opposite: A two-time Pro Bowler, Dwight White was a key, if not the best known, member of Pittsburgh's Steel Curtain defense throughout the decade.
MVP Books Collection

MALONE, WOODSON, AND MERRIWEATHER

Tough times plague Pittsburgh, as both the city and its football team lose their way. Cries of "One for the Thumb" peter out as the decade drags on.

"One for the Thumb in '81" became a rallying cry in Joe Greene's final season. *MVP Books Collection*

I f the fans were honest with themselves, they would've said they'd seen it coming, the inevitable letdown. Because simple logic—as well as the laws of the NFL—dictated that it was impossible to maintain the Steelers' '70s level of success over time. After all, those teams had played nearly perfect football for the better part of an entire decade.

So with a world made in balance, like Pittsburgh's own inclines, what went meteorically up sooner or later had to come crashing down.

The 1980s was the decade after. The town, the technology, the team all hit a trough. All got old at once. Industries that didn't retool dried up and blew away. As the economy dipped, then crumbled, Pittsburgh lost 100,000 manufacturing jobs along with uncountable ancillary jobs and businesses.

Arguably, the '80s were worse than the Great Depression, for this time Pittsburgh seemed to lose its purpose, its very identity. And the Steelers mirrored the times. Mired in mediocrity, they were unable to find the formula that would produce the plays and players that could win. And two NFL strikes didn't help.

The decade began with the fans' popular fashion statement, the bright yellow "One for the Thumb in '81" Joe Greene T-shirt. Clearly, the hopes were foolish and the bravado false.

Drafting near the bottom of the heap for so long made the Steelers talent poor. Yes, there were some good players. Wide receiver Louis Lipps (Steelers Nation bellowed "Loooooou" when he played), kicker Gary Anderson, and linebackers Bryan Hinkle and David Little drew cheers. But like the 1960s, there was not enough talent on the team for the Steelers to notch enough Ws. The Steelers were often competitive and occasionally exciting, but they were no longer champions.

And everybody knew it.

No one more than Mark Malone. A fine, agile quarterback, Malone brought glittering college credentials to the NFL. Perhaps with better sideman playing in his band, perhaps with a system more tailored to him, he might have succeeded. But unlike predecessor Terry Bradshaw, Malone simply couldn't get the job done—or done often enough—and endured the fans' displeasure. The Steelers Nation boos that echoed 'round Three Rivers Stadium were deafening.

No, Malone couldn't do it. Nor could David Woodley. Nor Bubby Brister. Nor much of anybody taking the snaps. The Steelers tripped, stumbled, and fell, racking up a decade of lackluster and losing seasons.

On the other side of the ball, the defense had its moments—and its stars. Pickoff artist Mike Merriweather, an able and adept linebacker, became a fan favorite. In Pittsburgh, with memberships in Steelers Nation dispensed with mother's milk, it was hardly uncommon for a 10-year-old fan to attend his first-ever Steelers game, witness a Merriweather pick-six, and holler, "I've been waiting all my life to see that!"

While the '80s left ashes in the fans' mouths—particularly with the 1988 death of founder Art Rooney and consecutive 51–0 and 41–10 losses to Cleveland and Cincinnati in '89—there were rays of hope. By decade's end, the Steelers once again began to stockpile talent: impossibly slick safety Carnell Lake, deliciously brutal linebacker Greg Lloyd, and Purdue's all-everything Rod Woodson. A brilliant play reader with sprinter speed, Woodson excelled as a quick, canny corner who covered the globe and picked off passes at will. In his spare time, he returned kickoffs and punts for serious yardage.

Suddenly, Steelers Nation had real stars to watch.

Somehow, once again, Steelers Nation would be able to sleep at night.

And hope for a brighter tomorrow.

—A. M.

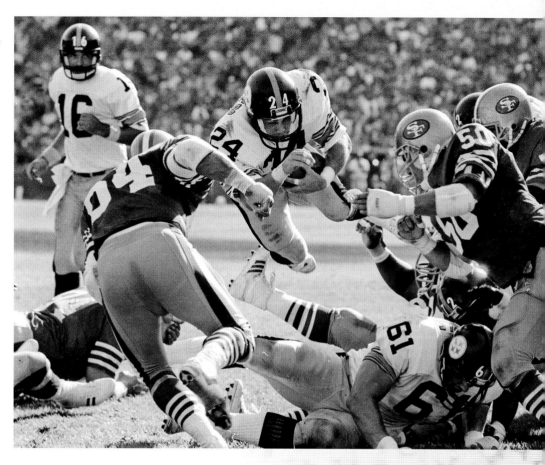

On October 14, 1984, in their gutsiest victory of the decade, running back Rich Erenberg and the injury-riddled Steelers handed the 49ers their only loss of the season. *Al Golub/AP Images*

1980

9–7   3rd place

Game-by-Game

9/7	W, 31–17, vs. Houston Oilers
9/14	W, 20–17, at Baltimore Colts
9/21	L, 28–30, at Cincinnati Bengals
9/28	W, 38–3, vs. Chicago Bears
10/5	W, 23–17, at Minnesota Vikings
10/12	L, 16–17, vs. Cincinnati Bengals
10/20	L, 34–45, vs. Oakland Raiders
10/26	L, 26–27, at Cleveland Browns
11/2	W, 22–20, vs. Green Bay Packers
11/9	W, 24–21, at Tampa Bay Buccaneers
11/16	W, 16–13, vs. Cleveland Browns
11/23	L, 13–28, at Buffalo Bills
11/30	W, 23–10, vs. Miami Dolphins
12/4	L, 0–6, at Houston Oilers
12/14	W, 21–16, vs. Kansas City Chiefs
12/22	L, 17–26, at San Diego Chargers

Team Scoring

352 points scored

313 points allowed

Theo Bell (left) gets a pregame hug from fellow receiver Lynn Swan. In addition to being the club's punt returner, Bell led all Steeler receivers with 748 receiving yards and 25.8 yards per catch in 1980. *Tony Tomsic/Getty Images*

INEVITABLE DROP-OFF

Aging Stars Can't Keep Up, Fall Short of Playoffs

Before the word *three-peat* had entered the sports lexicon, Terry Bradshaw had his sights set on a third straight Super Bowl title. "If there's any one team that can win three in a row, we can do it," he said. But they couldn't. The core players on the team were growing old and wearing down.

In 1980, the age of the average NFL player was 26. Yet these were the ages of the nine future Hall of Famers on the Steelers' roster: Joe Greene, 35; Terry Bradshaw, 32; Mel Blount, 32; Jack Ham, 31; Franco Harris, 30; Jack Lambert, 28; Mike Webster, 28; Lynn Swann, 28; and John Stallworth, 28.

All nine of the abovementioned had been drafted between 1969 and '74. In the second half of the decade, as perennial winners, the Steelers were always drafting in the bottom of the rounds. Moreover, they could no longer outsmart their competitors or find diamonds in the rough. Scouting around the NFL had become much more advanced; other teams caught up.

In 1980, Franco Harris dropped below 1,000 yards rushing for the first time in seven years, and fresh-legged backup Sidney Thornton amassed just 325 yards. John Stallworth missed most of the year due to injury. Terry Bradshaw & Co still found ways to put points on the board, but the defense was burned for 313 points (15th best in the league), including 45 to the Raiders. The overall result was 9–7, two games worse than Houston and Cleveland in the AFC Central.

The Shutdown CB: Mel Blount

Renaldo Nehemiah, the track star turned football player who had set eight world records in hurdle events, showed off his vertical leap to Steelers one day. Mel Blount then demonstrated what he could do. Despite wearing wing-tipped shoes and a three-piece suit, Blount outleapt the Olympic star.

"When you create a cornerback, the mold is Mel Blount," said linebacker Jack Ham. "He was the most incredible athlete I have ever seen. With Mel, you could take one wide receiver and just write him off. He could handle anybody in the league."

A third-round pick out of Southern University, Blount was unusually big for a cornerback: 6-foot-3 and more than 200 pounds. He ran the 40-yard dash in 4.5 seconds, and his arms were exceptionally long. His experience as a wide receiver helped him read the minds of his opponents, and he could catch the ball as well as they could. His 57 interceptions remain a Steelers record, and he led the NFL with 11 pickoffs in 1975.

"He was the best ever to play the game," former Steelers defensive coordinator Bud Carson once said. "There's no one who comes close. With Blount's speed, anticipation, height, and reach, nobody could get away from him."

In 1972, Blount didn't allow a single touchdown pass against him the entire season. His amazing talent went largely unrecognized until '75, when he made his first of five Pro Bowls and was named NFL Defensive Player of the Year by the Associated Press.

Though Blount did not invent bump-and-run coverage, he made it famous—so much so that the NFL rewrote the rules in 1978 so that receivers had a fighting chance. Still, Blount continued to shut down wideouts for six more years.

"I didn't want to be second to anyone," Blount said. "I wanted to set the standards for my position."

With his mission accomplished, Blount retired after the 1983 season, his 14th with the Steelers. He was inducted into the Pro Football Hall of Fame in his first year of eligibility.

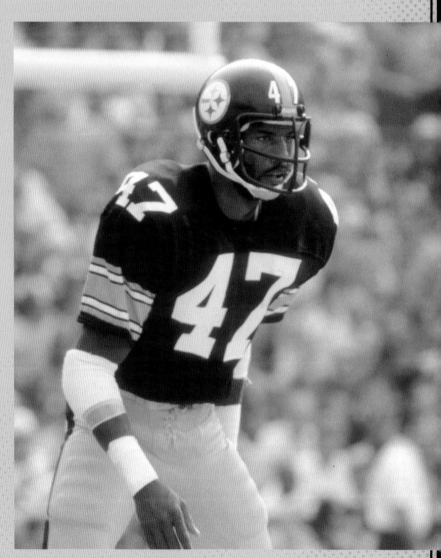

"My biggest strength," Mel Blount said, "was one-on-one man-to-man coverage." *Focus on Sport/Getty Images*

He Gave His All:
Mike Webster

Of the nine Steelers from the 1970s who are enshrined in the Pro Football Hall of Fame, eight have lived long, productive lives. The other was Mike Webster. The man who protected Terry Bradshaw and spearheaded the ground attack, who sacrificed his body, mind, and life for the good of the team and the fans of Pittsburgh, died at age 50 after living in chronic agony.

Born in Tomahawk, Wisconsin, Webster starred at the University of Wisconsin and was drafted by the Steelers in 1974. "Iron Mike," who was said to be the strongest player on the team, started nearly every game at center for Pittsburgh from 1976 to '88 and then played two more seasons with Kansas City. He earned nine trips to the Pro Bowl, and seven times he garnered All-Pro honors.

After he retired, Webster lived only 12 more years, most of which were spent in torment. He suffered from hearing loss as well as chronic pain to his back, knees, foot, shoulder, elbow, and hands—all of which had been injured or worn down on the gridiron. Most tragically, he suffered from chronic traumatic encephalopathy (CTE), a progressive degenerative disease of the brain.

Webster had taken so many blows to the helmet that his head ached constantly. He took medications for pain, seizure prevention, anxiety, and depression. Doctors also prescribed Eldepryl, commonly taken by those who suffer from Parkinson's disease. A father of four, Webster lived in such agony that he frequently Tasered himself multiple times. "The only way he could get to sleep," said his son, Garrett.

Delusional, Webster wrote dark, rambling diary entries and stockpiled weapons that he seriously considered using on NFL officials. Near the end, he could be found sleeping in his truck or hunched over in the Amtrak station in downtown Pittsburgh, munching on dry cereal. He died of heart failure on September 24, 2002, five years after his enshrinement in the Hall of Fame.

In 1988, Mike Webster was in his 15th year with the Steelers and had two more left to play. The long career would prove to have devastating effects on his body and his mind. *MVP Books Collection*

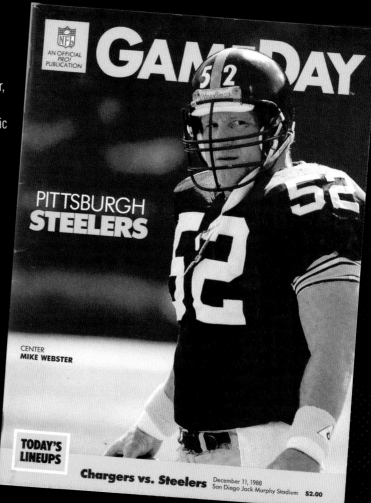

NFL
AN OFFICIAL
PRO!
PUBLICATION

GAME DAY

PITTSBURGH STEELERS

CENTER
MIKE WEBSTER

TODAY'S LINEUPS

Chargers vs. Steelers December 11, 1988 San Diego Jack Murphy Stadium $2.00

NONE FOR THE THUMB

Defense Disappoints in Mean Joe's Final Year

When the Steelers slumped to 9–7 in 1980, they took NFL oddsmakers by surprise. Against the Vegas line, Pittsburgh went 3–13 that year. In 1981, however, prognosticators expected the Steelers to wallow in mediocrity—and did they ever. Chuck Noll's crew went 8–8 on the season and 8–8 against the Vegas line.

Although Rocky Bleier had retired, Terry Bradshaw and Franco Harris once again lined up in the backfield. Bradshaw ranked sixth in the NFL with an 83.9 passer rating, thanks largely to 22 touchdown passes and just 14 interceptions. John Stallworth returned from injury to top 1,000 receiving yards, and Harris fell just 13 yards shy of quadruple digits in rushing.

The Steelers' defense finished eighth in the NFL against the run (and allowed just five rushing touchdowns) but ranked 26th against the pass. Perhaps most disheartening, the Steelers could no longer beat the league's good teams; of their eight victories, only one came against a club with a winning record.

After Pittsburgh's fourth NFL title in January 1980, Joe Greene popularized the phrase "One for the Thumb" in his quest for a fifth Super Bowl championship ring. T-shirts and pins, graced with an illustration of Greene with four rings on his right hand, proclaimed "One for the Thumb in '81." The dream was still alive when the Steelers closed November at 8–5, but they dropped three close ones to end the year. After the season, Joe Greene called it quits.

Quarterback Terry Bradshaw drops back to pass against the Cincinnatii Bengals. *Getty Images*

1981

8–8 2nd place

Game-by-Game

9/6	**L,** 33–37, vs. Kansas City Chiefs
9/10	**L,** 10–30, at Miami Dolphins
9/20	**W,** 38–10, vs. New York Jets
9/27	**W,** 27–21 (OT), vs. New England Patriots
10/4	**W,** 20–6, at New Orleans Saints
10/11	**W,** 13–7, vs. Cleveland Browns
10/18	**L,** 7–34, at Cincinnati Bengals
10/26	**W,** 26–13, vs. Houston Oilers
11/1	**L,** 14–17, vs. San Francisco 49ers
11/8	**L,** 21–24, at Seattle Seahawks
11/15	**W,** 34–20, at Atlanta Falcons
11/22	**W,** 32–10, at Cleveland Browns
11/29	**W,** 24–0, vs. L.A. Rams
12/7	**L,** 27–30, at Oakland Raiders
12/13	**L,** 10–17, vs. Cincinnati Bengals
12/20	**L,** 20–21, at Houston Oilers

Team Scoring

356 points scored
297 points allowed

6–3   4th place

Game-by-Game

9/13	**W, 36–28,**	at Dallas Cowboys
9/19	**W, 26–20 (OT),**	vs. Cincinnati Bengals
11/21	**W, 24–10,**	at Houston Oilers
11/28	**L, 0–16,**	at Seattle Seahawks
12/5	**W, 35–14,**	vs. Kansas City Chiefs
12/12	**L, 0–13,**	at Buffalo Bills
12/19	**L, 9–10,**	at Cleveland Browns
12/26	**W, 37–14,**	vs. New England Patriots
1/2	**W, 37–21,**	vs. Cleveland Browns

Playoffs

1/9	**L, 13–28,**	vs. San Diego Chargers

Team Scoring

204 points scored
146 points allowed

THE NINE-GAME SEASON

Steelers Go 6–3 in Strike-Shortened Campaign

The year 1982 was a troubled one in Pittsburgh. A national recession coupled with the continued struggles of the steel industry led to a 12-percent unemployment rate in Pennsylvania. As for the Steelers, an NFL players strike wiped out Week 3 through Week 10. Fans could fill their time by visiting the "Steelers 50 Seasons" exhibition at the David L. Lawrence Convention Center, where memorabilia, films, and photographs were on display and the team's four Lombardi trophies were mounted on a rotating platform. A grand banquet on October 9 attracted 2,600 people, including many current and former Steelers.

With all four members of the Steel Curtain defensive line now retired, Pittsburgh opened the season with a new and quite effective 3-4 defense. The Steelers won both pre-strike games, including a 26–20 overtime win over the reigning AFC champion Bengals, and amassed 74 points in the last two games of the season to finish at 6–3. Despite only two Pro Bowl players on defense—Jack Ham and Donnie Shell—Pittsburgh led the NFL in rushing defense.

Sixteen teams made the playoffs in this strike-marred season, and in what would be the last great game of his career, Terry Bradshaw riddled the Chargers for 325 yards in the playoff opener. But San Diego's Dan Fouts topped him with 333 aerial yards and three touchdown passes, while Chuck Muncie ran for 126 yards. Fouts connected with All-Pro tight end Kellen Winslow on two fourth-quarter touchdown throws to turn a 28–17 Steelers lead into a 31–28 Chargers triumph.

After the season, two more dynasty mainstays—Jack Ham and Lynn Swann—decided to hang 'em up.

Franco Harris couldn't find many holes during Pittsburgh's playoff meeting with the Chargers, gaining only 35 yards on 10 carries. The Steelers held a 28–17 fourth quarter lead before falling 31–28. *Focus on Sport/Getty Images*

LIFE AFTER BRADSHAW

Soft Schedule Helps Steelers Win the Central

10–6   1st place

With Terry Bradshaw sitting out virtually all of 1983 following elbow surgery, backup quarterback Cliff Stoudt needed to step up. He didn't. Yet thanks to a relentless ground attack and a nails-tough defense, the Steelers pulled out 10 victories in '83 and won the AFC Central.

Behind Stoudt, a clipboard holder his three previous seasons in Pittsburgh, the Steelers finished 27th in the NFL in passing yards. Stoudt fired 21 interceptions, fumbled 10 times, and suffered 51 sacks. The loss of wide receiver John Stallworth to injury for 12 games limited Stoudt's options, but 33-year-old Franco Harris picked up the slack with 279 rushes for 1,007 yards. Jack Lambert also seemed ageless, earning All-Pro honors as the spiritual leader of the third-best defense in the league. The defense excelled despite the tragic loss of Gabe "Senor Sack" Rivera, Pittsburgh's 1983 first-round pick who was paralyzed following a car crash on October 20.

Beginning October 2, the Steelers ripped off seven consecutive victories. Three straight losses followed, prompting center Mike Webster to fret. "We started 9–2 and all of a sudden we're 9–5. Are we going to give up and let everything slip away?" They didn't. The Steelers whipped the New York Jets 34–7 the next week to clinch a playoff spot.

Even though the Steelers posted a 10–6 record, they hadn't faced a good team all season; each opponent had finished at 9–7 or worse. When the Steelers played the Los Angeles Raiders in the opening playoff round, they were crushed 38–10. After the season, a sore-armed Bradshaw retired and Harris left for a swansong season in Seattle.

In his sole season as Pittsburgh's primary quarterback, Cliff Stoudt ranked 25th in the NFL in passer rating but went 9–6 as a starter. *Diamond Images/Getty Images*

Game-by-Game

Date	Result	Opponent
9/4	L, 10–14,	vs. Denver Broncos
9/11	W, 25–21,	at Green Bay Packers
9/18	W, 40–28,	at Houston Oilers
9/25	L, 23–28,	vs. New England Patriots
10/2	W, 17–10,	vs. Houston Oilers
10/10	W, 24–14,	at Cincinnati Bengals
10/16	W, 44–17,	vs. Cleveland Browns
10/23	W, 27–21,	at Seattle Seahawks
10/30	W, 17–12,	vs. Tampa Bay Buccaneers
11/6	W, 26–3,	vs. San Diego Chargers
11/13	W, 24–13,	at Baltimore Colts
11/20	L, 14–17,	vs. Minnesota Vikings
11/24	L, 3–45,	at Detroit Lions
12/4	L, 10–23,	vs. Cincinnati Bengals
12/10	W, 34–7,	at New York Jets
12/18	L, 17–30,	at Cleveland Browns

Playoffs

Date	Result	Opponent
1/1	L, 10–38,	at L.A. Raiders

Team Scoring

355 points scored
303 points allowed

9–7   1st place

Game-by-Game

9/2   **L, 27–37,**
vs. Kansas City Chiefs

9/6   **W, 23–17,**
at New York Jets

9/16   **W, 24–14,**
vs. L.A. Rams

9/23   **L, 10–20,**
at Cleveland Browns

10/1   **W, 38–17,**
vs. Cincinnati Bengals

10/7   **L, 7–31,**
vs. Miami Dolphins

10/14   **W, 20–17,**
at San Francisco 49ers

10/21   **L, 16–17,**
at Indianapolis Colts

10/28   **W, 35–10,**
vs. Atlanta Falcons

11/4   **W, 35–7,**
vs. Houston Oilers

11/11   **L, 20–22,**
at Cincinnati Bengals

11/19   **L, 24–27,**
at New Orleans Saints

11/25   **W, 52–24,**
vs. San Diego Chargers

12/2   **L, 20–23 (OT),**
at Houston Oilers

12/9   **W, 23–20,**
vs. Cleveland Browns

12/16   **W, 13–7,**
at L.A. Raiders

Playoffs

12/30   **W, 24–17,**
at Denver Broncos

1/6   **L, 28–45,**
at Miami Dolphins

Team Scoring

387 points scored
310 points allowed

Running back Frank Pollard grinded out 105 yards on 24 carries behind a patched-together offensive line in Pittsburgh's magical victory over the "unbeatable" 49ers. *Al Golub/AP Images*

OVERACHIEVERS

Steelers Stun Niners, Whip Broncos in Playoffs

On a warm, sunny October afternoon in 1984, the Steelers gutted out one of the most improbable victories in team history. Pittsburgh, just 3–3 at the time, lined up against the mighty San Francisco 49ers at Candlestick Park. Not only did the Steelers face the best defense in the NFL, they did so with three injured starters on their offensive line. It figured to be a slaughter, but somehow the Steelers were able to orchestrate long drives, and they prevailed 20–17. It would be the Niners' only loss of the year. Otherwise, they were 18–0, including the Super Bowl.

"Super Bowl victories are great," said Chuck Noll, referring to the four that *his* teams had won, "but I don't think I've ever been associated with a victory any better than this one. We had guys playing who were beat up and hurt. They wanted this very badly."

Without that victory, the Steelers wouldn't have made the playoffs in 1984. They finished at 9–7, one game ahead of Cincinnati. Though the Bengals defined the parity that the league sought—finishing at 8–8 with 339 points scored and 339 points allowed—they would have won the tiebreaker over Pittsburgh should both teams had finished at 8–8.

In terms of yardage, the Steelers finished the season eighth in the NFL in offense and fifth in defense. With center Mike Webster leading the charge, fullback Frank Pollard churned out 851 rushing yards and running backs Walter Abercrombie and Rich Erenberg combined for 1,015.

Three-year Steelers backup Mark Malone (nine starts) and former Dolphin David Woodley (seven starts) split time at quarterback. Though Woodley had been known for his running ability with Miami, he rarely left the pocket under Noll. He didn't have to—not with Pro Bowl receivers John Stallworth (career-high 1,395 receiving yards) and rookie Louis Lipps (860). Together, they caught 20 touchdown passes. Linebacker Mike Merriweather (15 sacks) spearheaded the defense.

The Steelers showed their character once again in their opening playoff game, when they defeated the 13–3 Broncos 24–17 in Denver. "Or attitude is simple," cornerback Dwayne Woodruff said after the game. "Teams aren't going to score on us. Period." Denver led the game 17–10 until Malone led the comeback. Malone said afterward: "I told the guys in the huddle, 'If you want to win this game, now's the time. You've got to win it right now.' . . . It was like someone shot them up with adrenaline. They went berserk and we went up the field."

A 10-yard scoring pass to Lipps tied the game. It remained 17–17 until Steelers free safety Eric Williams intercepted a John Elway pass and returned it to the Denver 2-yard-line with 2:45 left in the game. Pollard scored the game-winning touchdown.

In the AFC Championship Game, the Steelers were 10-point underdogs against the 15–2 Dolphins. Miami quarterback Dan Marino, who during the 1984 regular season had become the first NFL quarterback to throw for 5,000 yards, riddled the Steelers for 421 yards and four touchdowns—including a couple long back-breakers to wide receiver Mark "Super" Duper. The Dolphins punched their ticket to the Super Bowl with a 45–28 victory, but the overachieving Steelers had done themselves proud.

Mark Malone outperformed Denver's Hall of Fame quarterback John Elway in their 1984 playoff matchup. Malone completed 17 of 28 passes for 224 yards and one TD, while Elway went just 19 for 37 and had two interceptions, including one by Eric Williams with under three minutes left in the game, leading to Pittsburgh's winning touchdown. *George Gojkovich/Getty Images*

The Three Rivers Experience

In an interview with ESPN, Joe Greene spoke about playing at Three Rivers Stadium. "When you walked into that stadium and saw the sign 'You're in Steelers Country' . . . ." Mean Joe couldn't finish the sentence. He was choked up; tears rolled down his rugged face. "It was the fans and the people involved . . . ," he said.

Architecturally, Three Rivers was as dull as a concrete donut. It was the players and fans who brought the stadium to life. Though the venue opened in 1970, the Immaculate Reception in 1972 served as a christening celebration. When Franco Harris scored the winning touchdown, fans howled and roared, pumped their fists and jumped up and down. Footage of the game shows men hugging each other in the stands. The place was jumpin'—as it would for the next 28 years.

From 1973 to 2000, every Steelers game was sold out. From warm, sunny September afternoons to frigid, overcast December days, steelworkers and students, bricklayers and beauticians breathed life into Three Rivers. They waved their "Terrible Towels" and raised banners in support of their favorite players. "Franco's Italian Army" and "Gerela's Gorillas" were among the battalions of fans at home games. Such resounding support helped the Steelers go 182–73 in their 31 seasons at TRS.

Three Rivers Stadium arose during the era of multipurpose stadiums—large, enclosed, circular structures that could field both NFL and MLB teams. Lack of character was a common characteristic, as were artificial turf and huge parking lots, which were great for tailgating.

Veterans Stadium in Philadelphia, Riverfront Stadium in Cincinnati, and Busch Stadium are three other examples of "cookie-cutter" stadiums. They all had giant electronic scoreboards and glass-enclosed luxury suites. Red, yellow, and orange seats gave Three Rivers some rings of color. Dan Rooney wrote that the stadium "looked like a big layer cake, perfectly round."

Constructed at a cost of $55 million, Three Rivers opened in July 1970. Its name referred to its location—at the confluence of the Allegheny River and Monongahela River, which forms the Ohio River. It was built on the site of the old Exposition Park, where Art Rooney had played football in the early days of the sport.

The stadium's initial capacity for football was less than 49,000, but it was eventually expanded to 59,000. Though the team was middle-of-the-pack throughout the 1980s and early '90s, fans never wavered in their support. From 1992 through '97, they inspired the Steelers to the playoffs every season. Jerome Bettis called Three Rivers "a loud, noisy type of place. We capitalized on that—raising a ruckus, the crowd really fired up."

The Pirates and Steelers played their last games at Three Rivers Stadium in 2000 before moving to PNC Park and Heinz Field, respectively. The final football game, on December 17, was like old times. Fifty former Steelers were on hand, and Jack Lambert pumped up the team beforehand, shouting, "All right, defense! Let's kill. Let's go!" In wet, nasty weather, with the fans chanting "dee-fence, dee-fence," the Steelers crushed the Washington Redskins 24–3. Eight weeks later, the stadium was imploded.

The Steelers celebrated their final season at Three Rivers in 2000.
MVP Books Collection

Above: The "You're in Steeler Country" banner has been a source of immense pride in Pittsburgh for decades. *George Gojkovich/Getty Images*

1985

Game-by-Game

9/8	**W, 45–3,** vs. Indianapolis Colts
9/16	**L, 7–17,** at Cleveland Browns
9/22	**W, 20–0,** vs. Houston Oilers
9/30	**L, 24–37,** vs. Cincinnati Bengals
10/6	**L, 20–24,** at Miami Dolphins
10/13	**L, 13–27,** al Dallas Cowboys
10/20	**W, 23–10,** vs. St. Louis Cardinals
10/27	**L, 21–26,** at Cincinnati Bengals
11/3	**W, 10–9,** vs. Cleveland Browns
11/10	**W, 36–28,** at Kansas City Chiefs
11/17	**W, 30–7,** at Houston Oilers
11/24	**L, 23–30,** vs. Washington Redskins
12/1	**L, 23–31,** vs. Denver Broncos
12/8	**L, 44–54,** at San Diego Chargers
12/15	**W, 30–24,** vs. Buffalo Bills
12/21	**L, 10–28,** at New York Giants

Team Scoring

379 points scored
355 points allowed

John Stallworth corrals one of his 75 catches in 1985. The dynasty holdover was more of a possession receiver in '85, with his yards-per-catch down to 12.5. *Damian Strohmeyer/NFL/Getty Images*

SEVEN LOUSY WINS

Steelers Endure First Losing Season in 14 Years

Poor Tunch Ilkin. The offensive tackle was drafted by Pittsburgh three months after they won their fourth Super Bowl. "But my career coincided with the demise of the Steeler dynasty," he said. Ilkin gave 13 years of his life to the Black and Gold, but he never played in the ultimate game. "I had this fear that the year I retired the Steelers would win another Super Bowl," he said. "There'd be a certain symmetry to that." For Ilkin's sake, at least, that didn't happen either.

The Steelers opened the 1985 season looking like potential Super Bowl champions. On an 80-degree day at Three Rivers, Mark Malone fired five touchdown passes—three to Louis Lipps—and ran for another as Pittsburgh blew out Indianapolis 45–3. Due to injuries, however, Malone would make only eight starts on the year and throw only eight more touchdown passes. David Woodley won four of his six starts, but his passer rating was just 53.8. Scott Campbell, a second-year QB out of Purdue, started two games and lost them both.

Despite running the "Air Coryell" offense, the Steelers relied heavily on running backs Frank Pollard and Walter Abercrombie, who combined for 1,842 yards on a whopping 470 carries. But without a decent passing attack and a defense that sent only one player to the Pro Bowl—outside linebacker Mike Merriweather—the Steelers finished at 7–9, their first losing season since 1971.

Over the last five games, the once-dominant Steelers defense coughed up 167 points. Actually, not all the scoring came against the D. In a late-season game against San Diego, Jeffery Dale returned an interception for a touchdown to cap the scoring for the Chargers. They won 54–44.

Double Yoi!: Myron Cope

Myron Cope began his career as a print journalist, and with good reasons. His writing for such magazines as *Sports Illustrated* and *The Saturday Evening Post* won national awards. And then there was his voice. Cope's grating, nasally tone, combined with a strong Pittsburgh accent and his penchant for Yiddish phrases, made him an unlikely candidate for radio. Yet he broadcast Steelers games for 35 years (1970–2004), and fans loved every minute of it.

Born in Pittsburgh to Lithuanian Jewish parents, Cope was a streetwise, college-educated, witty, colorful character. He had no broadcast training. His method, as he wrote in his memoir, *Double Yoi!*, was: "Just tell me when to start talking and when to shut up."

As the analyst on the Steelers broadcasts, Cope mixed Yiddish expressions such as "feh" and "yoi" with his own creations, such as "mmm-hah" and "okel dokel." Cope was the man who invented the Terrible Towel, and he doled out such nicknames as "Jack Splat" (for Jack Lambert) and "Slash" (for Kordell Stewart). Chuck Noll was "Emperor Chaz," and the Bengals were the "Bungles." He even immortalized Franco Harris's famous catch, christening it the "Immaculate Reception."

Gene Collier of the *Pittsburgh Post-Gazette* described Cope's voice as a "signature irascible rasp, gentle and shrill, squeaky and yelpy, often in high emotion fueled by sometimes illogical bursts of excitability."

Though he became an A-list celebrity in Pittsburgh, Cope held strong to his roots. He was a modest man, Steelers executive Joe Gordon told the *Post-Gazette*, "always had time for people, always was patient." He also contributed greatly to charitable causes.

Cope said that when he died, he wanted to be known more than just the creator of the Terrible Towel. "I've often thought that when I kick the bucket, there'd be a story that said, 'Creator of towel, dead,'" Cope said. "I would like to be remembered as a pretty decent writer."

He was that, and a whole lot more.

Yoi is a Yiddish word expressing shock or joy. Cope used it often in the Steelers broadcast booth. *George Gojkovich/Getty Images*

1986

Game-by-Game

9/7   **L**, 0–30,
at Seattle Seahawks

9/15   **L**, 10–21,
vs. Denver Broncos

9/21   **L**, 7–31,
at Minnesota Vikings

9/28   **W**, 22–16 (OT),
at Houston Oilers

10/5   **L**, 24–27,
vs. Cleveland Browns

10/13   **L**, 22–24,
at Cincinnati Bengals

10/19   **L**, 0–34,
vs. New England Patriots

10/26   **W**, 30–9,
vs. Cincinnati Bengals

11/2   **W**, 27–3,
vs. Green Bay Packers

11/9   **L**, 12–16,
at Buffalo Bills

11/16   **W**, 21–10,
vs. Houston Oilers

11/23   **L**, 31–37 (OT),
at Cleveland Browns

11/30   **L**, 10–13 (OT),
at Chicago Bears

12/7   **W**, 27–17,
vs. Detroit Lions

12/13   **W**, 45–24,
at New York Jets

12/21   **L**, 19–24,
vs. Kansas City Chiefs

Team Scoring

307 points scored
336 points allowed

JACKSON STEADIES THE SHIP

Pro Bowl Back Helps Steelers Avert Disaster

After back-to-back 1,000-yard rushing seasons, running back Earnest Jackson was waived by Eagles coach Buddy Ryan in mid-September 1986 because, Ryan allegedly told Jackson, they wanted to go with "younger guys." Earnest was 26. Numerous teams wanted Jackson, who could also block and catch the ball, but he chose Pittsburgh. "Noll wants a guy who can carry the ball 35 to 50 times a game, a guy who can play with pain, and that's want Earnest can do," said his agent, Harold Lewis.

Three games into 1986, the Steelers were desperate for any offense they could get. While scoring just 17 total points in those three contests, all losses, Pittsburgh had averaged just 65 rushing yards per game. Jackson's 60 rushing yards the next week, in his Steelers debut, helped Pittsburgh beat Houston in overtime. In fact, while en route to 910 rushing yards and a trip to the Pro Bowl, Earnest helped keep the team competitive almost every week.

Unfortunately, the Steelers lost numerous heartbreakers. The Browns beat them 27–24 for their first win ever at Three Rivers. The Steelers fell to the Bengals by two, Bills by four, and Chiefs by five. In back-to-back weeks in November, they lost in overtime to the Bears and Browns. They finished at 6–10.

Early-season pickup Earnest Jackson rushed for 910 yards in 13 games, including a season-high 147 against Detroit. *Mike Powell/ Allsport/Getty Images*

Optimists could note that after Jackson arrived, the Steelers went 6–7, and six of those losses could have been wins if they had scored just one more time. Fans and players felt no reason to panic. "Despite the losses," Dan Rooney wrote, "Chuck Noll never lost the team."

THE REPLACEMENTS

"Scabs" Fill NFL Rosters While Players Strike

The year 1987 was a troubled one for the Rooney family. Most tragically, Dan Rooney lost his 31-year-old daughter, Kathleen, to lupus. After years of poor drafting, Art Rooney, Jr., was removed from his position as VP of player personnel. Top pick Rod Woodson held out for more money. And NFL players went on strike after the season's second game, demanding that free agency be included in their Collective Bargaining Agreement.

Led by Tex Schramm, who referred to the owners as the "ranchers" and players as the "cattle," the owners played hardball. Though no football was played in Week 3, the owners audaciously fielded replacement players for Weeks 4–6. Like every other team, the Steelers scrounged for talent, signing many players whom they had cut in August or in previous years. Steve Bono would be the starting quarterback. Since the Rooneys worried that the "scabs" would be harassed if they practiced in Pittsburgh, they set up camp in Johnstown.

Chuck Noll, who had no problem coaching the replacements, did not agree with the union's actions. "They want to change the system, and the system has been pretty good for a lot of people," he said.

After the first game with replacement players, Earnest Jackson and football-obsessed Mike Webster (whose body had already endured too much football brutality) returned to the Steelers. Pittsburgh's replacement players went 2–1, with the only home game drawing 34,627 fans. After Week 6, NFL players returned without a CBA, although they eventually would win their quest for free agency.

The Steelers finished the season at 8–7, one game behind the AFC's two wildcard teams. Ironically, Mike Webster was the club's only Pro Bowl representative.

Steelers quarterback Mark Malone leans on wide receiver Weegee Thompson's truck on September 23, 1987, the first day of the strike. *Gene Puskar/AP Images*

8–7   3rd place

Game-by-Game

9/13	W, 30–17, vs. San Francisco 49ers
9/20	L, 10–34, at Cleveland Browns
10/4	W, 28–12, at Atlanta Falcons
10/11	L, 21–31, at L.A. Rams
10/18	W, 21–7, vs. Indianapolis Colts
10/25	W, 23–20, vs. Cincinnati Bengals
11/1	L, 24–35, at Miami Dolphins
11/8	W, 17–16, at Kansas City Chiefs
11/15	L, 3–23, vs. Houston Oilers
11/22	W, 30–16, at Cincinnati Bengals
11/29	L, 16–20, vs. New Orleans Saints
12/6	W, 13–9, vs. Seattle Seahawks
12/13	W, 20–16, at San Diego Chargers
12/20	L, 16–24, at Houston Oilers
12/26	L, 13–19, vs. Cleveland Browns

Team Scoring

285 points scored
299 points allowed

Pickoff Artist:
Rod Woodson

In retrospect, it's stunning that the Steelers were able to land Rod Woodson with the 10th overall pick in the 1987 draft. Not only had he been timed in the 40-yard dash at 4.29 seconds, but he was masterful in workouts at the NFL Scouting Combine. "He was so efficient in his movement, no wasted motion at all," said Tom Donahue, who would become the Steelers' director of pro personnel and development. "It was almost hard to believe."

At Purdue University, Woodson had become the first Big Ten athlete to win four conference 55-meter hurdles titles. This was a skill that came in handy on the gridiron, when he leapt over diving, flailing bodies en route to the end zone.

For the Boilermakers, this biracial, multi-threat talent played running back, wide receiver, cornerback, and safety, and he returned punts and kickoffs. Though he didn't line up on offense in his 10 years with the Steelers (1987–96) and 17 seasons in the NFL, Woodson often had his hands on the ball. In his pro career, he amassed 7,256 yards in punt and kickoff returns. Moreover, he returned his 71 interceptions (third in NFL history) for 1,483 yards, a record that stood until 2012. In 2013, the only player who was close to matching Rod Woodson's 12 career pick-sixes was Charles Woodson (11).

Steelers coach Bill Cowher called Woodson the best athlete he ever coached and "an unbelievable student of the game." "I enjoy the game," Woodson said. "I've dedicated myself to it—studying film, understanding offenses, getting a feel for it. Then letting go."

Woodson, the first NFL cornerback to garner 11 Pro Bowl invitations, peaked in the early '90s. He logged a career-high 100 tackles in 1992, intercepted eight passes in '93, and earned first-team All-Pro honors for the fifth time in '94. In 1995, he became the first NFL player to come back from reconstructive knee surgery in the same season, and he went on to make the Pro Bowl the following year. Woodson was inducted into the Pro Football Hall of Fame in 2009, his first year of eligibility.

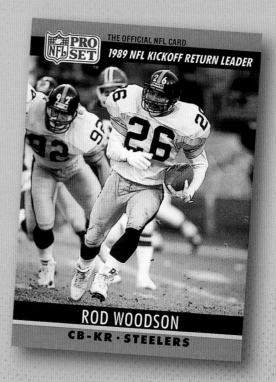

In addition to his skills as a defensive back, Rod Woodson was a record-breaking kick returner through his first eight seasons in Pittsburgh. *MVP Books Collection*

FAREWELL TO THE CHIEF

Pittsburgh Mourns the Loss of Art Rooney

On August 17, 1988, during a record-breaking heat wave in Pittsburgh, 87-year-old Art Rooney, Sr., suffered a devastating stroke. Eight days later, he was dead. Flags flew at half-mast in Pittsburgh, and hundreds of mourners swarmed St. Peter's Church for the funeral. All of the current Steelers were there, as was the mayor and governor. As the funeral procession wound through the North Side, thousands of residents lined the streets, many wiping tears and others raising signs saying "Goodbye Art" and "Thanks Chief."

Mourners remembered Rooney as a man of the people, even after winning four Super Bowls. "He was a very humble person," said Terry Bradshaw. "Losing or winning, he was no different."

The Steelers played the 1988 season with an "AJR" patch on their jerseys. Unfortunately, they stumbled through the worst season of Chuck Noll's 23 years as head coach. The Steelers lost 10 of their first 12 games, and they finished at 5–11.

Under defensive coordinator Tony Dungy (who would become one of the NFL's great head coaches), Pittsburgh finished 28th in the NFL in points allowed with 421. On September 11, the Redskins burned the Steelers' secondary for 422 aerial yards. On November 6, the Bengals ran for 221 yards and threw for 338.

Pittsburgh had a potent running attack (4.5 yards per carry) thanks to hard-charging Merril Hoge (705 yards) and rookie Warren Williams (409). But strong-armed Bubby Brister, in his third year with the Steelers and first as a starter, completed just 47.3 percent of his passes. Like Bradshaw in the early '70s, the Louisiana-born Brister was mocked for his southern accent and perceived lack of sophistication.

All in all, it was a lousy year.

"How would I like to be remembered after I die?" Art Rooney once asked. "I'd like to be remembered as a good guy." He will also be remembered for leading the Steelers to four Super Bowl titles, the spoils from which he proudly poses with coach Chuck Noll (second from right) and his sons Dan (left) and Art Jr. (right). *AP Images*

1988

5–11   4th place

Game-by-Game

9/4	W, 24–21,	vs. Dallas Cowboys
9/11	L, 29–30,	at Washington Redskins
9/18	L, 12–17,	vs. Cincinnati Bengals
9/25	L, 28–36,	at Buffalo Bills
10/2	L, 9–23,	vs. Cleveland Browns
10/9	L, 14–31,	at Phoenix Cardinals
10/16	L, 14–34,	vs. Houston Oilers
10/23	W, 39–21,	vs. Denver Broncos
10/30	L, 20–24,	at New York Jets
11/6	L, 7–42,	at Cincinnati Bengals
11/13	L, 26–27,	vs. Philadelphia Eagles
11/20	L, 7–27,	at Cleveland Browns
11/27	W, 16–10,	vs. Kansas City Chiefs
12/4	W, 37–34,	at Houston Oilers
12/11	L, 14–20,	at San Diego Chargers
12/18	W, 40–24,	vs. Miami Dolphins

Team Scoring

336 points scored
421 points allowed

1989

9–7   2nd place

Game-by-Game

9/10	**L, 0–51,** vs. Cleveland Browns
9/17	**L, 10–41,** at Cincinnati Bengals
9/24	**W, 27–14,** vs. Minnesota Vikings
10/1	**W, 23–3,** at Detroit Lions
10/8	**L, 16–26,** vs. Cincinnati Bengals
10/15	**W, 17–7,** at Cleveland Browns
10/22	**L, 0–27,** at Houston Oilers
10/29	**W, 23–17,** vs. Kansas City Chiefs
11/5	**L, 7–34,** at Denver Broncos
11/12	**L, 0–20,** vs. Chicago Bears
11/19	**W, 20–17,** vs. San Diego Chargers
11/26	**W, 34–14,** at Miami Dolphins
12/3	**L, 16–23,** vs. Houston Oilers
12/10	**W, 13–0,** at New York Jets
12/17	**W, 28–10,** vs. New England Patriots
12/24	**W, 31–22,** at Tampa Bay Buccaneers

Playoffs

12/31	**W, 26–23 (OT), at Houston Oilers**
1/7	**L, 23–24, at Denver Broncos**

Team Scoring

265 points scored
326 points allowed

132

STUNNING TURNAROUND

Steelers Make the Playoffs After Disastrous Start

In front of a shell-shocked Three Rivers crowd, the Steelers lost the 1989 season opener to the Browns 51–0. "It was the worst I've ever seen as a coach," said Chuck Noll. In fact, it was the most lopsided loss in Steelers history. Pittsburgh committed eight turnovers, managed just five first downs, and mustered only 53 yards of offense. The next week, the Steelers lost 41–10 at Cincinnati as quarterback Bubby Brister was sacked six times. "We either just played two of the best teams in the AFC," Noll said, "or this is going to be a long season."

Neither was the case. The next week, the Steelers' D came alive under new defensive coordinator Rod Rust, shutting out Minnesota in the second half for a 27–14 victory. Brister completed 15 consecutive passes in Week 4, a 23–3 win in Detroit, and Pittsburgh amazingly avenged their opening-day blowout by defeating the Browns 17–7 in Cleveland.

On the year, Pittsburgh finished last in the NFL in third-down conversions. Brister ranked among the league's lowest-rated quarterbacks, and the Steelers' running game chugged along at a 3.6-yards-per-carry clip. But the defense carried the team to a 9–7 record, highlighted by a 13–0 shutout over the Jets. Outside linebacker Greg Lloyd led Pittsburgh with 92 tackles and seven sacks, and cornerback Rod Woodson—who returned a kickoff for a touchdown to key a victory over San Diego—earned first-team All-Pro honors. Recognizing the Steelers' remarkable turnaround, the Maxwell Football Club honored Noll as the league's Coach of the Year.

The Steelers snuck into the playoffs as a wildcard team, and their fans were rewarded—or punished, depending on how you look at it—with two heart-pounding postseason games. Opening in the Astrodome, Pittsburgh trailed Houston 23–16 until fullback Merril Hoge plunged into the end zone with just 46 seconds left in the game. The Oilers looked primed to win it in sudden-death until Woodson forced and recovered a fumble on

The Steelers were back in the playoffs in 1989 after a four-year absence. They defeated the Oilers in the opening round, hoping to grasp once more for the Super Bowl trophy. *MVP Books Collection*

the Houston 46. Gary Anderson, a South African native who would become the Steelers' all-time scoring leader, booted a 50-yard field goal to win the game.

The Steelers played their guts out the following week in Denver, particularly Hoge. In a game that went down to the wire, he ran for 120 yards on 16 carries and caught eight passes for 60 yards. "As much yardage as he got, it was all hard yards," said Steelers assistant coach Dick Hoak, as quoted in the *Pittsburgh Press*. "Even when there were people in the holes, he was running over them, breaking tackle after tackle."

The Steelers were leading 23–17 until Broncos quarterback John Elway led one of his patented late-game comebacks, culminated by a one-yard Mel Bratton touchdown run. Down 24–23, the Steelers had enough time to get into field goal range. But Mark Stock dropped a pass and Brister fumbled the ball away, ending a remarkable season.

"It was like that little train going up, up, almost over the hill, only to get pushed back," said Steelers linebacker David Little. "It's harder to lose this way than to get blown out."

Merril Hoge romped for 120 yards on 16 carries and caught eight passes for 60 yards in Pittsburgh's 24–23 playoff loss to Denver. *Tim DeFrisco/Getty Images*

the Record Book

Team Leaders

(**Boldface** indicates league leader)

Scoring Leaders (Points)

1980: Matt Bahr, 96
1981: Dave Trout, 74
1982: Gary Anderson, 52
1983: Gary Anderson, 119
1984: Gary Anderson, 117
1985: Gary Anderson, 139
1986: Gary Anderson, 95
1987: Gary Anderson, 87
1988: Gary Anderson, 118
1989: Gary Anderson, 91

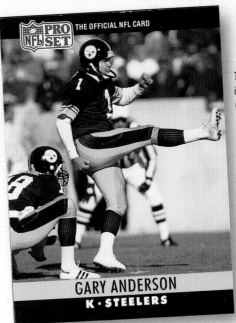

The second-leading scorer in NFL history (2,434), Gary Anderson is also the Steelers' all-time scoring leader (1,343). He played for Pittsburgh from 1982 to 1994. *MVP Books Collection*

Passing Leaders

(Completions / Attempts / Yards)

1980: Terry Bradshaw, 218 / 424 / 3,339
1981: Terry Bradshaw, 201 / 370 / 2,887
1982: Terry Bradshaw, 127 / 240 / 1,768
1983: Cliff Stoudt, 197 / 381 / 2,553
1984: Mark Malone, 147 / 272 / 2,137
1985: Mark Malone, 117 / 233 / 1,428
1986: Mark Malone, 216 / 425 / 2,444
1987: Mark Malone, 156 / 336 / 1,896
1988: Bubby Brister, 175 / 370 / 2,634
1989: Bubby Brister, 187 / 342 / 2,365

Rushing Leaders (Carries / Yards / TDs)

1980: Franco Harris, 208 / 789 / 4
1981: Franco Harris, 242 / 987 / 8
1982: Franco Harris, 140 / 604 / 2
1983: Franco Harris, 279 / 1,007 / 5
1984: Frank Pollard, 213 / 851 / 6
1985: Frank Pollard, 233 / 991 / 3
1986: Earnest Jackson, 216 / 910 / 5
1987: Earnest Jackson, 180 / 696 / 1
1988: Merril Hoge, 170 / 705 / 3
1989: Tim Worley, 195 / 770 / 5

Receiving Leaders

(Receptions / Yards / TDs)

1980: Lynn Swann, 44 / 710 / 7
1981: John Stallworth, 63 / 1,098 / 5
1982: Franco Harris, 31 / 249 / 0
1983: Calvin Sweeney, 39 / 577 / 5
1984: John Stallworth, 80 / 1,395 / 11
1985: John Stallworth, 75 / 937 / 5
1986: Walter Abercrombie, 47 / 395 / 2
1987: John Stallworth, 41 / 521 / 2
1988: Louis Lipps, 50 / 973 / 5;
 Merril Hoge, 50 / 487 / 3
1989: Louis Lipps, 50 / 944 / 5

Interceptions

(Number / Yards / TDs)

1980: Donnie Shell, 7 / 135 / 0
1981: Mel Blount, 6 / 106 / 1;
 Jack Lambert, 6 / 76 / 0
1982: Dwayne Woodruff, 5 / 53 / 0;
 Donnie Shell, 5 / 27 / 0
1983: Rick Woods, 5 / 53 / 0;
 Donnie Shell, 5 / 8 / 0
1984: Donnie Shell, 7 / 71 / 1

1985: Dwayne Woodruff, 5 / 80 / 0
1986: Lupe Sanchez, 3 / 71 / 1;
    Eric Williams, 3 / 44 / 0;
    Donnie Shell, 3 / 29 / 0;
    Rick Woods, 3 / 26 / 0;
    Harvey Clayton, 3 / 18 / 0;
    Bryan Hinkle, 3 / 7 / 0
1987: Dwayne Woodruff, 5 / 91 / 1
1988: Dwayne Woodruff, 4 / 109 / 1;
    Rod Woodson, 4 / 98 / 0
1989: Dwayne Woodruff, 4 / 57 / 0

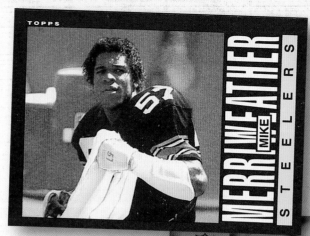

Linebacker Mike Merriweather, featured on this Topps card after logging 15 sacks in 1984, was named to three consecutive Pro Bowls. *MVP Books Collection*

First-Team All-Pros

1980: Jack Lambert, LB
1980: Donnie Shell, SS
1980: Mike Webster, C
1981: Mel Blount, CB
1981: Jack Lambert, LB
1981: Mike Webster, C
1982: Jack Lambert, LB
1982: Donnie Shell, SS
1983: Jack Lambert, LB
1983: Mike Webster, C
1989: Rod Woodson, KR/PR/CB

Pro Bowl Selections

1980: Jack Ham, LB
1980: Franco Harris, RB
1980: Jack Lambert, LB
1980: Donnie Shell, SS
1980: Mike Webster, C
1981: Mel Blount, CB
1981: Jack Lambert, LB
1981: Donnie Shell, SS
1981: Mike Webster, C
1982: Larry Brown, DT
1982: Jack Lambert, LB
1982: Donnie Shell, SS
1982: John Stallworth, WR
1982: Mike Webster, C
1983: Gary Anderson, K
1983: Jack Lambert, LB
1983: John Stallworth, WR
1983: Mike Webster, C

1984: Robin Cole, LB
1984: Louis Lipps, PR/WR
1984: Mike Merriweather, LB
1984: John Stallworth, WR
1984: Mike Webster, C
1985: Gary Anderson, K
1985: Louis Lipps, PR/WR
1985: Mike Merriweather, LB
1985: Mike Webster, C
1986: Earnest Jackson, FB
1986: Mike Merriweather, LB
1987: Mike Webster, C
1988: Tunch Ilkin, OT
1989: Tunch Ilkin, OT
1989: Rod Woodson,
    KR/PR/CB

1st-Round Draft Picks

1980: Mark Malone (28), QB,
    Arizona St.
1981: Keith Gary (17), DE,
    Oklahoma
1982: Walter Abercrombie
    (12), RB, Baylor
1983: Gabe Rivera (21), NT,
    Texas Tech
1984: Louis Lipps (23), WR,
    Southern Mississippi
1985: Darryl Sims (20), DE, Wisconsin
1986: John Rienstra (9), G, Temple
1987: Rod Woodson (10), DB, Purdue
1988: Aaron Jones (18), DE, Eastern
    Kentucky
1989: Tim Worley (7), RB, Georgia;
    Tom Ricketts (24), G, Pittsburgh

Wide Receiver LOUIS LIPPS

PITTSBURGH STEELERS

TODAY'S LINEUPS

Steelers vs. Broncos September 15, 1986 Three Rivers Stadium $2.00

Louis Lipps was coming off back-to-back Pro Bowl years when he was featured on this game program for an early-season matchup with the Broncos in 1986. *MVP Books Collection*

THE *1990s*

COWHER POWER, SLASH, AND THE BUS

Inspiring coaching, rugged defense, and perennial 1,000-yard seasons by Jerome Bettis result in six straight playoff seasons and a trip to the Super Bowl.

The fans of Steelers Nation knew it early in the decade: It was only a matter of time for Chuck Noll. He had collected a core of good players, but greatness eluded them. And the game had left the Master behind. Clearly, the Steelers needed a new hand at the helm.

Change came from one of Pittsburgh's own. Bill Cowher had grown up in a house with its own Steelers shrine. He embodied Pittsburgh rough and rugged. He was one of us.

Steelers Nation embraced "Cowher Power," and the team began to win again. First, it was on the legs of running back Barry Foster—the kind of big power back that had fueled the team's best offenses since John Henry Johnson. Drafted in 1990, Foster was setting Steelers rushing records just two years later. Steelers Nation rose as one and cheered. But injuries crippled Foster, and after '94 he was gone.

Now what?

Next on stage was quarterback Neil O'Donnell. Throwing behind an offensive line that averaged 300 pounds, O'Donnell excelled at flares and screens, racking up high completion rates, *moving* the ball.

With the Ws piling up faster than "Blitzburgh!" T-shirts, Cowher's relentless defenses put the Steelers in the playoffs six years running—and into another Super Bowl.

Super Bowl XXX came mid-decade, and Steelers fans, convinced of the team's invincibility, had plenty to cheer about. At Super Bowl parties, fans fell for the Southwest flavor, serving salsa and nachos, chili and cheese, even switching to Dos Equis to celebrate "One for the Thumb" in sun-drenched Tempe.

But the only thing triple-X-rated about the game was the Steelers' loss to the same Cowboys that Pittsburgh had trounced twice in the '70s. Worse, the L came on a brace of interceptions tossed by quickly out-of-favor Neil O'Donnell.

Steelers Nation was *so* unforgiving that the quarterback simply left town—which was good, because waiting in the wings was something the Steelers hadn't seen since the Great Depression: a four-tool QB. Kordell Stewart could pass—long, *very* long, with pinpoint accuracy—run, catch, even punt. Immediately nicknamed "Slash" for his multiple roles, he became the symbol of an entirely recast, rejuvenated Steelers team.

Bill Cowher loved that moniker, Slash. Stewart didn't. Ultimately, for all his talent, Stewart couldn't get the Steelers back to the Super Bowl. Playing in two AFC Championship Games, he didn't have the one attribute that Steelers fans value above vital signs.

The Steelers enjoyed great success with head coach Bill Cowher. *Jeff Haynes / AFP / Getty Images*

Kordell Stewart wasn't a winner.

But running back Jerome Bettis was.

Coming in a 1996 trade with St. Louis, big, bruising Bettis bowled over defenders, breaking second and third tackles before being hauled to earth. Nicknamed "The Bus," Bettis inflicted the licks, not the other way around.

Inducted immediately into Steelers Nation's all-time pantheon, The Bus picked up 1,000-yard seasons like Turnpike toll tickets. "Jerome epitomized what Pittsburgh is all about," player-turned-broadcaster Tunch Ilkin said. "This town loves tough guys. Jerome is a *bona fide* tough guy."

"Coming to the Steelers was a dream come true," Bettis said. "I came to a place that appreciated big running backs even more than quarterbacks. That helped, because I *loved* to play." That was obvious, because when The Bus bounced off the turf, he did a trademark dance, feet flying one way, head the other.

A natural leader, Bettis complemented a team that starred center Dermontti Dawson, wide receiver Yancey Thigpen, and linebacker Levon Kirkland. Overall, the '90s Steelers were the greatest collection of Pittsburgh football talent that didn't win it all.

Still, that team set the stage for championships to come in the new century. Cowher Power and The Bus would see to that.

—A. M.

1990

9–7   3rd place

Game-by-Game

9/9	L, 3–13, at Cleveland Browns
9/16	W, 20–9, vs. Houston Oilers
9/23	L, 3–20, at L.A. Raiders
9/30	L, 6–28, vs. Miami Dolphins
10/7	W, 36–14, vs. San Diego Chargers
10/14	W, 34–17, at Denver Broncos
10/21	L, 7–27, at San Francisco 49ers
10/29	W, 41–10, vs. L.A. Rams
11/4	W, 21–9, vs. Atlanta Falcons
11/18	L, 3–27, at Cincinnati Bengals
11/25	W, 24–7, at New York Jets
12/2	L, 12–16, vs. Cincinnati Bengals
12/9	W, 24–3, vs. New England Patriots
12/16	W, 9–6, at New Orleans Saints
12/23	W, 35–0, vs. Cleveland Browns
12/30	L, 14–34, at Houston Oilers

Team Scoring

292 points scored
240 points allowed

FROM BOOS TO WS

Steelers Overcome TD Drought, Win Nine Games

Where was the Pittsburgh offense? Certainly not in the end zone. Through the first four games of the 1990 season, Bubby Brister & Co. failed to score a single touchdown. In a 20–9 win over Houston, Rod Woodson returned a punt for a score and D. J. Johnson took an interception to the house. But the offense was averaging just 175 yards per game, and the Steelers were 1–3.

During the fourth game, a 28–6 home loss to Miami in which Brister fired three interceptions, fans practically booed the quarterback off the field. "If I were them, I'd be booing too," Brister said. "They really had something to boo about today."

But like the previous season, the coaching staff adjusted and the Steelers came alive, going 8–4 the rest of the way. Against Denver, Brister threw for 353 yards and four touchdowns, including three to tight end Eric Green. In a raucous 35–0 crushing of Cleveland on December 23, rookie power back Barry Foster emerged with 100 yards rushing.

Still, it was the defense—which stunningly ranked first in the league in yardage against—that carried the team. It was a group effort; Woodson, Johnson, strong safety Carnell Lake, and linebackers Hardy Nickerson and Greg Lloyd all logged between 62 and 69 tackles. Under first-year defensive coordinator Dave Brazil, the Steelers didn't allow more than 324 yards per game until the season finale against Houston.

Unfortunately, the 34–14 loss to the Oilers dropped the Steelers to 9–7, costing them both the division title and a berth in the playoffs. Considering their dreadful start, it was amazing they had even come that close.

Rod Woodson runs with the ball after an interception against the San Francisco 49ers at Candlestick Park in San Francisco, California. *Photo by Focus on Sport/Getty Images*

NOLL TAKES FINAL BOW

Coach Retires with 193 Wins, Four Super Bowl Rings

By the end of the 1991 season, Chuck Noll knew it was time to retire. Perhaps his first inkling came in Week 2, when the Steelers defense—so reliable the year before—coughed up 537 yards and 52 points to Buffalo. Perhaps he knew the season was lost on November 3. Trailing Denver 20–13 in the waning seconds, Steelers quarterback Neil O'Donnell fired a fourth-down pass in the end zone to tight end Eric Green. The ball hit him between the 8 and the 6 and fell to the ground, dropping Pittsburgh to 3–6.

The Steelers, who won their last two games to finish at 7–9, were mediocre in all phases of the game in 1991. O'Donnell, a rookie out of Maryland, went 2–6 in eight starts compared to 5–3 for Bubby Brister, although their stats were similar. Merril Hoge led the team with 610 rushing yards, but at just 3.7 per carry. Pro Bowl linebacker Greg Lloyd anchored a defense that allowed 1,053 yards more than the previous season's group.

On the day after Christmas, Noll announced his retirement. "The end has to come sometime for everyone," Noll said. "For me, this is it." Noll had coached the Steelers for 23 years, winning 193 games—at the time, the sixth most in NFL history. By 2013, no coach had matched his four Super Bowl wins.

At the press conference, Steelers President Dan Rooney had tears in his eyes. "He taught the Steelers and the city of Pittsburgh what it meant to be special," Rooney said. Nothing further needed to be said.

Chuck Noll runs onto the field for the last time as Steelers head coach, on December 22, 1991, at Three Rivers Stadium. Dan Rooney said he was surprised when Noll told him he wanted to retire, despite his 23 years at the helm. *Bill Amatucci Collection/Diamond Images/Getty Images*

7–9   2nd place

Game-by-Game

9/1	W, 26–20,	vs. San Diego Chargers
9/8	L, 34–52,	at Buffalo Bills
9/15	W, 20–6,	vs. New England Patriots
9/22	L, 14–23,	at Philadelphia Eagles
10/6	W, 21–3,	at Indianapolis Colts
10/14	L, 20–23,	vs. New York Giants
10/20	L, 7–27,	vs. Seattle Seahawks
10/27	L, 14–17,	at Cleveland Browns
11/3	L, 13–20,	at Denver Broncos
11/10	W, 33–27 (OT),	at Cincinnati Bengals
11/17	L, 14–41,	vs. Washington Redskins
11/24	W, 26–14,	vs. Houston Oilers
11/28	L, 10–20,	at Dallas Cowboys
12/8	L, 6–31,	at Houston Oilers
12/15	W, 17–10,	vs. Cincinnati Bengals
12/22	W, 17–10,	vs. Cleveland Browns

Team Scoring

292 points scored
344 points allowed

The Terrible Towel and Steelers Nation

Two years before *Star Wars*, the Steelers almost had a stadium full of Darth Vaders. For the 1975 playoffs, executives for the team's flagship radio station, WTAE, wanted to create a gimmick that would rouse the fans. Someone suggested that patrons be given black masks with Chuck Noll's motto, "Whatever it takes," inscribed on the masks in gold lettering. But that would cost too much.

"What we need here," Steelers analyst Myron Cope said, "is something that's lightweight and portable and already is owned by just about every fan."

"How about towels?" suggested sales executive Larry Garrett.

Cope suddenly had a brainstorm. "We could call it the Terrible Towel," he said.

And with that, one of the greatest gimmicks in sports history was born. Fans waved thousands of yellow Terrible Towels in that week's playoff win over the Colts, and the tradition has continued ever since. More than six million official Terrible Towels have been sold, raising several million dollars for the Allegheny Valley School, which cares for the mentally disabled, including Cope's son, Danny.

Since the 1970s, the Steelers have built one of the strongest fan bases in North America. It started, of course, with the sudden rush of success in the 1970s. Fans went bonkers, creating not just the aforementioned Franco's Italian Army and Gerela's Gorillas but such fan clubs as Lambert's Lunatics, Bradshaw's Brigade, Russell's Raiders, Shell's Bombers, and Rocky and the Flying Squirrels.

With the struggles of the steel industry, most notably during the recession of the early 1980s, many Pittsburghers relocated to other regions of the country. Their loyalty to the Steelers never waned, and thus emerged "Steelers Nation"—a fan base that stretched from coast to coast. In reference to the Terrible Towel, Steelers safety Troy Polamalu noted that "every great nation has a flag. I think [for] the Steelers Nation, it's obvious that that's our flag."

Steelers fans have been known to swaddle newborns in Terrible Towels. This "flag" has flown at the summit of Mt. Everest, at the South Pole, in Vatican City, and even in space. Astronaut Mike Fincke, a Pittsburgh native, waved the Terrible Towel from the International Space Station.

Not only have the Steelers sold out every game since 1972, but close to 90,000 names are on their season-ticket waiting list, with an approximate wait time of 50 years. In a recent analysis by *Forbes* magazine, the Steelers tied the Packers for the second-best fans in the NFL, trailing only the Cowboys. Steelers merchandise, *Forbes* stated, outsold every other team's. According to a *Sports Illustrated* poll of 321 NFL players, the Steelers had the second-most intimidating fans in the NFL, behind the Eagles.

Of course, the Steelers faithful make their presence felt at road games. For Super Bowl XL in Detroit, Pittsburgh fans outnumbered Seahawks supporters 25 to 1, according to ESPN.com reporter Greg Garber. When a Steeler is enshrined in the Pro Football Hall of Fame, thousands make the road trip to Canton.

"How fortunate I was to play for the Pittsburgh fans," Jack Lambert proclaimed during his induction speech in 1990, "a proud and hard-working people who love their football and their players." Fans roared their approval and waved their Terrible Towels.

With a painted face, a hard hat, and the Terrible Towel, this fan is a certified member of Steelers Nation. *Al Bello/Getty Images*

MYRON COPE'S OFFICIAL

The terrible towel ™

A PITTSBURGH ORIGINAL

MVP Books Collection

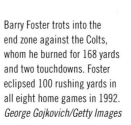

1992

11–5   1st place

Game-by-Game

9/6	W, 29–24, at Houston Oilers
9/13	W, 27–10, vs. New York Jets
9/20	W, 23–6, at San Diego Chargers
9/27	L, 3–17, at Green Bay Packers
10/11	L, 9–17, at Cleveland Browns
10/19	W, 20–0, vs. Cincinnati Bengals
10/25	W, 27–3, at Kansas City Chiefs
11/1	W, 21–20, vs. Houston Oilers
11/8	L, 20–28, at Buffalo Bills
11/15	W, 17–14, vs. Detroit Lions
11/22	W, 30–14, vs. Indianapolis Colts
11/29	W, 21–9, at Cincinnati Bengals
12/6	W, 20–14, vs. Seattle Seahawks
12/13	L, 6–30, at Chicago Bears
12/20	L, 3–6, vs. Minnesota Vikings
12/27	W, 23–13, vs. Cleveland Browns

Playoffs

1/9	L, 3–24, vs. Buffalo Bills

Team Scoring

299 points scored
225 points allowed

COWHER'S THE MAN

New Coach Leads Steelers to Division Crown

Dan Rooney strongly considered Joe Greene to succeed head coach Chuck Noll, but Bill Cowher—the 34-year-old defensive coordinator of the Kansas City Chiefs—impressed Rooney the most. A native of western Pennsylvania, Cowher's "self-discipline and integrity shone through," Rooney wrote. According to Steelers Director of Football Operations Tom Donahue, Cowher "had a plan for what he wanted to do, and could articulate that plan. He was also very enthusiastic, very consistent, and confident."

Those traits bode well for the Steelers, who were beginning to brim with young talent. Under Cowher and his defensive coordinator, Dom Capers, the 1992 Steelers improved to second in the NFL in fewest points allowed, highlighted by a shutout of Cincinnati on *Monday Night Football*. Hardy Nickerson (114 tackles) and Pro Bowl selections Greg Lloyd and Rod Woodson spearheaded a fired-up defense that led the league in takeaways.

Offensively, Pro Bowl linemen Dermontti Dawson (a Hall of Fame–bound center) and Carlton Hasselrig (right guard) opened holes for Barry Foster, who turned an NFL-high 390 carries into a Steelers-record 1,690 rushing yards. Despite modest numbers, sophomore quarterback Neil O'Donnell earned a Pro Bowl trip due to his game-management skills.

The Steelers won the AFC Central with a record of 11–5. A 27–10 mugging of the Jets in Week 2, in which the Steelers recovered seven turnovers and Foster ran for 190 yards, set the tone for the season. Foster topped 100 yards rushing in 13 games, including the playoff opener versus Buffalo at Three Rivers. However, he couldn't crack the goal line, and the Steelers lost 24–3. Still, for the first time in years, optimism was sky-high in Pittsburgh.

Barry Foster trots into the end zone against the Colts, whom he burned for 168 yards and two touchdowns. Foster eclipsed 100 rushing yards in all eight home games in 1992.
George Gojkovich/Getty Images

SNEAKING IN

Pittsburgh Nabs a Playoff Berth—Then Loses in OT

The emerging Steelers suffered some growing pains in 1993. They finished at 9–7, and a 2–4 stretch late in the season was marked by sacks, dropped passes, and a lack of touchdowns. Yet in a trio of statement games, the Steelers signaled to the league that they were a team on the rise.

The first came on November 15, when Pittsburgh avenged its blowout playoff loss to Buffalo (7–1 coming in) with a 23–0 smoking. "The difference was we came out and shoved it down their throat in the second half," said fullback Merril Hoge. "We have not done that since I've been here."

In the season finale, the Steelers showed their mettle with a 16–9 win over Cleveland. Credit linebacker Greg Lloyd, who gave the offense a tongue-lashing at halftime (when they trailed 9–3) and then forced two fumbles in the second half. The win, coupled with losses by the Jets and Dolphins, allowed Pittsburgh to snatch a wildcard berth.

The Steelers were an eight-point underdog at Kansas City in the opening playoff game, yet they took the Chiefs to overtime. Actually, they should have won it earlier. A 22-yard touchdown pass by Neil O'Donnell to Eric Green put the Steelers up 24–17 with 4:11 to go. Pittsburgh had the ball with three minutes left, but a dropped pass on third down and a blocked Mark Royals punt was followed by a Joe Montana touchdown pass. Eleven minutes into overtime, Kansas City's Nick Lowery booted a 32-yard field goal. "It hurts," said Steelers safety Darren Perry, "but it's typical of the whole year—up and down."

Tight end Adrian Cooper soars into the end zone in Pittsburgh's opening playoff game against Kansas City. His TD reception opened the scoring, but the Chiefs won the game in overtime. *Joseph Patronite/NFL/Getty Images*

1993

9–7   2nd place

Game-by-Game

9/5	L, 13–24, vs. San Francisco 49ers
9/12	L, 0–27, at L.A. Rams
9/19	W, 34–7, vs. Cincinnati Bengals
9/27	W, 45–17, at Atlanta Falcons
10/10	W, 16–3, vs. San Diego Chargers
10/17	W, 37–14, vs. New Orleans Saints
10/24	L, 23–28, at Cleveland Browns
11/7	W, 24–16, at Cincinnati Bengals
11/15	W, 23–0, vs. Buffalo Bills
11/21	L, 13–37, at Denver Broncos
11/28	L, 3–23, at Houston Oilers
12/5	W, 17–14, vs. New England Patriots
12/13	W, 21–20, at Miami Dolphins
12/19	L, 17–26, vs. Houston Oilers
12/26	L, 6–16, at Seattle Seahawks
1/2	W, 16–9, vs. Cleveland Browns

Playoffs

1/8	L, 24–27 (OT), at Kansas City Chiefs

Team Scoring

308 points scored
281 points allowed

143

12–4   1st place

Game-by-Game

9/4	**L**, 9–26, vs. Dallas Cowboys
9/11	**W**, 17–10, at Cleveland Browns
9/18	**W**, 31–21, vs. Indianapolis Colts
9/25	**L**, 13–30, at Seattle Seahawks
10/3	**W**, 30–14, vs. Houston Oilers
10/16	**W**, 14–10, vs. Cincinnati Bengals
10/23	**W**, 10–6, at New York Giants
10/30	**L**, 17–20 (OT), at Arizona Cardinals
11/6	**W**, 12–9 (OT), at Houston Oilers
11/14	**W**, 23–10, vs. Buffalo Bills
11/20	**W**, 16–13 (OT), vs. Miami Dolphins
11/27	**W**, 21–3, at L.A. Raiders
12/4	**W**, 38–15, at Cincinnati Bengals
12/11	**W**, 14–3, vs. Philadelphia Eagles
12/18	**W**, 17–7, vs. Cleveland Browns
12/24	**L**, 34–37, at San Diego Chargers

Playoffs

1/7	**W**, 29–9, vs. Cleveland Browns
1/15	**L**, 13–17, vs. San Diego Chargers

Team Scoring

316 points scored
234 points allowed

CHAMPIONSHIP-STYLE FOOTBALL

Steelers Fall Just Three Yards Short of the Super Bowl

Prior to their playoff matchup in January 1995, Cleveland's Earnest Byner tried to taunt Steelers defensive end Brentson Buckner by stomping on his Terrible Towel.

"I'm supposed to be scared because he's doing this?" Buckner asked afterward.

Hardly. Although the fans who waved their Terrible Towels inspired Pittsburgh to eight home victories in 1994, it was the Steelers' talent and determination that helped them go an AFC-best 12–4—and beat Cleveland three times, including in the playoffs.

The Steelers prevailed with old-school, smash-mouth football. A massive offensive line, led by Pro Bowlers Dermontti Dawson and Duval Love, paved the way for the top running game in the NFL. Power backs Barry Foster and Bam Morris each topped 800 yards.

Defensively, Pittsburgh ranked second in the league in both points and yardage. Outside linebacker Kevin Greene led the NFL with 14 quarterback sacks, while fellow OLB Greg Lloyd—an All-Pro in '94—chalked up 10 sacks. Inside linebackers Chad Brown and Levon Kirkland led the team with 119 and 100 total tackles, respectively. Strong safety Carnell Lake joined fellow defensive back Rod Woodson in the Pro Bowl. "He's the ultimate warrior," Steelers receiver Ernie Mills said of Lake. "He's big, strong, and fast . . . the best strong safety in the game."

After losing in overtime to Arizona to drop to 5–3, Bill Cowher's Steelers ripped off seven consecutive victories. Two came in sudden-death, as Gary Anderson booted walk-off field goals against Houston and Miami. The most satisfying win of the regular season may have come against the rival Browns on December 18. Pittsburgh scored two quick touchdowns and cruised to a 17–7 victory to clinch home-field advantage in the playoffs. A record-setting Three Rivers crowd was rockin', and Santa Claus gave Cowher a

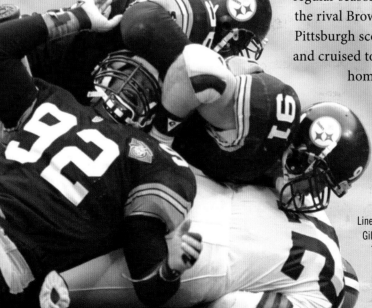

Linebackers Kevin Greene (91) and Jason Gildon (92) bury quarterback Vinny Testaverde in the turf during Pittsburgh's convincing 29–9 playoff win over the Browns. *Simon Bruty/Getty Images*

congratulatory handshake as he trotted off the field.

By winning its opening playoff game, Cleveland earned the right to lose to Pittsburgh yet again. This time, the Steelers steamrolled the Browns 29–9, as Foster ran for 133 of the team's 238 yards. "They blocked the world," said Morris. Steelers President Dan Rooney could sense that championship-style football had finally returned to Pittsburgh. "This is a new time," he said, as quoted in the *Pittsburgh Post-Gazette*, "a wonderful time."

The Steelers should have beaten San Diego in the AFC Championship Game; after all, they outgained the Chargers 415 yards to 226. In freakish 60-degree weather, Neil O'Donnell opened the scoring with a 16-yard touchdown pass to John Williams. Pittsburgh led 13–3 until San Diego's Stan Humphries threw 43-yard touchdown passes in both the third and fourth quarters, putting the Chargers ahead 17–13.

On the Steelers' final drive, O'Donnell completed seven consecutive passes to move the ball to the 9-yard line. A third-down pass to Williams got the Steelers to the 3, but it was fourth down. It all came down to one play. O'Donnell fired the ball to Foster in the end zone, but it was broken up by linebacker Dennis Gibson. The Chargers ran out the clock and advanced to the Super Bowl.

"There's a very empty feeling right now," Cowher said afterward. "I guess you can say the further you come, the harder it is to fall."

Neil O'Donnell threw for 349 yards and no interceptions in the AFC Championship Game against San Diego, yet the Steelers scored only one touchdown. They shot themselves in the foot with eight penalties for 111 yards. *Greg Crisp/Getty Images*

Passion and Pride:
Bill Cowher

On January 21, 1992, Bill Cowher was full of can-do confidence. The energetic 34-year-old had just been named the Steelers' new head coach, replacing the legendary Chuck Noll, and already he was talking Super Bowl. "My goal is to put a fifth trophy out there," he told the press.

"Chuck Noll was Chuck Noll. . . . Bill Cowher is going to be Bill Cowher," he said. "I'm going to be me. I've prepared myself to handle adversity, and I've prepared myself to handle success."

But as Ed Bouchette of the *Pittsburgh Post-Gazette* reported, Cowher was not as self-assured as he appeared to be. "I don't know what I've gotten into," Cowher told his wife, Kaye, on the phone a few hours after his initial press conference. "Honey, I may have gotten myself in too deep over my head."

Though he may have confided his insecurities to his wife, Cowher made his players feel that everything would be all right. "Coach Cowher came in very motivated, very personable . . . ," safety Carnell Lake said. "He came and saw—and instilled a greater sense of team unity."

In his initial interview with Cowher, Steelers President Dan Rooney knew he was the right coach for the Steelers. "Bill's self-discipline and integrity shone through . . . ," Rooney wrote in his autobiography. "Cowher also had an infectious enthusiasm. He wanted to win. What's more, he even looked like a Steeler. With his jutting jaw and chiseled features, he reminded me of our old logo, the one that depicted a rough, tough, brawny steelworker walking an I-beam."

Born in Pittsburgh, Cowher starred in multiple sports at Carlynton High School. Though he wanted to play at Penn State, he ended up starring for North Carolina State, where he was named team MVP. The 6-foot-3, 225-pound linebacker made it in the NFL, but just barely. He played two years

apiece, as a deep reserve and special teams player, with Cleveland and Philadelphia in the early 1980s.

"I was always that guy who had to sweat out the 47-man roster to make the cut . . . ," he said. "I spent the extra time studying, working, trying to find that little edge that would get me up to the gifted guy. That work ethic that I had to bring as a marginal athlete is one that I took over to coaching."

Cowher rose quickly through the NFL coaching ranks, first as a special teams and secondary coach with Cleveland and then, beginning in 1989, as the defensive coordinator for Kansas City.

With the Steelers, Cowher inherited a slew of talented players and fused them into an instant winner. Players lauded him as communicative, respectful, and inspiring. He could also be a demanding SOB, especially when guys committed mental mistakes on the field. "When he gets in your face, you know the saliva's going to fly," linebacker Greg Lloyd told *Sports Illustrated*. "When he gives you that shower, you just hope it's raining so you can't tell if it's rain or spit."

In his first six seasons as Steelers head coach, Cowher led Pittsburgh to the playoffs every year, including a Super Bowl trip during the 1995–96 campaign. In his 15 seasons at the post, Cowher made the postseason 10 times, including a 15–1 season in 2004 and a Super Bowl triumph a year later. Under Cowher, the Steelers went 149–90–1. His commitment to building a tough defense paid off handsomely. His teams finished in the NFL's top three in fewest yards allowed six times.

After an 8–8 season in 2006, Cowher stepped down to spend more time with his family. They turned out to be precious years, as Kaye battled cancer and died in 2010. As late as 2013, Cowher said he likely would return to coaching again. If so, the line of interested GMs would be out the door.

The fiery Bill Cowher wasn't shy about telling off the zebras. In 2003, he was fined $10,000 for criticizing a replay official. *Don Emmert/AFP/Getty Images*

11–5   1st place

Game-by-Game

9/3	**W, 23–20,** vs. Detroit Lions
9/10	**W, 34–17,** at Houston Oilers
9/18	**L, 10–23,** at Miami Dolphins
9/24	**L, 24–44,** vs. Minnesota Vikings
10/1	**W, 31–16,** vs. San Diego Chargers
10/8	**L, 16–20,** at Jacksonville
10/19	**L, 9–27,** vs. Cincinnati Bengals
10/29	**W, 24–7,** vs. Jacksonville
11/5	**W, 37–34 (OT),** at Chicago Bears
11/13	**W, 20–3,** vs. Cleveland Browns
11/19	**W, 49–31,** at Cincinnati Bengals
11/26	**W, 20–17,** at Cleveland Browns
12/3	**W, 21–7,** vs. Houston Oilers
12/10	**W, 29–10,** at Oakland Raiders
12/16	**W, 41–27,** vs. New England Patriots
12/24	**L, 19–24,** at Green Bay Packers

Playoffs

1/6	**W, 40–21,** vs. Buffalo Bills
1/14	**W, 20–16,** vs. Indianapolis Colts
1/28	**Super Bowl: L, 17–27,** vs. Dallas Cowboys

Team Scoring

407 points scored

327 points allowed

The AFC Championship Game ended when Colts receiver Aaron Bailey couldn't corral this "Hail Mary" pass from quarterback Jim Harbaugh. *Keith Srakocic/AP Images*

A BLITZ TO THE SUPER BOWL

Steelers Win Eight Straight, Overcome Playoff Scares

" Three More Yards." After falling that much short of a Super Bowl the previous season, "Three More Yards" became the rallying cry in 1995. But seven games into the new season, with Pittsburgh struggling at 3–4, grinding out a little extra yardage wasn't the problem. The issues were Rod Woodson's torn ACL and Neil O'Donnell's broken finger, both suffered in a season-opening win over Detroit.

Backup quarterback Mike Tomczak may have misinterpreted the rallying cry as "Three More Picks." In O'Donnell's absence, he threw three interceptions each against Detroit, Miami, and Minnesota. Jim Miller entered the Vikings game and fired three picks, too. The most frustrating loss of all may have been the one that dropped the Steelers to 3–4. In a Thursday night game against Cincinnati, Pittsburgh amassed 468 yards and committed just one turnover but lost 27–9.

"We just can't score," said Steelers running back Morris. "We're kicking field goals or not even doing that. It's frustrating, and we've got to start getting it right."

The Steelers got it right in the next two games, crushing Jacksonville 24–7 and beating the Bears in overtime 37–34. In Chicago, O'Donnell fired a fourth-down touchdown pass to Ernie Mills with 1:06 left, and Norm Johnson won it with a 24-yard field goal in sudden-death. "This," O'Donnell said afterward, "is just the start of a lot of big things to come."

O'Donnell delivered on his prophecy, extending the Steelers' winning streak to eight games. The defense—one of the league's finest—keyed victories over Cleveland, Houston, and Oakland, yielding just 27 first downs *combined* in those games. All-Pro linebacker Greg Lloyd led the "Blitzburgh" defense in '95 with 116 total tackles and six forced fumbles. Willie Williams, who replaced Woodson at cornerback, was second on the club with 69 solo tackles and third in the NFL with seven interceptions.

While scatback Erric Pegram led the Steelers with 813 rushing yards, O'Donnell—known as a conservative game manager—ranked ninth in the league with 247.5 yards per game. O'Donnell found a jackpot in athletic wide receiver Yancey Thigpen, who set a Pittsburgh record with 85 receptions, good for 1,307 yards. The Steelers' second battle against Cincinnati showed how far the offense had improved. They upped their yardage from 468 to 556 and their points from nine to 49. O'Donnell threw for a career-high 377 yards.

The Steelers finished with an 11–5 record, winning the AFC Central by four games. In the playoff opener at Three Rivers, with the wind chill dipping toward zero, the Steelers opened up a 26–7 lead on Buffalo in the third quarter. After the Bills cut the lead to 26–21, Bam Morris scored two late touchdowns for a 40–21 win.

Pittsburgh caught a break when Indianapolis (9–7 in the regular season) upset Kansas City (13–3) in the playoffs. That gave the Steelers the home-field advantage in the AFC Championship Game. Pittsburgh, an 11-point favorite, led 13–9 in the fourth quarter when Colts quarterback Jim Harbaugh quieted the crowd with a 47-yard touchdown pass to Floyd Turner.

O'Donnell countered with his own theatrics, hitting Mills with a 37-yard pass to the Colts' 1-yard line with 1:51 left. Morris scored, and the Steelers went ahead 20–16. Harbaugh could have won the game with his last-second heave to the end zone, but his tipped pass fell on prone Colts receiver Aaron Bailey and rolled off his chest.

"It was almost another Immaculate Reception," Bailey said.

Key word: *almost*.

For the first time in 16 years, the Steelers were headed to the Super Bowl.

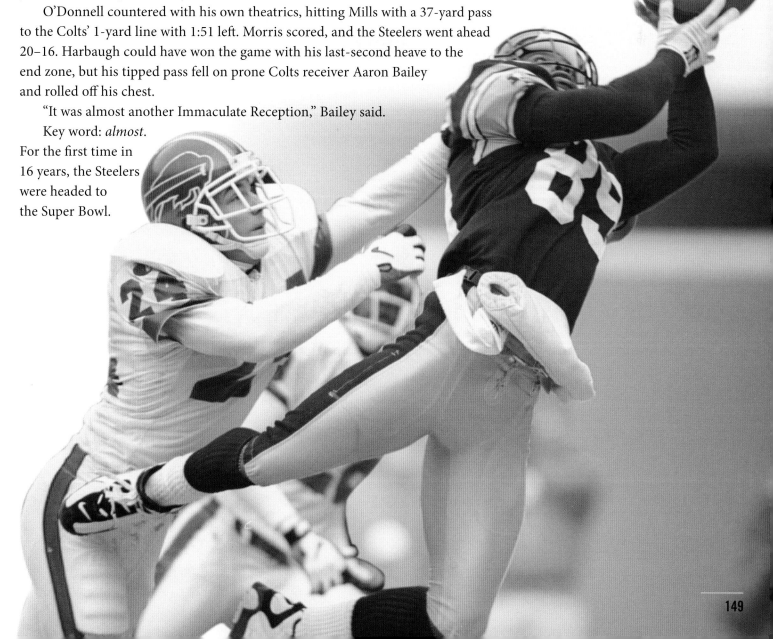

Ernie Mills caught six passes, including one for a touchdown, in Pittsburgh's 40–21 playoff thumping of the Bills to advance to the AFC title game. *Don Pensinger/Getty Images*

Super Bowl XXX:
Throwing It All Away

As the "XXX" label implied, a lot was "hot" about the January 1996 Super Bowl. The game was played for the first time in Arizona (Sun Devil Stadium in Tempe), beauty queen Vanessa Williams sang the National Anthem, and the contest featured two of the NFL's marquee brands—the Steelers and Dallas Cowboys, who were gunning for their third straight Super Bowl title. No wonder the game attracted a record 95.1 million U.S. viewers.

Besides the Hall of Fame–bound "Triplets"—quarterback Troy Aikman, wide receiver Michael Irvin, and running back Emmett Smith—the Cowboys had added glitzy cornerback "Neon" Deion Sanders. Led by coach Barry Switzer, Dallas went 12–4 during the season and entered the game as a 13 ½-point favorite—in part because NFC teams had won 11 straight Super Bowls. Rod Woodson, despite tearing his ACL in the season opener, returned to play for Pittsburgh,

Odds-makers were feeling smug when Dallas took a 13–0 lead. But a six-yard touchdown pass by Neil O'Donnell to Yancey Thigpen with 13 seconds left in the first half put Pittsburgh back in the game. Dallas cornerback Larry Brown, whose infant son had died in November, proved the hero in the second half, intercepting two passes. In the third quarter, Brown's 44-yard interception return set up a Cowboys touchdown, putting them ahead 20–7.

Pittsburgh rallied in the fourth quarter, scoring first on a 46-yard Norm Johnson field goal to make it 20–10. Though more than 11 minutes remained, Bill Cowher called for an onside kick. The Steelers recovered, and nine plays later Bam Morris powered in from the 1. The extra point made it 20–17, and after Pittsburgh forced Dallas to punt, the Steelers had a chance to tie or go ahead.

That's when O'Donnell and receiver Andre Hastings miscommunicated on their route. "I did a hook and Neil ran an out," Hastings said. The ball sailed right to Brown, who returned it 33 yards to the 6. Two plays later, Emmitt Smith scored the clinching touchdown, as Dallas won 27–17.

"We gave away the Super Bowl," said running back Erric Pegram. "We gave the darn thing away."

Except for one player, none of these Steelers would have a chance to redeem themselves. Cornerback Willie Williams was the only man on the 1995 roster who would win a Super Bowl with Pittsburgh 10 years later.

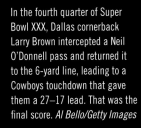

In the fourth quarter of Super Bowl XXX, Dallas cornerback Larry Brown intercepted a Neil O'Donnell pass and returned it to the 6-yard line, leading to a Cowboys touchdown that gave them a 27–17 lead. That was the final score. *Al Bello/Getty Images*

Lights Out:
Dermontti Dawson

As her baby started crying, Brandy Jurkovic nudged her husband to get up and handle the feeding. John Jurkovic, a defensive tackle for Jacksonville, didn't mind doing so on this night; he was already awake. "I'd been tossing and turning before he started crying," Jurkovic told *Sports Illustrated*, because in two days he would face a certain Steelers center named Dermontti. "Dawson has that effect on your sleep," Jurkovic said.

Jerome Bettis called Dawson the quickest lineman in the league, so quick that he could pull and lead a sweep. "He's as nimble as a defensive back," Steelers offensive lineman Roger Duffy told *SI*. "I've played center, but when I watch Dermontti, it's like the tape's on a different speed."

Bill Cowher dubbed Dawson the best center in NFL history. "The greatest thing about Dermontti is, he epitomized what you want in a player," Cowher told the *Pittsburgh Post-Gazette*. "When he came to work, he had a smile on his face. He loved life; he loved practice. He was one of those guys—you talk about tempo—he was running out of the huddle every play. Everyone had to keep up with him."

While growing up in Lexington, Kentucky, Dermontti was so dutiful that he made sure the house was spic-and-span before his mother returned home from work. In track, he won the state title in both the discus throw and shot put. Despite his freakish quickness and speed, and 290 pounds of solid muscle, Dawson wasn't taken out of Kentucky until the 44th pick in the 1988 draft.

A year later, Dawson replaced Mike Webster as Pittsburgh's starting center. That meant that the Steelers had a Hall of Famer at the position continuously for 27 years. Dawson, who was inducted in 2012, played in 170 consecutive games and was named first-team All-Pro six consecutive years (1993–98). He retired in 2000, finally allowing opposing nose tackles to get a good night's sleep.

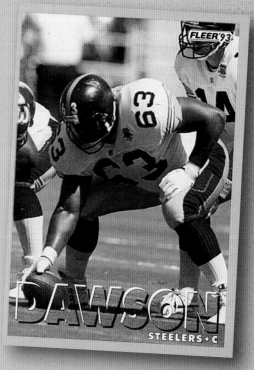

In high school, Dermontti Dawson was timed in the 40-yard-dash in 4.4 seconds—jaw-dropping for a guy whose listed NFL playing weight was 288 pounds. *MVP Books Collection*

Game-by-Game

Date	Result	Opponent
9/1	L, 9–24,	at Jacksonville Jaguars
9/8	W, 31–17,	vs. Baltimore Ravens
9/16	W, 24–6,	vs. Buffalo Bills
9/29	W, 30–16,	vs. Houston Oilers
10/7	W, 17–7,	at Kansas City Chiefs
10/13	W, 20–10,	vs. Cincinnati Bengals
10/20	L, 13–23,	at Houston Texans
10/27	W, 20–17,	at Atlanta Falcons
11/3	W, 42–6,	vs. St. Louis Rams
11/10	L, 24–34,	at Cincinnati Bengals
11/17	W, 28–3,	vs. Jacksonville Jaguars
11/25	W, 24–17,	at Miami Dolphins
12/1	L, 17–31,	at Baltimore Ravens
12/8	W, 16–3,	vs. San Diego Chargers
12/15	L, 15–25,	vs. San Francisco 49ers
12/22	L, 14–18,	at Carolina Panthers

Playoffs

Date	Result	Opponent
12/29	W, 42–14,	vs. Indianapolis Colts
1/5	L, 3–28,	at New England Patriots

Team Scoring

344 points scored
257 points allowed

POWER FOOTBALL

Bettis, Defense Muscle Steelers to Division Title

If the Steelers were to repeat as AFC champions in 1996, they'd have to do so without three of their best players. Quarterback Neil O'Donnell, offensive tackle Leon Searcy, and linebacker Kevin Greene—all former or future Pro Bowlers—left as free agents.

Steelers fans were dreading life under new starting quarterback Mike Tomczak, a 33-year-old journeyman who had thrown nine interceptions and just one touchdown pass a year earlier for Pittsburgh. Tomczak was no Tom Brady during his 15 starts in 1996, ranking 23rd in the NFL in passer rating, but he did win 10 games, a feat achieved by only four other quarterbacks that year.

Really, it was the running game—which ranked second in the NFL—that powered the Steelers offense. Big, bruising Jerome Bettis, acquired in a trade with St. Louis, bulldozed his way to 1,431 yards and 11 touchdowns. Speedy Erric Pegram offered a change of pace, compiling 509 yards (5.2 per carry) behind Pittsburgh's stellar offensive line. Kordell Stewart, a backup quarterback with sprinter speed, blazed an 80-yard path to glory during the season finale against Carolina.

On the strength of a 7–1 home record, the Steelers went 10–6 in '96, clinching the AFC Central title in their 14th game before dropping the last two.

Steelers defenders Jerry Olsavsky (55) and Kevin Henry sack Colts quarterback Jim Harbaugh in a 42–14 playoff rout of Indianapolis. Harbaugh was held to 140 yards on 33 throws, and he was sacked four times. *Henry Abrams/AFP/Getty Images*

The "Blitzburgh" defense, which held five opponents under 10 points, ranked second in the NFL in both takeaways and fewest yards allowed. Darren Perry and Pro Bowlers Rod Woodson and Carnell Lake all recorded pick-sixes. Inside linebacker Levon Kirkland, who blended the heft of a defensive tackle with the feet of a safety, led the team with 113 total tackles. All-Pro linebacker Chad Brown rang up 13 sacks.

Entering the playoffs, fans still worried about Tomczak, whose passer rating over the last three games was a woeful 54.2. He sputtered in the wildcard game against Indianapolis (176 yards, two picks), but the running game (231 rushing yards) and defense (eight first downs allowed) carried Pittsburgh to a resounding 42–14 win at Three Rivers. The Steelers actually trailed 14–13 at halftime, but they opened the second half with a 16-play, 91-yard drive that took 9:30 off the clock. "We just started to pound it and pound it," said Bettis, who rushed for 102 yards. "That drive exemplified what this offense can do."

In the Colts game, Bill Cowher platooned Tomczak with Stewart, who threw just one pass but ran nine times, scoring two touchdowns. Cowher tried the same combo the next week at New England, but with dismal results.

In what was dubbed the "Fog Bowl," the Patriots opened up a 21–0 first-half lead and cruised to a 28–3 victory. Tomczak completed 16 of 29 passes, but for just 110 yards, while Stewart went 0-for-10. The Steelers ran for a modest 123 yards. "Their defensive line did some stunts and caught our offensive line off guard," said Bettis, who was hampered by a groin injury. "I wasn't 100 percent, so it was a rough day out there."

Uncertainty about the Steelers' quarterback situation would continue throughout the winter—and into the spring and summer.

The Steelers were enveloped by fog and the Patriots defense in the divisional playoff game at New England, where the Patriots marched to a 28–3 victory.
Al Bello/Getty Images

11–5   1st place

Game-by-Game

8/31	**L, 7–37,**	vs. Dallas Cowboys
9/7	**W, 14–13,**	vs. Washington Redskins
9/22	**L, 21–30,**	at Jacksonville Jaguars
9/28	**W, 37–24,**	vs. Tennessee Titans
10/5	**W, 42–34,**	at Baltimore Ravens
10/12	**W, 24–22,**	vs. Indianapolis Colts
10/19	**W, 26–10,**	at Cincinnati Bengals
10/26	**W, 23–17 (OT),**	vs. Jacksonville Jaguars
11/3	**L, 10–13,**	at Kansas City Chiefs
11/9	**W, 37–0,**	vs. Baltimore Ravens
11/16	**W, 20–3,**	vs. Cincinnati Bengals
11/23	**L, 20–23,**	at Philadelphia Eagles
11/30	**W, 26–20 (OT),**	at Arizona Cardinals
12/7	**W, 35–24,**	vs. Denver Broncos
12/13	**W, 24–21 (OT),**	at New England Patriots
12/21	**L, 6–16,**	at Tennessee Titans

Playoffs

1/3	**W, 7–6, vs. New England Patriots**
1/11	**L, 21–24, vs. Denver Broncos**

Team Scoring

372 points scored

307 points allowed

RUNNER/PASSER/WINNER

"Slash" Leads Pittsburgh to AFC Title Game

In July 1997, Bill Cowher announced that Kordell Stewart would be his starting quarterback for the upcoming season. Fans didn't know what to expect from the extraordinarily gifted but unproven QB. Stewart possessed blazing speed and could chuck the ball 75 yards, as he had done for Colorado against Michigan with a successful "Hail Mary" pass in 1994. In his first two seasons with Pittsburgh (1995–96), Stewart was called "Slash" because of the keyboard symbol; he lined up at quarterback/running back/wide receiver. Yet as a passer, including the playoffs, he completed only 17 of 48 attempts in those two seasons.

Stewart struggled early in 1997, as the Steelers opened at 1–2. But in the next five games—all wins—"Slash" completed 58 percent of his passes, threw for eight touchdowns, and ran for five. With Stewart hitting his targets—including Yancey Thigpen, who set a team record with 1,398 receiving yards—and averaging 5.4 yards per carry on the season, defenses were spread thin. That pleased Jerome "The Bus" Bettis, who amassed 1,665 rushing yards.

On the season, Stewart threw for 3,020 yards and 21 touchdowns while running for 476 yards and 11 scores. Moreover, he led the NFL with five game-winning drives, three of which came in overtime. In sudden-deaths, Pittsburgh beat Jacksonville on a Stewart-to-Bettis touchdown pass, Arizona on a Bettis TD run, and New England on a Norm Johnson field goal. All the while, the Steelers utterly dominated the line of scrimmage, leading the NFL in both rushing yards (2,479)—behind nose tackle Joel Steed and inside linebacker Levon Kirkland—and fewest rushing yards allowed (1,318).

Pittsburgh finished at 11–5 and won the AFC Central, edging 11–5 Jacksonville. The teams had gone 1–1 against each other and 6–2 in the division, but the Steelers won the tiebreaker because they had defeated division opponents by a larger margin than the Jaguars had.

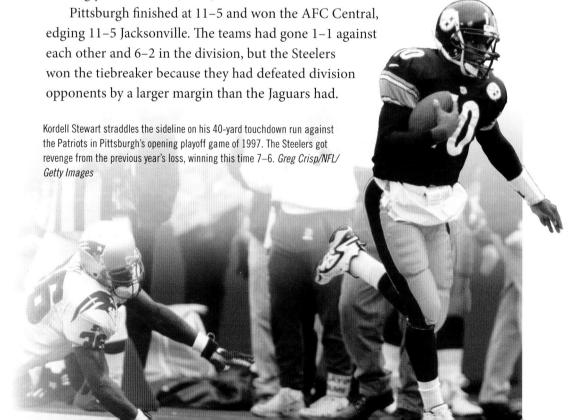

Kordell Stewart straddles the sideline on his 40-yard touchdown run against the Patriots in Pittsburgh's opening playoff game of 1997. The Steelers got revenge from the previous year's loss, winning this time 7–6. *Greg Crisp/NFL/ Getty Images*

Pittsburgh also earned the AFC's No. 2 seed, which meant a first-round bye, and hosted New England in their first playoff game.

Stewart opened the scoring early with a 40-yard touchdown run. From there, it was a white-knuckle ride to the finish line, as Pittsburgh prevailed 7–6. With 3:24 to go, New England stuffed Stewart at the 1 on fourth down. "I should have kicked the field goal," Cowher said afterward. "I'm a young coach and I screwed up." The Steelers defense, however, saved its coach's hide. Defensive end Mike Vrabel forced a fumble, and Kirkland picked off a Drew Bledsoe "Hail Mary" pass to end the game.

Hosting Denver in the AFC Championship Game, the Steelers went ahead 14–7 early in the second quarter thanks to a 33-yard touchdown run by Stewart and a 1-yard plow by Bettis. But John Elway led the Broncos to a 24–14 lead by halftime, and that scored remained unchanged until Stewart fired a 14-yard touchdown pass to Charles Johnson with 2:46 remaining. Denver then faced third-and-six at its own 15, but Elway completed a first-down pass to Shannon Sharpe to seal the deal. The Broncos won 24–21.

Afterward, Denver linebacker Bill Romanowski showed no mercy for his conquered foes. "The Steelers said they wanted to ride The Bus," he said. "Well, they can—home for the off-season."

Yancey Thigpen hauled in six catches for 92 yards, but it wasn't enough in the Steelers' 24–21 loss to Denver in the AFC Championship Game. Thigpen was coming off a career season in which he led the team in catches, receiving yards, and receiving touchdowns. *Greg Crisp/Getty Images*

The Bus: Jerome Bettis

On Draft Day 1996, the Steelers stole the keys to "The Bus," then climbed aboard for a 10-year joy ride.

Pittsburgh's acquisition of Jerome Bettis from St. Louis was more like highway robbery. In three seasons with the Rams, the 5-foot-11, 250-pound monster back had rushed for 3,091 yards and earned two Pro Bowl invitations. But Rams coach Rich Brooks said he "wanted a little more speed at the position," so St. Louis traded Bettis and a third-round pick to Pittsburgh for second- and fourth-round selections.

Bettis may not have been a speed-burner, but he fit in perfectly with Bill Cowher's offense. Bettis was like Bam Morris on steroids—figuratively speaking. While the Steelers' massive offensive line could push defenders two yards up field, Bettis could carry the pile for several more. He even had surprisingly quick feet for his size.

Bettis was an immediate sensation with the Steelers. He topped 100 yards rushing 10 times in 1996, including 129 yards and two first-quarter touchdowns against the Rams. He had plenty of "speed at the position" when he raced 50 yards for a touchdown that afternoon. "That season," wrote Myron Cope in his autobiography, "he battered his way to 1,431 yards, leaving would-be tacklers prone as if hit by a bus." So Cope started calling Bettis "The Bus." His uniform colors, which resembled those of a school bus, added to the appeal of the nickname.

Jerome had grown up in Detroit, where he excelled in the classroom and, for fun, liked to bowl and ice skate. Bettis was diagnosed with asthma as a teenager, but that didn't stop him from pursuing his football dreams. With Notre Dame, St. Louis,

and Pittsburgh, Bettis impressed everyone with his caring nature, maturity, and positive attitude. "He's upbeat," Cowher said. "He's bubbly. He's smart. He's committed."

Everyone loved The Bus, especially in 1997 when he ran for a career-high 1,665 yards on a league-topping 375 carries. In his first six seasons with Pittsburgh, Bettis surpassed 1,000 yards every year, averaging 1,298 per. His 10,571 career rushing yards with the Steelers rank second in team history behind Franco Harris's 11,950. Jerome's NFL career totals of 3,479 carries and 13,662 yards rank fourth and sixth, respectively. Only three running backs in NFL history tallied more carries than Jerome

Bettis explained how he piled up the yards. "I tried to inflict punishment on the defenders instead of just taking it," he said. "When I did that, I got defenders to turn away. After getting hit so many times, their mentality changed from being aggressive to just trying to get me on the ground. Then they had to play my game. I was able to make them miss me, or bounce off them and keep going."

In the community and in the locker room, Bettis was a charismatic leader. Quarterback Ben Roethlisberger remembered how Jerome took him under his wing right after he was drafted in 2004. "He opens up my notebook to the first page and writes down his phone numbers," Roethlisberger recalled in *The Bus: My Life in and out of a Helmet*. "He says, 'This is my home number; this is my cell number. If you ever need anything, give me a call. . . .' When he walked away I was like, 'Wow, I can't believe that just happened.' I was so in awe."

Late in his career, Bettis's body was so battered that he had trouble getting out of bed and walking down stairs. Yet in 2005, he came back for one final season. In a fairytale campaign, he helped lead the Steelers to a Super Bowl victory, with the ultimate game played in his hometown of Detroit. After the win, Bettis stood next to Hines Ward, the Super Bowl MVP. "I'm going to Disneyland, baby," Ward announced, "and I'm taking The Bus!"

Left: Bettis has always found time for fans, even those who can't afford Heinz Field tickets. His Bus Stops Here Foundation attempts to improve the overall quality of life for troubled and underprivileged children. *Keith Srakocic/AP Images*

Right: In the first postseason game of his career, Jerome Bettis busted through the Colts defense to the tune of 102 yards and two touchdowns on December 29, 1996. *Tony Tomsic/Getty Images*

1998

7–9 3rd place

Game-by-Game

9/6	**W, 20–13,** at Baltimore Ravens
9/13	**W, 17–12,** vs. Chicago Bears
9/20	**L, 0–21,** at Miami Dolphins
9/27	**W, 13–10,** vs. Seattle Seahawks
10/11	**L, 20–25,** at Cincinnati Bengals
10/18	**W, 16–6,** vs. Baltimore Ravens
10/26	**W, 20–13,** at Kansas City Chiefs
11/1	**L, 31–41,** vs. Tennessee Titans
11/9	**W, 27–20,** vs. Green Bay Packers
11/15	**L, 14–23,** at Tennessee Titans
11/22	**W, 30–15,** vs. Jacksonville Jaguars
11/26	**L, 16–19 (OT),** at Detroit Lions
12/6	**L, 9–23,** vs. New England Patriots
12/13	**L, 3–16,** at Tampa Bay Buccaneers
12/20	**L, 24–25,** vs. Cincinnati Bengals
12/28	**L, 3–21,** at Jacksonville Jaguars

Team Scoring

263 points scored
303 points allowed

Steelers tight end Mark Bruener catches a Thanksgiving Day pass while defended by Detroit's Rob Fredrickson. The infamous overtime coin toss was forthcoming. *Duane Burleson/AP Images*

HEADS . . . YOU LOSE

Steelers Tank After Turkey Day Coin-Toss Fiasco

Even though Pittsburgh entered 1998 without offensive coordinator Chan Gailey and wide receiver Yancey Thigpen (lost to free agency), the season started well enough. The Steelers opened at 7–4, including wins over playoff-bound Green Bay and Jacksonville. But then, with a flip of a coin, the season turned.

As Steelers and Lions captains met for a pre-overtime coin flip on Thanksgiving Day in Detroit, Jerome Bettis called "tails" and referee Phil Luckett misinterpreted his call as "heads." The Lions received, drove downfield, and kicked a field goal. Game over. Afterward, Luckett said that Bettis had called "heads . . . tails." "I did not say 'heads-tails,'" Bettis retorted. "That is a lie. That's a bald-faced lie."

Regardless, the "Curse of the Coin Toss" seemed to haunt the Steelers the rest of the season. They lost each of the next four weeks to fall to 7–9, missing the playoffs for the first time in Bill Cowher's seven-year tenure. It was hard to tell which hurt more—the 25–24 loss to the rival Bengals or the other three defeats, in which Pittsburgh mustered a total of five field goals and no touchdowns. Kordell Stewart struggled mightily in the last four games, throwing seven interceptions and no touchdown passes.

After a season-ending loss to Jacksonville, the Steelers were blaming themselves, not officials. "We ought to take a look in the mirror and make sure something like this doesn't happen again," Steelers halfback Fred McAfee said. "We have to come back with a fire and a vigor that no one has ever seen."

The Steelers Nation was not exactly proud of its team during the 1999 season, as evidenced by this fan who opted to hide his face under a bag. Pittsburgh lost seven of its last eight games to finish at 6–10. *Ezra Shaw/Getty Images*

Game-by-Game

9/12	W, 43–0, at Cleveland Browns
9/19	W, 23–20, at Baltimore Ravens
9/26	L, 10–29, vs. Seattle Seahawks
10/3	L, 3–17, vs. Jacksonville Jaguars
10/10	L, 21–24, at Buffalo Bills
10/17	W, 17–3, at Cincinnati Bengals
10/25	W, 13–9, vs. Atlanta Falcons
11/7	W, 27–6, at San Francisco 49ers
11/14	L, 15–16, vs. Cleveland Browns
11/21	L, 10–16, at Tennessee Titans
11/28	L, 20–27, vs. Cincinnati Bengals
12/2	L, 6–20, at Jacksonville Jaguars
12/12	L, 24–31, vs. Baltimore Ravens
12/18	L, 19–35, at Kansas City Chiefs
12/26	W, 30–20, vs. Carolina Panthers
1/2	L, 27–36, vs. Tennessee Titans

Team Scoring

317 points scored
320 points allowed

LATE-SEASON COLLAPSE

Steelers Take a Tumble After 5–3 Start

When the Steelers ventured into Candlestick Park in 1999 and whipped the 49ers 27–6, to improve to 5–3, it looked like they were primed for a playoff run. "We're going forward," said Steelers safety Lee Flowers. "We have the momentum, and we're definitely playing well."

That was November 7. By Christmas Day, the Steelers had yet to win another game. They lost six straight, and they finished the season at 6–10. What Flowers didn't count on was a pair of four-turnover games, three matchups against really tough opponents (Tennessee twice and Jacksonville), and the unexpected demise of the defense.

The Steelers opened the season with a 43–0 mauling of Cleveland. Kordell Stewart threw for a touchdown and ran for one, and Mike Tomczak went 8-for-8 with two touchdown passes in relief—including one to second-year wide receiver Hines Ward, his first of 85 career TD catches. While Stewart struggled during the year (just one 200-yard passing game), Tomczak made five starts at age 37 and performed well (12 touchdowns, eight interceptions). The defense was more troubling than Stewart. After allowing just 18 total points during a midseason three-game winning streak, it coughed up 133 over the last four games.

The season finale against Tennessee turned ugly. After Pittsburgh's Joey Porter scored on a 46-yard fumble return to cut the Titans' lead to 40–29, Tennessee's Denard Walker returned a fumble 83 yards to pretty much wrap it up. After the play, frustrated Steelers receiver Troy Edwards punched Titans defensive end Danion Sidney; both were ejected.

"Very frustrating," coach Bill Cowher said about the season. "Very disappointing."

THE 1990s RECORD BOOK

Team Leaders

(**Boldface** indicates league leader)

Scoring Leaders (Points)

1990: Gary Anderson, 92
1991: Gary Anderson, 100
1992: Gary Anderson, 113
1993: Gary Anderson, 116
1994: Gary Anderson, 104
1995: Norm Johnson, 141
1996: Norm Johnson, 106
1997: Norm Johnson, 106
1998: Norm Johnson, 99
1999: Kris Brown, 105

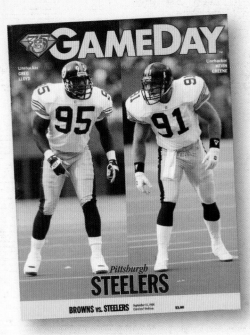

The Steelers ranked among the NFL's top three in defense five times in the 1990s, thanks in large part to linebackers Greg Lloyd and Kevin Greene. *MVP Books Collection*

Passing Leaders

(Completions / Attempts / Yards)

1990: Bubby Brister, 223 / 387 / 2,725
1991: Neil O'Donnell, 156 / 286 / 1,963
1992: Neil O'Donnell, 185 / 313 / 2,283
1993: Neil O'Donnell, 270 / 486 / 3,208
1994: Neil O'Donnell, 212 / 370 / 2,443
1995: Neil O'Donnell, 246 / 416 / 2,970
1996: Mike Tomczak, 222 / 401 / 2,767
1997: Kordell Stewart, 236 / 440 / 3,020
1998: Kordell Stewart, 252 / 458 / 2,560
1999: Mike Tomczak, 139 / 258 1,625

Rushing Leaders

(Carries / Yards / TDs)

1990: Merril Hoge, 203 / 772 / 7
1991: Merril Hoge, 165 / 610 / 2
1992: Barry Foster, **390** / 1,690 / 11
1993: Leroy Thompson, 205 / 763 / 3
1994: Barry Foster, 216 / 851 / 5
1995: Erric Pegram, 213 / 813 / 5
1996: Jerome Bettis, 320 / 1,431 / 11
1997: Jerome Bettis, **375** / 1,665 / 7
1998: Jerome Bettis, 316 / 1,185 / 3
1999: Jerome Bettis, 299 / 1,091 / 7

Receiving Leaders

(Receptions / Yards / TDs)

1990: Louis Lipps, 50 / 682 / 3
1991: Louis Lipps, 55 / 671 / 2
1992: Jeff Graham, 49 / 711 / 1
1993: Eric Green, 63 / 942 / 5
1994: John L. Williams, 51 / 378 / 2
1995: Yancey Thigpen, 85 / 1,307 / 5
1996: Andre Hastings, 72 / 739 / 6
1997: Yancey Thigpen, 79 / 1,398 / 7
1998: Courtney Hawkins, 66 / 751 / 1
1999: Troy Edwards, 61 / 714 / 5;
Hines Ward, 61 / 638 / 7

Interceptions

(Number / Yards / TDs)

1990: Rod Woodson, 5 / 67 / 0
1991: Thomas Everett, 4 / 53 / 0
1992: Darren Perry, 6 / 69 / 0
1993: Rod Woodson, 8 / 138 / 1
1994: Darren Perry, 7 / 112 / 0
1995: Willie Williams, 7 / 122 / 1
1996: Rod Woodson, 6 / 121 / 1
1997: Donnell Woolford, 4 / 91 / 0;
Darren Perry, 4 / 77 / 0
1998: Dewayne Washington, 5 / 178 / 2
1999: Scott Shields, 4 / 75 / 0;
Dewayne Washington, 4 / 1 / 0

When the Steelers arrived in Arizona for Super Bowl XXX, it had been 16 years since they last appeared in the big game—and they were back facing their old '70s foes, the Cowboys. *MVP Books Collection*

First-Team All-Pros

1990: Rod Woodson, CB/KR/PR
1992: Barry Foster, RB
1992: Rod Woodson, CB/KR/PR
1993: Dermontti Dawson, C
1993: Greg Lloyd, LB
1993: Rod Woodson, CB/KR/PR
1994: Dermontti Dawson, C
1994: Kevin Greene, LB
1994: Greg Lloyd, LB
1994: Rod Woodson, CB/PR
1995: Dermontti Dawson, C
1995: Greg Lloyd, LB
1996: Jerome Bettis, RB
1996: Chad Brown, LB
1996: Dermontti Dawson, C
1997: Dermontti Dawson, C
1997: Levon Kirkland, LB
1997: Carnell Lake, CB/SS
1998: Dermontti Dawson, C

Pro Bowl Selections

1990: David Little, LB
1990: Rod Woodson, CB/KR/PR
1991: Greg Lloyd, LB
1991: Rod Woodson, CB/KR/PR
1992: Dermontti Dawson, C
1992: Barry Foster, RB
1992: Carlton Haselrig, G
1992: Greg Lloyd, LB
1992: Neil O'Donnell, QB
1992: Rod Woodson, CB/KR/PR
1993: Gary Anderson, K

1993: Dermontti Dawson, C
1993: Barry Foster, RB
1993: Eric Green, TE
1993: Greg Lloyd, LB
1993: Rod Woodson, CB/KR/PR
1994: Dermontti Dawson, C
1994: Eric Green, TE
1994: Kevin Greene, LB
1994: Carnell Lake, SS
1994: Greg Lloyd, LB
1994: Duval Love, G
1994: Rod Woodson, CB/PR
1995: Dermontti Dawson, C
1995: Kevin Greene, LB
1995: Carnell Lake, CB/SS
1995: Greg Lloyd, LB
1995: Yancey Thigpen, WR
1996: Jerome Bettis, RB
1996: Chad Brown, LB
1996: Dermontti Dawson, C
1996: Levon Kirkland, LB
1996: Carnell Lake, SS
1996: Rod Woodson, CB
1997: Jerome Bettis, RB
1997: Dermontti Dawson, C
1997: Levon Kirkland, LB
1997: Carnell Lake, CB/SS
1997: Joel Steed, NT
1997: Yancey Thigpen, WR
1998: Dermontti Dawson, C

1st-Round Draft Picks

1990: Eric Green (21), TE, Liberty
1991: Huey Richardson (15), LB, Florida
1992: Leon Searcy (11), T, Miami (FL)
1993: Deon Figures (23), DB, Colorado
1994: Charles Johnson (17), WR, Colorado
1995: Mark Bruener (27), TE, Washington
1996: Jamain Stephens (29), T, North Carolina A&T
1997: Chad Scott (24), DB, Maryland
1998: Alan Faneca (26), G, Louisiana St.
1999: Troy Edwards (13), WR, Louisiana Tech

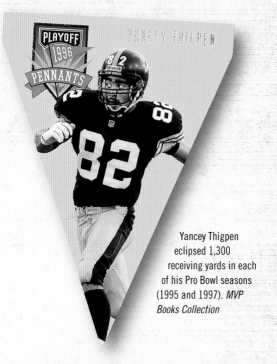

Yancey Thigpen eclipsed 1,300 receiving yards in each of his Pro Bowl seasons (1995 and 1997). *MVP Books Collection*

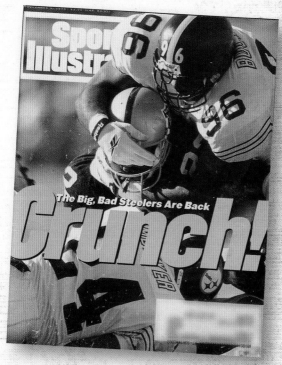

Defensive end Brentson Buckner and defensive back Tim McKyer made the cover of *Sports Illustrated* in 1994, when the team allowed just seven rushing touchdowns. *MVP Books Collection*

THE 2000s

HEINZ FIELD, BIG BEN, AND SUPER SUCCESS

Supreme leadership and two plays for the ages help the Steelers win their fifth and record-setting sixth Super Bowl titles.

Santonio Holmes is on top of the world after making a spectacular game-winning catch and earning the MVP Award in Super Bowl XLIII. *NY Daily News Archive via Getty Images*

SPORTS ★ FINAL

Sports starts on page 46

February 2, 2009

DAILY SPORTS NEWS!

SWEET HOLMES

Miracle TD catch makes Steelers Super for record sixth time

14 SUPER PAGES INSIDE

Most Valuable Player Santonio Holmes celebrates as touchdown catch in corner of end zone with 35 seconds left gives Steelers 27-23 victory over Cardinals and a record sixth Super Bowl championship last night in Tampa. **COVERAGE BEGINS ON PAGE 46**

As the century and millennium turned, Pittsburgh and the Steelers saw big changes and big wins—more, perhaps, in the 2000s than in any other decade in Steelers history except for the '70s.

As blue collars turned increasingly white, and industry morphed from heavy metal to high-tech, tailgaters and partiers were just as likely to serve pâté and piña coladas as kielbasa and kraut. Pittsburgh traded one 30-year-old stadium (Three Rivers) for two new ballyards, the Pirates' PNC Park and the Steelers' Heinz Field.

Bigger, bolder, better, Heinz Field featured many more luxury accommodations, huge catering halls, and endless food and souvenir concessions. Opening on October 7, 2001, and dubbed the "Mustard Palace" for Heinz and the sea of yellow seats, it cost a cool $281 million.

Steelers Nation couldn't have cared less about the price tag, or about the seat licenses they had to buy, just as long as the *experience* continued and the team kept winning. The Steelers did, all through the decade, adding a deuce of Lombardis—Nos. 5 and 6—to the trophy case.

It was "One for the Thumb" and "Sixburgh!" all in one breath.

While the "Immaculate Reception" did not lead to a championship in 1972, it did brand *immaculate* into Steelers jargon. The 2000s brought two championships and two miracle plays—or splash plays, as coach Mike Tomlin has taught Steelers Nation to say.

Pre-Super Bowl XL: the "Immaculate Redemption."

Super Bowl XLIII: the "Immaculate Interception."

Before all that, though, the Steelers needed a miracle quarterback. By 2004, Kordell Stewart had been replaced by Arena Football vet Tommy Maddox. When Maddox went down, coach Bill Cowher gave snap-calling to rookie Ben Roethlisberger. By the time the ice was scraped off the windshields, Ben had won 13 consecutive starts.

Whoa.

The following year, 2005, that arm, that incredible agility and field command, was combined with an emotional plea from veteran Jerome Bettis to take the Steelers to Super Bowl Extra Large in The Bus's hometown, Detroit, and give him the one thing he lacked: a ring. It's hard to say what Steelers Nation liked more, the football or the story.

In Indianapolis during the 2005 playoffs, the Steelers needed a miracle win. Impossibly, Bettis fumbled within breathing distance of the Indy end zone. Colts cornerback Nick Harper grabbed the ball and headed for Steelers pay dirt. Miraculously, Big Ben managed to snag Harper's ankle and bring him down. *Voila!* The Immaculate Redemption entered Steelers Nation lore.

The Super Bowl victory over Seattle was anticlimactic, although the winning gadget play—Ben to scat back Willie Parker to receiver Antwaan Randle El to Hines Ward, who scampered in for six—will linger in fans' hearts forever.

It was coach Cowher's finest hour.

A year later, he was gone.

Enter Mike Tomlin, tough, defense-minded, and the Steelers' first African American head coach. With bone-crushing NFL Defensive Player of the Year James Harrison leading the best D in football, the 2008 Steelers stuffed *everything*.

Super Bowl XLIII, against the Cardinals, brought the miracle. With the Birds on the Pittsburgh 1-yard line, Harrison grabbed a pass and then motored all the way down the line. His 100-yard dash, the Immaculate Interception, was the longest play in Super Bowl history.

Brilliant Roethlisberger to Santonio Holmes completions made "Sixburgh!" a reality—and the Steelers the all-time Super Bowl champs.

For Steelers Nation, the real prize came two weeks earlier. Beating the Ravens in the AFC Championship Game, a triumphant Mike Tomlin pointed the trophy to the fans: "I just love you guys," he gushed.

For Steelers Nation, the feeling was mutual.

—A. M.

With Ben Roethlisberger (2004 first-round pick) heading the offense and Troy Polamalu (2003 first-round pick) leading the defense, the Steelers brought another dynasty era to Pittsburgh in the new millennium. Here the two share in the celebration following their Super Bowl XLIII victory in February 2009. *Chris McGrath/Getty* Images

9–7   3rd place

Game-by-Game

9/3	**L, 0–16,** vs. Baltimore Ravens
9/17	**L, 20–23,** at Cleveland Browns
9/24	**L, 20–23,** vs. Tennessee Titans
10/1	**W, 24–13,** at Jacksonville Jaguars
10/8	**W, 20–3,** at New York Jets
10/15	**W, 15–0,** vs. Cincinnati Bengals
10/22	**W, 22–0,** vs. Cleveland Browns
10/29	**W, 9–6,** at Baltimore Ravens
11/5	**L, 7–9,** at Tennessee Titans
11/12	**L, 23–26 (OT),** vs. Philadelphia Eagles
11/19	**L, 24–34,** vs. Jacksonville Jaguars
11/26	**W, 48–28,** at Cincinnati Bengals
12/3	**W, 21–20,** vs. Oakland Raiders
12/10	**L, 10–30,** at New York Giants
12/16	**W, 24–3,** vs. Washington Redskins
12/24	**W, 34–21,** at San Diego Chargers

Team Scoring

321 points scored

255 points allowed

Linebacker Joey Porter takes Baltimore quarterback Trent Dilfer to the ground during Pittsburgh's 9–6 victory over the Ravens in October. It was one of 10.5 sacks in 2000 for Porter, who is the third player in Steelers history to record 60 sacks with the franchise. *Steve Gross/AP Images*

VOTE OF CONFIDENCE

Rooney Believes in Cowher; Team Responds

Despite the Steelers' collapse in 1999, coach Bill Cowher "never lost my confidence," wrote Dan Rooney. When Cowher offered his resignation, Rooney didn't accept it. When Cowher butted heads with Tom Donahoe, the team's director of football operations, it was Donahoe who was sent packing.

Rooney still had faith in Cowher after the Steelers got shut out 16–0 by Baltimore in the season opener—and after they dropped the next two games by identical 23–20 scores, losses that could have been victories if officials hadn't blown some calls. Eventually, Rooney's faith paid off. After the 0–3 start, the Steelers went 9–4 the rest of the way and began a half decade of success that would rival the heyday of the '70s dynasty.

Typical of the Steelers, the defense turned the season around. Over a five-game stretch, they held opponents to six field goals and zero touchdowns. "Right now, we're the bullies on the block," said safety Lee Flowers after Pittsburgh's second straight shutout. Earl Holmes led the Steelers with 128 total tackles, and fellow linebackers Jason Gildon and Joey Porter reached double digits in sacks.

The Steelers still had quarterback issues, as Kordell Stewart ranked 26th in the NFL in passer rating and journeyman Kent Graham started five games. More significantly, the Black and Gold had issues with the black-and-whites. In addition to the two blown-call games early in the season, Pittsburgh would have beaten Philadelphia had officials called an obvious penalty during the Eagles' last-ditch onside kick attempt. Turn those three losses into wins and Pittsburgh would have finished at 12–4—second best record in the NFL. As it was, in the Steelers' last year ever at Three Rivers Stadium, they didn't make the playoffs.

Butting Heads with Baltimore

In a 2007 matchup, Steelers receiver Hines Ward crashed into unsuspecting Baltimore free safety Ed Reed at full speed, hitting him under the facemask and lifting him off his feet. In the same game, Ward also nailed linebacker Bart Scott with a brutal hit. Scott sought revenge.

"His time will come," Scott told the *Pittsburgh Post-Gazette*, stating that a player would someday take out Ward's knee. "No one will care," Scott said. "No one will send him any cards saying they're sorry. Not to that guy."

With the Ravens and Steelers, vicious hits and hostile rhetoric were not uncommon. From 2001 through '12, when Pittsburgh won seven AFC Central titles and the Ravens four, their rivalry was the fiercest in the NFL. Their games were hard-hitting and closely contested, with 13 contests in those dozen years decided by three points or fewer.

The games were more than just intense; a genuine hatred of one another developed. Some say the animosity dates back to when the Ravens were the Cleveland Browns. "Hey, Cleveland . . . Season's Beatings!" proclaimed a Three Rivers banner at Christmastime.

With the Ravens and Steelers, the beatings were literal. In 2006, Scott gloated after slamming Steelers quarterback Ben Roethlisberger to the turf. "I jumped up and did my bird dance, then looked back and saw Ben was still down, and I'm like, 'Yeah, I knocked him out of the game,'" Scott boasted. In 2008, Ravens linebacker Ray Lewis—the nastiest hitter in NFL history—fractured the shoulder of running back Rashard Mendenhall. The Ravens followed by claiming they would put "bounties" on the Steelers.

In 2009, Steelers strong safety Ryan Clark delivered a helmet-to-helmet blow that knocked out Ravens running back Willis McGahee. In 2010, Baltimore linebacker Jameel McClain clocked Steelers tight end Heath Miller in the head with his helmet and forearm. At least McClain was apologetic, calling such hits "horrible types of plays."

As long as the Ravens and Steelers battle twice each year in the AFC Central, bad blood will continue to flow.

There's no love lost between the Baltimore Ravens and the Pittsburgh Steelers.
Patrick Smith / Getty Images

The Heinz Field Experience

When Steelers officials met with the architects who would build their new stadium, they asked that the new structure be "distinctively Pittsburgh." Apparently, fans grumbled, that meant ketchup and mustard.

After three decades in multipurpose Three Rivers Stadium, the Pirates sought a new, baseball-only ballpark. The Steelers also coveted a 21st-century venue. Not only would the Steelers and taxpayers fund the $281 million, football-only stadium, shared with the University of Pittsburgh Panthers, but so too would the H. J. Heinz Company, which agreed to pour $57 million into the pot over a period of 20 years.

But the company won more than just naming rights to Heinz Field. Two enormous Heinz ketchup bottles tilted over the 27- by 96-foot Sony JumboTron, at the time the largest scoreboard in the NFL. When the Steelers would enter the Red Zone (inside the 20-yard line), the ketchup bottles would "pour" red into the video screen, which proclaimed "Heinz Red Zone." Moreover, in an unfortunate coincidence, the choice of seat color seemed to be Heinz related. The vast majority of the 65,050 seats were meant to be "Steeler gold," but they wound up looking like mustard yellow.

The Heinz theme was a source of irritation to fans, who otherwise were treated to a first-class venue. HOK Sport, the architectural firm, did acknowledge Pittsburgh's heritage with a steel- and glass-themed design. Most impressively, Heinz Field is the only open-ended field in the NFL. Instead of staring at an oval of fellow fans, patrons enjoy a spectacular panorama of skyscrapers, rivers, and the soaring fountain of Point State Park.

The Steelers were scheduled to play their first regular-season game at Heinz Field on September 16, 2001, but the first game was postponed due to the September 11 terrorist attacks. The home opener, played on October 7 against the Bengals, was met with mostly positive reviews. Some fans griped about the clogged escalators, and others were a little skittish about the steep upper deck. Most, however, raved about the scenery, clear views of the field, state-of-the-art sound system, and modern amenities. Others enjoyed the enormous Great Hall that housed a collection of Steelers memorabilia, including replica lockers of such legends as Terry Bradshaw and Jack Lambert.

Over the years, opposing teams have complained about Heinz Field's natural grass, which can get mucked up pretty badly by the Steelers, Panthers, and high school teams that play there. But Steelers players have lobbied to keep it, no matter how sloppy it gets.

In the end, it's not the stadium but the people who populate it that makes Heinz Field special. Dressed in Ben Roethlisberger and Troy Polamalu jerseys, wearing hard hats or other Steelers headwear, waving Terrible Towels, and hoisting banners such as "You're in Steeler Country," Heinz Field has become hostile territory to opposing players. ESPN ranked it as the second most feared venue in the NFL, behind Green Bay's Lambeau Field. Visiting teams don't have even pockets of fans support, because Steelers fans don't sell their tickets.

In the Steelers' first 12 years at Heinz Field, fans were treated to victories nearly three-quarters of the time. Playoffs included, Pittsburgh went 77–27–1 at home during that span, logging at least seven wins in a season an incredible six times. Highlights came in 2008 and 2010, when fans cheered the Black and Gold to victories in the AFC Championship Game.

Above: Situated downriver of the Pirates' PNC Park, Heinz Field rests along the Ohio River at the confluence of the Allegheny River (left) and Monongahela River (right). *iofoto/ Shutterstock*

Right: Heinz Field is the only NFL stadium with an open view of its host city. *John S. Zeedick/AP Images*

Left: The cover of the Steelers' 2001 Media Guide pictured the design for the new stadium. *MVP Books Collection*

13–3   1st place

Game-by-Game

9/9	**L**, 3–21, at Jacksonville Jaguars
9/30	**W**, 20–3, at Buffalo Bills
10/7	**W**, 16–7, vs. Cincinnati Bengals
10/14	**W**, 20–17, at Kansas City Chiefs
10/21	**W**, 17–10, at Tampa Bay Buccaneers
10/29	**W**, 34–7, vs. Tennessee Titans
11/4	**L**, 10–13, vs. Baltimore Ravens
11/11	**W**, 15–12 (OT), at Cleveland Browns
11/18	**W**, 20–7, vs. Jacksonville Jaguars
11/25	**W**, 34–24, at Tennessee Titans
12/2	**W**, 21–16, vs. Minnesota Vikings
12/9	**W**, 18–7, vs. New York Jets
12/16	**W**, 26–21, at Baltimore Ravens
12/23	**W**, 47–14, vs. Detroit Lions
12/30	**L**, 23–26 (OT), at Cincinnati Bengals
1/6	**W**, 28–7, vs. Cleveland Browns

Playoffs

1/20	**W**, 27–10, vs. Baltimore Ravens
1/27	**L**, 17–24, vs. New England Patriots

Team Scoring

352 points scored
212 points allowed

A CHRISTENING BASH

Steelers Reach AFC Title Game at the New Heinz Field

After the Steelers' first-ever preseason game at Heinz Field, safety Lee Flowers bubbled with enthusiasm. "We're kind of giddy right now about our new place," he told reporters. "We wanted to establish ourselves here right away. Look at Tennessee: They won all of their home games in their new stadium their first year, and that's eight wins right there."

As it turned out, the Steelers did win eight games at Heinz Field in 2001, playoffs included. In the home opener, which was postponed until October 7 following the 9/11 attacks, Pittsburgh steamrolled Cincinnati 16–7. Jerome Bettis ran for 153 yards and surpassed 10,000 for his career. The Steelers won five consecutive games before losing a 13–10 squeaker at home to Baltimore, then won seven in a row. Their 13–3 record was their best since 1978.

The Steelers, who went 11–4–1 against the spread, were at times electrifying. In a win at Tampa Bay, Bettis ran for a 46-yard touchdown and threw a 32-yard TD pass to Jerame Tuman. Ten times the Steelers sacked quarterback Brad Johnson, with Joey Porter logging four of them.

Kordell Stewart regained his 1997 glory, completing 60.2 percent of his passes for a career-high 3,109 yards—including 333 in an upset over the reigning Super Bowl–champion Ravens. Against the spread in 2001, the Steelers went 11–4–1. Stewart, Bettis, and wide receiver Hines Ward (Steelers-record 94 catches, 1,003

Running back Amos Zereoue dives over the line of scrimmage and into the end zone during Pittsburgh's opening playoff game against Baltimore. His two first-half touchdowns helped give the Steelers a 17–0 lead en route to a 27–10 final. *Timothy A. Clary/AFP/Getty Images*

Despite a strong 13-3 regular season finish, Pittsburgh couldn't hold on against New England in the AFC Championship Game. Here, Steelers players Chris Fuamatu-Ma'afala (#45) and Plaxico Burress (#80) watch from the sidelines as Pittsburgh loses to the Patriots 17-24. *David Maxwell/ AFP / Getty Images*

yards) all made the Pro Bowl. Bettis was leading the NFL with 1,072 rushing yards through 11 games, but he missed the remainder of the regular season and the first playoff game with an injury.

Porter and fellow linebackers Kendrell Bell and Jason Gildon (both Pro Bowl picks) combined for 30 sacks. On the season, the Steelers defense led the NFL in fewest rushing yards, fewest total yards, and fewest first downs allowed. They held six foes to exactly one score.

As the AFC's No. 1 seed, the Steelers hoped to ride a Heinz Field high all the way to the Super Bowl. Against the rival Ravens in Pittsburgh's playoff opener, 5-foot-8 running back Amos Zereoue scored two first-half touchdowns, helping the Steelers build a 20–3 lead at intermission. A 32-yard Stewart-to-Plaxico Burress touchdown pass punctuated the 27–10 Pittsburgh victory. "That was our most dominating performance, by far," Porter said afterward. "They kept talking about how they had their swagger back. Well, I didn't see any swagger."

Unfortunately, the New England Patriots had some swagger in the AFC Championship Game, particularly on special teams. New England's Troy Brown returned a punt 55 yards for a touchdown, and Antwan Harris returned a 49-yard blocked field goal for a score. Former Pro Bowl quarterback Drew Bledsoe combined with hot shot rookie Tom Brady (who was injured late in the first half) for 22 completions and no interceptions. Stewart was picked off three times, which turned out to be pivotal in the 24–17 Patriots victory.

For the Steelers, who had entered the game as 9 ½-point favorites, it was their third loss in AFC Championship Games under Bill Cowher, all at home. Fans were particularly frustrated with Stewart, who had thrown six interceptions and just one touchdown pass in his two AFC title games. His days as Pittsburgh's starting quarterback were numbered.

10–5–1   **1st place**

Game-by-Game

9/9	**L, 14–30,** at New England Patriots
9/15	**L, 17–30,** vs. Oakland Raiders
9/29	**W, 16–13 (OT),** vs. Cleveland Browns
10/6	**L, 29–32,** at New Orleans Saints
10/13	**W, 34–7,** at Cincinnati Bengals
10/21	**W, 28–10,** vs. Indianapolis Colts
10/27	**W, 31–18,** at Baltimore Ravens
11/3	**W, 23–20,** at Cleveland Browns
11/10	**T, 34–34 (OT),** vs. Atlanta Falcons
11/17	**L, 23–31,** at Tennessee Titans
11/24	**W, 29–21,** vs. Cincinnati Bengals
12/1	**W, 25–23,** at Jacksonville Jaguars
12/8	**L, 6–24,** vs. Houston Texans
12/15	**W, 30–14,** vs. Carolina Panthers
12/23	**W, 17–7,** at Tampa Bay Buccaneers
12/29	**W, 34–31,** vs. Baltimore Ravens

Playoffs

1/5	**W, 36–33,** vs. Cleveland Browns
1/11	**L, 31–34 (OT),** at Tennessee Titans

Team Scoring

390 points scored
345 points allowed

"TOMMY GUN" RELOADS

Maddox Takes the Team on a Playoff-Bound Joyride

It appeared that Tommy Maddox had been a colossal Draft Day bust. Turns out, he was just a late bloomer.

Drafted out of UCLA by Denver in the first round in 2002, Maddox was supposed to be the heir apparent to John Elway. But after going 0–4 as a rookie starter that year, "Tommy Gun" lasted just one more season with the Broncos before bouncing to the Rams and the Giants and then out of the league by 1997. After reemerging with the Arena Football League's New Jersey Red Dogs in 2000, Maddox signed as a backup with the Steelers in 2001 and replaced Kordell Stewart in the middle of the team's third game of 2002.

Pittsburgh was in danger of falling to 0–3 that afternoon, but Maddox completed 11 of 13 passes to captain an overtime victory over the Browns. Including that triumph, the Steelers went 10–3–1 the rest of the way, with Maddox starting 11 games. The NFL's Comeback Player of the Year piloted three comeback victories, completed 62.1 percent of his passes, and ranked fourth in the league in yards per pass attempt (7.5).

Maddox took advantage of the spectacular receiving tandem of Hines Ward and Plaxico Burress. Ward caught a team-record 112 passes for 1,329 yards, while the 6-foot-5 Burress grabbed 78 for 1,325. In a 34–34 tie with Atlanta on November 10, Maddox threw for a team-record 473 yards, with Burress setting a club mark with 253 receiving yards.

Maddox was taken off the field by ambulance the following week after suffering a concussion at Tennessee. However, he led Pittsburgh to victory in the final three games, as the Steelers clinched the top spot in the new AFC North, a quartet of teams that included all of Pittsburgh's big rivals: Cleveland, Cincinnati, and Baltimore.

Hosting the Browns in the wildcard game, the Steelers fell behind 14–7 at intermission. "Tommy brought the whole team together at halftime and told us what we were going to do," wide receiver Terance Mathis said. "He said if you don't think we're going to win this game, you need to go back into the locker room."

Few thought the Steelers would prevail when they fell behind 24–7. But Maddox responded with three touchdown passes, and Chris Fuamatu-Ma'afala scored the winning TD on a three-yard run with 54 seconds left. After the Steelers' most dramatic comeback playoff victory since the Immaculate Reception, they moved on to play the Titans in Tennessee.

Pittsburgh trailed the Titans 28–20 in the fourth quarter, but Maddox had one last comeback in him. His 21-yard touchdown pass to Ward, followed by a Ward-to-Burress pass for a two-point conversion, tied the score at 28–28. After the teams traded field goals, Tennessee's Joe Nedney missed a 48-yarder at the end of regulation.

In overtime, Nedney blew a 31-yard chip shot—only to get second life due to a controversial running-into-the-kicker call on Dewayne Washington. Nedney's 26-yard boot split the uprights. "For a game to be decided on that call is ludicrous," Bill Cowher fumed afterward. "A game can't be decided because a kicker takes two steps and we have someone slide into him."

But it was, and a season filled with comebacks ended in another playoff heartache.

Referee Ron Blum calls a running-into-the-kicker penalty against Pittsburgh in overtime of their playoff game against Tennessee. The call gave the Titans a second chance at a field goal, which they made. *Amy Sancetta/AP Images*

Opposite page: Tommy Maddox flung three touchdown passes in the final 19 minutes to overcome a 17-point deficit against the Browns in the 2002 AFC wildcard game. *Tami Tomsic/ Getty Images*

6–10   3rd place

Game-by-Game

9/7	**W, 34–15,** vs. Baltimore Ravens
9/14	**L, 20–41,** at Kansas City Chiefs
9/21	**W, 17–10,** at Cincinnati Bengals
9/28	**L, 13–30,** vs. Tennessee Titans
10/5	**L, 13–33,** vs. Cleveland Browns
10/12	**L, 14–17,** at Denver Broncos
10/26	**L, 21–33,** vs. St. Louis Rams
11/2	**L, 16–23,** at Seattle Seahawks
11/9	**W, 28–15,** vs. Arizona Cardinals
11/17	**L, 14–30,** at San Francisco 49ers
11/23	**W, 13–6,** at Cleveland Browns
11/30	**L, 20–24,** vs. Cincinnati Bengals
12/7	**W, 27–7,** vs. Oakland Raiders
12/14	**L, 0–6,** at New York Jets
12/21	**W, 40–24,** vs. San Diego Chargers
12/28	**L, 10–13 (OT),** at Baltimore Ravens

Team Scoring

300 points scored
327 points allowed

On December 14, the snow fell and the players slid as the weather conditions kept the score in the single digits. The New York Jets defeated the Pittsburgh Steelers 6–0 in a comedy of errors borne of weather. *Ezra Shaw/Getty Images*

RUNNING IN QUICKSAND

Steelers Can't Move the Ball, Finish 6–10

Bill Cowher had always been a high-strung coach, particularly when things weren't going his way. After railing against the officials on the final play of the 2002 season, he turned his wrath on the 2003 schedule makers. Why in the world were the Steelers forced to play a road game in Cleveland on November 23, he wanted to know, after playing a Monday night road game in San Francisco? As it turned out, Cowher's frustrations lasted throughout the year.

In a season plagued by injuries to the offensive line, the Steelers went 6–10. Cowher shuffled linemen in the hopes of finding a cohesive unit, but it didn't work. Despite ranking 16th in the NFL in carries, the Steelers finished 31st in rushing yards, averaging a league-low 3.3 per lug. Jerome Bettis needed 246 carries to amass his 811 yards.

The offensive line allowed 41 sacks, and Tommy Maddox's passer rating dropped from 85.2 in 2002 to 75.3. Hines Ward continued as his favorite target, snatching 95 passes. Although the defense was terrific, ranking ninth in the league in yards allowed—with linebacker James Farrior leading the team with 141 total tackles—the Steelers never won even two consecutive games.

Cowher's frustrations literally snowballed on December 14 against the Jets. On a snowy, then rainy day in New Jersey, the Steelers were shut out 6–0. Cowher tensed up in the fourth quarter as New York running back Curtis Martin slogged 56 yards on a play that seemed to take an hour and a half. The Steelers got the ball back, but their hopes of a comeback kept falling incomplete, as "Tommy Gun" ended the game with eight consecutive misfires.

Epic Overachiever: Hines Ward

For many years, Hines Ward hated who he was, and his shame brought his mother to tears.

Shunned in Korea for marrying an African American GI, Kim Young He faced greater challenges when she moved with her husband and one-year-old Hines to Georgia. The couple soon divorced, and Kim worked up to three jobs to take care of her son.

Despite Kim's efforts, a young, confused Hines felt ashamed of his Korean mother. When she drove him to school, he slunk in his seat "because I didn't want them [schoolmates] to know she was my mom," he told *Sports Illustrated*. When he turned to look back at the car, he'd see his mother crying. "I was lost," he said.

Burning with shame, anger, and confusion, Ward became an epic overachiever. He excelled in football and baseball as well as the classroom. At the University of Georgia, he amassed nearly 4,000 yards as a wide receiver, tailback, and quarterback. After the Steelers drafted him in the third round in 1998, he became the most prolific receiver in team history.

In 14 seasons with Pittsburgh, Ward set franchise records for receptions (1,000), receiving yards (12,083), and touchdown catches (85). From 2001 to '04, he topped 1,000 yards and made the Pro Bowl each year, with career highs of 112 receptions and 1,329 receiving yards in '02. Along the way, Ward earned a reputation as the best blocking wide receiver in the NFL as well as one of the game's nastiest hitters. His takedown of Baltimore's Ed Reed in 2010—in which he rammed his helmet into Reed's chest—prompted Reed to call Ward a "dirty player" who "tried to cheap-shot" me. Such accusations were not the first against Ward.

After catching his 1,000th pass in his final game in 2011, Ward retired from football. However, he has continued to push himself, delving into broadcasting and acting, competing in the Ironman Triathlon, and winning *Dancing with the Stars*. His many charitable ventures include the Helping Hands Korea Foundation. Formed as a tribute to his mother, the foundation targets biracial discrimination, especially as it occurs among the children of his native country.

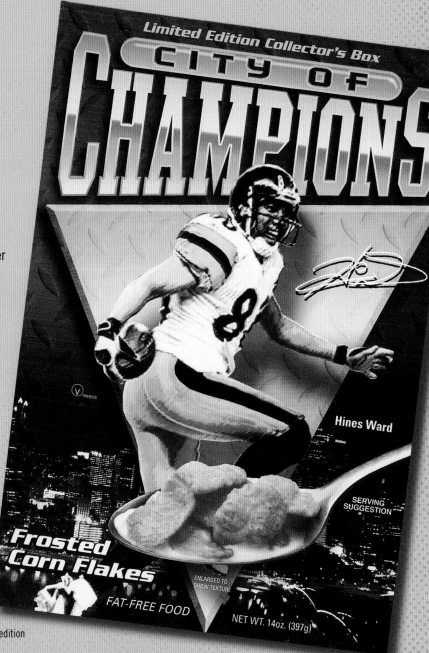

Hines Ward graced the box of this special championship edition of Frosted Corn Flakes cereal. *MVP Books Collection*

15–1   1st place

Game-by-Game

9/12	W, 24–21, vs. Oakland Raiders
9/19	L, 13–30, at Baltimore Ravens
9/26	W, 13–3, at Miami Dolphins
10/3	W, 28–17, vs. Cincinnati Bengals
10/10	W, 34–23, vs. Cleveland Browns
10/17	W, 24–20, at Dallas Cowboys
10/31	W, 34–20, vs. New England Patriots
11/7	W, 27–3, vs. Philadelphia Eagles
11/14	W, 24–10, at Cleveland Browns
11/21	W, 19–14, at Cincinnati Bengals
11/28	W, 16–7, vs. Washington Redskins
12/5	W, 17–16, at Jacksonville Jaguars
12/12	W, 17–6, vs. New York Jets
12/18	W, 33–30, at New York Giants
12/26	W, 20–7, vs. Baltimore Ravens
1/2	W, 29–24, at Buffalo Bills

Playoffs

1/15	W, 20–17 (OT), vs. New York Jets
1/23	L, 27–41, vs. New England Patriots

Team Scoring

372 points scored
251 points allowed

BEN-SATIONAL!

Rookie QB Leads Steelers to 14 Straight Wins

Same old Steelers . . . . That's what fans must have muttered in Week 2 of 2004. After its dismal 6–10 campaign, Pittsburgh barely squeaked by a subpar Oakland team in the '04 opener and got blown out 30–13 by the Ravens. Worse, Steelers quarterback Tommy Maddox was lost to an elbow injury in the Baltimore game, forcing Pittsburgh to use a raw rookie named Ben Roethlisberger.

"Big Ben" (6-foot-5, 240 pounds) was a first-round draft pick, but he came out of Miami of Ohio, which played in the second-tier Mid-American Conference. Yet what the casual fan didn't realize was that Roethlisberger had worked magic at Miami, winning his last 13 games while averaging 48 points per outing. Roethlisberger was some kind of miracle man, and he proved it his rookie year by winning 13 consecutive starts as the Steelers went a shocking 15–1.

Dallas coach Bill Parcells compared the rugged, tough, extremely accurate Roethlisberger to Dan Marino, and that was before Big Ben riddled the Cowboys for 21-of-25 passing and a comeback victory on October 17. Though his yardage totals were generally low, the rookie ranked fourth in the NFL in completion percentage (66.4) and fifth in passer rating (98.1).

Meanwhile, a healthier offensive line led to a dramatically improved running game, as Jerome Bettis, Duce Staley, and Co. ranked second in the NFL in rushing. Tackle Marvel Smith joined first-team All-Pros Alan Faneca (guard) and Jeff Hartings (center) in the Pro Bowl. The Steelers led the league in average drive time, which helped the defense lead the NFL in fewest yards and points allowed. Pro Bowlers on defense included linebackers James Farrior and Joey Porter, defensive end Aaron Smith, and dynamic strong safety Troy Polamalu.

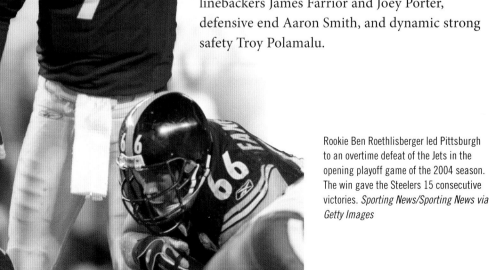

Rookie Ben Roethlisberger led Pittsburgh to an overtime defeat of the Jets in the opening playoff game of the 2004 season. The win gave the Steelers 15 consecutive victories. *Sporting News/Sporting News via Getty Images*

The defense, offensive line, and Roethlisberger controlled the action so thoroughly that there were only a handful of scares during the regular season. Against Jacksonville, the Steelers needed a late drive and 37-yard field goal by Jeff Reed with 18 seconds left to prevail 17–16. In the closing minutes against the Giants on December 18, Big Ben led the team on a 67-yard, game-winning touchdown drive. "In the fourth quarter," said coach Bill Cowher, "he has a feel for the game and an understanding of the game, and he manages it well."

That poise carried over to Pittsburgh's opening playoff game against the Jets. On a 20-degree, late-afternoon game at Heinz Field, the Jets went ahead 17–10 thanks to long punt and interception returns for touchdowns. A 12-play Steelers drive, ending with a touchdown with 6:00 remaining, tied it. Pittsburgh survived two scares when New York's Doug Brien missed two field goals in the final two minutes, one of which hit the goal post. "God gave us another chance," said Hartings. The Steelers won in overtime on a 33-yard field goal—the culmination of a 14-play drive.

Though the Steelers hosted the AFC Championship Game, they faced the favored—and reigning Super Bowl–champion—New England Patriots. With a game-time temperature of nine degrees, and winds howling at 20 mph, the Pats jumped ahead 24–3 by halftime and cruised 41–27. Though Tom Brady and Roethlisberger each completed 14 passes and two touchdown tosses, Brady threw zero interceptions to Big Ben's three, which included a disastrous 87-yard pick-six that put New England up by 21. The Patriots did all they could to rattle and confuse the rookie QB. "They threw the book at us," Roethlisberger said.

For Big Ben, who had won 28 consecutive starts, greater things lay ahead.

The Steelers did not have enough to stay with New England in the AFC title game in January 2005. *Andy Lyons/Getty Images*

2005

11–5 2nd place

Game-by-Game

9/11 **W,** 34–7,
vs. Tennessee Titans

9/18 **W,** 27–7,
at Houston Texans

9/25 **L,** 20–23,
vs. New England Patriots

10/10 **W,** 24–22,
at San Diego Chargers

10/16 **L,** 17–23 (OT),
vs. Jacksonville Jaguars

10/23 **W,** 27–13,
at Cincinnati Bengals

10/31 **W,** 20–19,
vs. Baltimore Ravens

11/6 **W,** 20–10,
at Green Bay Packers

11/13 **W,** 34–21,
vs. Cleveland Browns

11/20 **L,** 13–16,
at Baltimore Ravens

11/28 **L,** 7–26,
at Indianapolis Colts

12/4 **L,** 31–38,
vs. Cincinnati Bengals

12/11 **W,** 21–9,
vs. Chicago Bears

12/18 **W,** 18–3,
at Minnesota Vikings

12/24 **W,** 41–0,
at Cleveland Browns

1/1 **W,** 35–21,
vs. Detroit Lions

Playoffs

1/8 **W,** 31–17,
at Cincinnati Bengals

1/15 **W,** 21–18,
at Indianapolis Colts

1/22 **W,** 34–17,
at Denver Broncos

2/5 **Super Bowl:** W, 21–10,
vs. Seattle Seahawks

Team Scoring

389 points scored
258 points allowed

A HARD DRIVE TO DETROIT

Wildcard Steelers Prevail in Three Road Playoff Games

Since their last Super Bowl season in 1979, the Steelers had made the playoffs 13 times, been to six AFC title games, and won one conference championship. But they still had not fulfilled Joe Greene's dream of winning "One for the Thumb." With a team that excelled in all phases of the game, the 2005 Steelers seemed poised to slip a fifth ring on their fingers. They would indeed arrive at Super Bowl XL in Detroit, but they would have to travel a long, bumpy road to get there.

Part of the problem was that The Bus was breaking down. Jerome Bettis, in what would be his last NFL season, rumbled for just 368 yards. First-year starter "Fast" Willie Parker picked up the slack with 1,202 rushing yards for a team that finished first in the NFL in rushing attempts and last in throws.

Ben Roethlisberger was even more efficient in 2005 than during his sensational rookie year, throwing just nine interceptions, leading the league in yards per

With just over a minute to go in their playoff battle and Pittsburgh up 21–18, Indy's Nick Harper scooped up a fumble and was headed for a 96-yard touchdown—until Ben Roethlisberger saved the day. *Michael Conroy/AP Images*

attempt (8.9), and finishing third in passer rating (98.6). The Steelers went 9–3 in his 12 games and 2–2 (behind Tommy Maddox and Charlie Batch) when he was sidelined by injury.

The Steelers were 7–2 through nine games, with the only losses coming to New England, on a last-second field goal, and Jacksonville, in overtime. Against the Jaguars, Maddox fumbled the snap of a sure game-winning field goal and then threw a pick-six in OT. The Steelers plummeted from 7–2 to 7–5 by losing to Baltimore in sudden-death (Maddox was sacked six times) and then falling to the Colts and Bengals—their main contender in the AFC North. "We have four games left," Bill Cowher said. "We have to play this thing out every week."

The Steelers proceeded to run the table. The Bus inspired the team to victory with 101 rushing yards in the snow against Chicago, and the defense came alive in 18–3 and 41–0 routs of Minnesota and Cleveland, respectively. A 35–21 thumping of a woeful Lions team on New Year's Day put the Steelers at 11–5. Unfortunately for Pittsburgh, the Bengals finished with the same record and won the tiebreaker. To reach the Super Bowl, the wildcard Steelers would have to win three playoff games on the road—a feat no NFL team had ever achieved.

The Steelers opened in Cincinnati, where Roethlisberger threw three touchdown passes in a 31–17 victory. But that was nothing compared to his heroics the next week at Indianapolis. With just over a minute to go, and Pittsburgh up 21–18, Bettis shockingly fumbled on the Colts' 2-yard line. In a stunning turnaround, Indy's Nick Harper scooped up the loose ball and raced toward the Steelers' end zone, only to be caught from behind by Roethlisberger—who grabbed his ankle—at the Colts' 42. When Mike Vanderjagt missed a 46-yard field goal, Pittsburgh escaped with the victory. "There was no way I could let Jerome's career end that way," Big Ben said.

Roethlisberger again proved his fortitude in the AFC Championship Game, as he completed 21 of 29 passes for 275 yards and two touchdowns at Denver. Though an underdog against the 14–3 Broncos, the Steelers scored on their first four possessions and breezed to a 24–3 halftime lead and a 34–17 victory.

"We traveled a hard road and grew as a football team," Cowher said. "Now we need to win one more game. No one ever remembers who lost the Super Bowl."

Jerome Bettis and the Steelers rushed for only 90 yards on 33 carries against Denver in the AFC Championship Game, but Pittsburgh won the takeaway battle 4–0 and prevailed 34–17. *Jonathan Daniel/Getty Images*

Super Bowl XL: One for The Bus

Just days before Super Bowl XL in Detroit, Jerome Bettis informed Steelers Chairman Dan Rooney and President Art Rooney, Jr., that he would retire after the game. Then he told his teammates. "Jerome's our guy," said nose tackle Casey Hampton. "He asked us to bring him home. That touched us. That's what we fought for."

For 10 years, Bettis had sacrificed his body, devoted his personal time, and even took pay cuts for the sake of the Steelers. Now, as Pittsburgh squared off against Seattle in the Super Bowl—staged in Jerome's hometown of Detroit—his teammates strove to win one for The Bus.

Such motivation, as well as a virtual home-field advantage considering all the Steelers fans who packed Ford Field, gave Pittsburgh an edge against a powerful Seahawks team. Seattle (13–3) had led the NFL with 452 points behind running back Shaun Alexander (1,880 rushing yards) and quarterback Matt Hasselbeck, and its defense was just as stout as Pittsburgh's.

Fans sat through a relatively uneventful first half. A 12-play Steelers drive late in the second quarter, highlighted by a 37-yard pass from Ben Roethlisberger to Hines Ward,

put Pittsburgh up 7–3 at intermission. Then, after the Rolling Stones rocked the halftime show with "Start Me Up," Willie Parker *did*. The speedy halfback blew through a hole created by All-Pro guard Alan Faneca and took it 75 yards to the house for a 14–3 Steelers lead.

Pittsburgh was on the verge of scoring again when Seattle's Kelly Herndon picked off a Roethlisberger pass and returned it 76 yards, setting up a Hasselbeck touchdown pass. The score remained 14–10 until nine minutes remained in the fourth quarter, when coach Bill Cowher reached deep into his bag of tricks. Big Ben pitched to Parker, who handed off to wide receiver (and former quarterback) Antwaan Randle El, who fired a perfect 43-yard touchdown pass to Ward. Seattle couldn't score on its final two drives, and the Steelers prevailed 21–10.

"It's been an incredible ride," The Bus said after the game. "I'm probably the luckiest football player who ever played."

With 9:04 remaining in the game and the Steelers up 14–10, wide receiver Antwaan Randle El fired the ball to Hines Ward, who skipped into the end zone to complete the 43-yard scoring pass play. *Harry How/Getty Images*

In 2006, Willie Parker rushed for 1,494 yards, fourth most in Steelers history. He went off for 213 yards against New Orleans and 223 versus Cleveland. *Grant Halverson/Getty Images*

CRASH

Steelers Slow to Recover After Big Ben's Accident

On June 12, 2006, while riding his Suzuki Hayabusa motorcycle without a helmet, Ben Roethlisberger suffered the worst hit of his life. Rammed by a Chrysler New Yorker, Ben crashed into the car's windshield and fell to the pavement. Paramedics and surgeons worked to repair the life-threatening damage: multiple facial fractures including a broken jaw and nose, lost and chipped teeth, a ruptured blood vessel, and a nine-inch gash on his head.

Seven weeks later, Big Ben pronounced himself fit and ready to go for the first preseason game. "Ben's a competitor, a warrior," Hines Ward said. Roethlisberger played throughout the preseason, but four days before the season opener, he underwent an emergency appendectomy. Quarterback Charlie Batch led the Steelers to victory that day over Miami, and a week later Roethlisberger was back in the starting lineup.

Clearly, though, Big Ben was not the same. In his first game back, Pittsburgh was shut out, and in his first three games he threw seven interceptions and no touchdown passes. Roethlisberger improved dramatically over his next four outings (72.0 completion percentage, seven touchdowns, seven picks), but due to his slow start and other injuries, Pittsburgh fell to 2–6.

The Steelers were their championship selves in the second half, going 6–2. Willie Parker ran for 223 yards against Cleveland, and the defense held opponents to single digits in three consecutive games. However, the 8–8 finish left Pittsburgh a game behind the AFC's two wildcard teams.

If only Ben had worn a helmet, fans muttered week after week, the Steelers would have made the playoffs. After the season, Bill Cowher retired, saying he wanted to spend more time with his family.

8–8   3rd place

Game-by-Game

9/7	**W**, 28–17, vs. Miami Dolphins
9/18	**L**, 0–9, at Jacksonville Jaguars
9/24	**L**, 20–28, vs. Cincinnati Bengals
10/8	**L**, 13–23, at San Diego Chargers
10/15	**W**, 45–7, vs. Kansas City Chiefs
10/22	**L**, 38–41 (OT), at Atlanta Falcons
10/29	**L**, 13–20, at Oakland Raiders
11/5	**L**, 20–31, vs. Denver Broncos
11/12	**W**, 38–31, vs. New Orleans Saints
11/19	**W**, 24–20, at Cleveland Browns
11/26	**L**, 0–27, at Baltimore Ravens
12/3	**W**, 20–3, vs. Tampa Bay Buccaneers
12/7	**W**, 27–7, vs. Cleveland Browns
12/17	**W**, 37–3, at Carolina Panthers
12/24	**L**, 7–31, vs. Baltimore Ravens
12/31	**W**, 23–17 (OT), at Cincinnati Bengals

Team Scoring

353 points scored
315 points allowed

Steeler Tough: Ben Roethlisberger

In 2006, Ben Roethlisberger was nearly killed in a motorcycle crash that resulted in gruesome injuries to his face, teeth, and skull. During that season, he suffered an emergency appendectomy and then a concussion. All told, he missed *one game*. If not indestructible, "Big Ben" is one of the toughest SOBs ever to play quarterback in the NFL.

"I saw the guy play on a broken ankle when he came down here, and we even broke his nose, and the guy continued to play," Ravens linebacker Terrell Suggs told the Baltimore media in 2012. "You can never question this guy's toughness. Guys like that are what this game is about."

Roethlisberger grew up just outside Findlay, Ohio, where he indulged in football, basketball, and baseball—sports in which he would earn all-district honors in high school. "I absolutely hate to lose in anything," Ben told *USA Today*. "Hate it. It burns me, drives me crazy."

In the fall of 1999, just five years before going 13–0 as the Steelers' rookie quarterback, Roethlisberger was learning the position as a senior at Findlay High School in Ohio. Previously, Ben had been a tall, lanky wide receiver, but he proved to be a quick study at quarterback, to say the least. In his sole season as Findlay's QB, he shattered state records with 4,041 aerial yards and 54 touchdown passes.

Roethlisberger chose Miami of Ohio over Ohio State and rewrote the RedHawks' record books. As a redshirt junior, he threw for 4,486 yards and led the humble little MAC school to a No. 10 ranking in the final AP poll. After forgoing a fourth college season, Ben was drafted 11th overall in 2004 and signed a six-year, $40 million contract. "This is a franchise type quarterback," his agent, Leigh Steinberg, told AP. "I think he's a Troy Aikman, John Elway type of quarterback. He's that good."

At first, Steelers All-Pro guard Alan Faneca didn't buy the hype. When Roethlisberger was forced to start the third game of his rookie season, due to an injury to starter Tommy Maddox, the *Pittsburgh Post-Gazette* asked the All-Pro guard if he was excited to have the promising Roethlisberger in the lineup. "No, it's not exciting," Faneca said. "Do you want to go work with some little young kid who's just out of college?"

In this case, the answer was yes. Setting NFL rookie records for completion percentage (66.4) and passer rating (98.1), Roethlisberger led the Steelers to a 15–1 record—the first 15-win season ever by an AFC team. Ben impressed coaches with his ability to execute his passes even against complex defensive schemes. His composure in the pocket was extraordinary for a rookie. He would follow through with precision even with defenders bearing down on him.

Year after year, Roethlisberger achieved amazing feats. In the 2005 season, he became the youngest quarterback to lead a team to a Super Bowl title. In 2006, he played 15 games despite the trauma to his body—and threw for 433 yards against Denver. The next season, Ben set a Steelers record with 32 touchdown passes and made the Pro Bowl. In 2008, he led Pittsburgh to another Super Bowl title. In '09, he threw for a Steelers-record 4,328 yards. The next year, he returned to the Super Bowl yet again, losing to Green Bay. In 2011, he played through a badly injured ankle and led Pittsburgh to a 12–4 record, earning a second Pro Bowl berth.

Critics of Roethlisberger—and there are few—have said that he hasn't put up the dazzling numbers of Tom Brady, Payton Manning, Drew Brees, and Aaron Rodgers. But as Mike Ditka said on the *Mike & Mike* radio show, "If you're gonna tell me that Ben Roethlisberger is not an elite quarterback, then you don't know what you're talking about!"

Entering 2013, his 10th NFL season, Roethlisberger held Steelers career records for completions, completion percentage, and passing yards. His career record as a starting quarterback, including playoffs: 97–43.

Showing his versatility, Ben Roethlisberger scrambles for extra yards against Green Bay in 2009—in a game in which he threw for a career-best 503 yards. *George Gojkovich/Getty Images*

As this Score trading card from 2013 suggests, Roethlisberger has been the heart and soul of the Steelers franchise for a decade and counting. *MVP Books Collection*

Game-by-Game

9/9	W, 34–7, at Cleveland Browns
9/16	W, 26–3, vs. Buffalo Bills
9/23	W, 37–16, vs. San Francisco 49ers
9/30	L, 14–21, at Arizona Cardinals
10/7	W, 21–0, vs. Seattle Seahawks
10/21	L, 28–31, at Denver Broncos
10/28	W, 24–13, at Cincinnati Bengals
11/5	W, 38–7, vs. Baltimore Ravens
11/11	W, 31–28, vs. Cleveland Browns
11/18	L, 16–19 (OT), at New York Jets
11/26	W, 3–0, vs. Miami Dolphins
12/2	W, 24–10, vs. Cincinnati Bengals
12/9	L, 13–34, at New England Patriots
12/16	L, 22–29, vs. Jacksonville Jaguars
12/20	W, 41–24, at St. Louis Rams
12/30	L, 21–27, at Baltimore Ravens

Playoffs

1/5	L, 29–31, vs. Jacksonville Jaguars

Team Scoring

393 points scored
269 points allowed

THE TOMLIN TURNAROUND

New Coach Leads Steelers to AFC North Crown

"Mike Tomlin," said Steelers President Art Rooney II upon introducing the team's new head coach in 2007, "is first and foremost a good person. That is the first test you have to pass." Apparently so, since that is the same message that Dan Rooney pronounced after signing Bill Cowher for the job in 1992. There were two other similarities between Tomlin and Cowher: both had a background in defense, and both were 34 years old when they took the job.

Unlike Cowher, Tomlin didn't talk about winning a Super Bowl right away. "We intend to make no bold predictions about what we are going to do," Tomlin said. "What we are going to do is promise to have a first-class, blue-collar work ethic."

Tomlin immediately captured the attention of his team in 2007. The defense performed at optimal level, leading the league in fewest yards against. Linebacker James Harrison, who paced the Steelers with 98 total tackles, made the Pro Bowl for the first time. On offense, Ben Roethlisberger ranked among the NFL's top three in touchdown passes (32) and passer rating (104.1). Willie Parker ran for 1,316 yards.

Pittsburgh opened at 7–2 before stumbling to the finish line. Following an overtime loss to a 1–8 Jets team, the Steelers survived a 3–0 scare against winless Miami during heavy rain at Heinz Field. When the Patriots crushed the Gold and Black 34–13 en route to a perfect 16–0 season, Pittsburghers realized that a Super Bowl might not be in the cards.

Nor was a playoff win. Though the Steelers won the AFC North at 10–6, Jacksonville edged them in the wildcard round 31–29. Pittsburgh had scored 19 points in the fourth quarter to go ahead, but Josh Scobee won it with a 25-yard field goal with 37 seconds remaining.

Rookie head coach Mike Tomlin had the Steelers clicking on both sides of the ball, but the team lost four of its last five games, including a heartbreaker against Jacksonville in the playoffs. *Gene J. Puskar/AP Images*

The X Factor:
Troy Polamalu

In 2003, for the first time in franchise history, the Steelers traded up in the draft. They had a darn good reason to do so. USC safety Troy Polamalu was scheduled to go in the middle of Round 1, and Pittsburgh had the No. 20 pick. They needed to move up to No. 16 to have a shot at the player whom they knew would be a star. By his second year, Troy was bound for the Pro Bowl.

"Troy Polamalu is a freak," said NFL quarterback Charlie Frye. "They'll line him up at safety, at linebacker, or up on the line. You can't get a good read on where he's coming from."

Of Samoan descent, Troy left his mother and siblings in Los Angeles at age eight and moved in with relatives in Oregon, where he embraced the beauty of the countryside. In high school, he starred in baseball, basketball, and especially football, once hitting a player so hard that he was penalized even though it was a clean, legal hit. At Southern Cal, Troy twice was named a first-team All-American. In his first scrimmage under head coach Pete Carroll, Polamalu mugged the running back of the ball and took it in for a touchdown. "He's as good a safety as I've ever coached," Carroll said.

Bill Cower and Mike Tomlin could make the same claim. With 4.33 speed, a 43-inch vertical leap, and tremendous instincts, Troy covers seemingly the whole field. In 2004, his first season as a starter, Polamalu ranked second on the Steelers with 97 total tackles while logging five interceptions and 15 defended passes. In his first decade in the league, Troy was invited to seven Pro Bowls, earned first-team All-Pro honors four times, and was often the "X factor" on a team that went to three Super Bowls.

With his supreme talent and long, flowing locks, Polamalu has been one of the most recognizable defensive players of the 21st century. Off the field, he is deeply spiritual, intellectually curious, and, said quarterback Carson Palmer, "nice to everybody . . . respectful, humble." Troy's hobbies include surfing, growing flowers, making furniture, and playing the piano. He says he keeps his trophies, which are many, stored in the attic.

A highly spiritual man, Polamalu prays after each play and named his children, Paisios and Ephraim, after Greek Orthodox Christian saints. *Joe Robbins/Getty Images*

Game-by-Game

9/7	**W**, 38–17, vs. Houston Texans
9/14	**W**, 10–6, at Cleveland Browns
9/21	**L**, 6–15, at Philadelphia Eagles
9/29	**W**, 23–20, vs. Baltimore Ravens
10/5	**W**, 26–21, at Jacksonville Jaguars
10/19	**W**, 38–10, at Cincinnati Bengals
10/26	**L**, 14–21, vs. New York Giants
11/3	**W**, 23–6, at Washington Redskins
11/9	**L**, 20–24, vs. Indianapolis Colts
11/16	**W**, 11–10, vs. San Diego Chargers
11/20	**W**, 27–10, vs. Cincinnati Bengals
11/30	**W**, 33–10, at New England Patriots
12/7	**W**, 20–13, vs. Dallas Cowboys
12/14	**W**, 13–9, at Baltimore Ravens
12/21	**L**, 14–31, at Tennessee Titans
12/28	**W**, 31–0, vs. Cleveland Browns

Playoffs

1/11	**W**, 35–24, vs. San Diego Chargers
1/18	**W**, 23–24, vs. Baltimore Ravens
2/1	**Super Bowl:** W, 27–23, vs. Arizona Cardinals

Team Scoring

347 points scored
223 points allowed

BEATING THE BEST

Despite Brutal Schedule, Steelers Roll to Super Bowl

The Steelers entered the 2008 season facing the toughest schedule imaginable. Not one of their non-division opponents had a losing record in 2007, and their slate included games against New England (16–0 the previous season), Dallas (13–3), Indianapolis (13–3), and the New York Giants (reigning Super Bowl champions). Moreover, five of the games were at night and two were against the improved Ravens, Pittsburgh's bitter division rival.

The Black and Gold, however, were up for the challenge, especially the defense under coordinator Dick LeBeau. In 2008, the Steelers led the NFL in fewest points allowed, fewest total yards, and fewest passing yards, and they were No. 2 against the run. Incredibly, the Steelers limited 10 opponents to zero or one touchdowns, including the mighty Patriots in a 33–10 whooping. While linebacker James Farrior led the team in total tackles with 133, All-Pro Troy Polamalu picked off seven passes. Linebacker James Harrison, the AP NFL Defensive Player of the Year, compiled a team-record 16 sacks and a league-best seven forced fumbles.

San Diego safety Eric Weddle is called for pass interference against wide receiver Nate Washington in the 2008 divisional playoff matchup. The Steelers won 35–24 to advance to the AFC Championship Game. *Rob Tringali/Getty Images*

Against stout competition, Ben Roethlisberger had an off year (17 TDs, 15 picks) and leading rusher Willie Parker (791 yards) averaged just 3.8 yards per carry. However, the D carried Pittsburgh to a 12–4 record, the AFC North title, and a No. 2 seed in the playoffs, which meant a first-round bye. After No. 1 seed Tennessee lost its divisional playoff game on Saturday, the Steelers were guaranteed home field in the AFC Championship Game if they could beat San Diego on Sunday.

Pittsburgh led the Chargers 14–10 at the half thanks in part to a 67-yard punt return by Santonio Holmes. The Steelers rolled up a 35–17 lead before a late San Diego touchdown made the final score 35–24. Parker finished the game with 146 rushing yards on 27 carries. "Pound them down," Holmes said. "Once we get them down, we can do whatever we want to do with them."

With bad blood brewing, the Steelers hosted the Ravens in the AFC title game. On a cold Pittsburgh night, the home team went ahead 13–0 on a 65-yard pass from Roethlisberger to Holmes. The Steelers led 16–14 late in the fourth quarter when a Polamalu pick-six iced a 23–14 victory. The game featured 14 punts and just 24 first downs. "It's the way every Baltimore–Pittsburgh game is," Steelers receiver Hines Ward said. "Sometimes guys get hit so hard, you don't know if they're going to get up."

The Steelers got up and stood proud. For the first time under coach Mike Tomlin, they were going to the Super Bowl.

Polamalu's Return

Thanks to a spectacular play by No. 43, the Steelers were off to Super Bowl 43. With 4:42 remaining in the AFC Championship Game, Pittsburgh led the Ravens by just two points, 16–14. Baltimore faced a third-and-13 on its own 28 when rookie quarterback Joe Flacco threw to the right flat. Reading Flacco's eyes, Troy Polamalu jumped in front of the intended receiver and picked off the pass at the Baltimore 40.

With his long locks flying, Troy raced down the left sideline before reversing field completely and finding a path to the end zone on the right side of the field. Heinz Field went bonkers, as fans knew that the pick-six had pretty much clinched the Steelers' trip to the Super Bowl, especially the way the defense had played all evening long. Ben Roethlisberger sympathized with Flacco after the game. "He went against the No. 1 defense in the world," Ben said.

Troy Polamalu celebrates his 40-yard interception return in the 2008 conference title game. *Getty Images*

Super Bowl XLIII: Holmes Schooled

With the world in the throes of a financial crisis, and Pittsburgh facing an Arizona Cardinals team that had gone 9–7, sponsors worried about viewership of Super Bowl XLIII in Tampa. Yet a record-setting 98.7 million Americans tuned in, and those who didn't go to bed when the score was 20–7 were treated to a dandy finish.

Empowered by a 38-yard pass from Ben Roethlisberger to Hines Ward, but stuffed at the goal line, Pittsburgh opened the scoring with an 18-yard field goal. On the first play of the second quarter, Big Ben hit tight end Heath "Big Money" Miller for a four-yard touchdown. Arizona, behind 37-year-old quarterback Kurt Warner, quickly cut the deficit to 10–7. That's how it remained until the last play of the half, when Steelers James Harrison stunned the nation.

With the Cardinals on the Pittsburgh 1-yard line, Warner was picked off over the middle by the All-Pro linebacker. With an army of blockers ahead of him, Harrison rumbled 100 yards down the right sideline. Instead of trailing 14–10 entering the Bruce Springsteen halftime show, the Steelers miraculously were up 17–7. It was dubbed the "Immaculate Interception."

Pittsburgh went ahead 20–7 in the third quarter, but the Cards didn't fold. After Arizona's 87-yard, fourth-quarter drive cut the deficit to 20–14, Steelers center Justin Hartwig was flagged for holding in the end zone—a safety. Two plays later, with just 2:47 remaining, Warner hooked up with All-Pro receiver Larry Fitzgerald for a 64-yard touchdown. Just like that, Arizona led 23–20.

That's when Roethlisberger and Santonio Holmes put on a show for the ages. On a nine-play drive, Ben and Holmes connected on passes of 14, 13, and 40 yards. Then, with Pittsburgh facing second-and-goal at the 6 with 42 seconds to go, Holmes—while on the run—caught a high pass in the right corner of the end zone. Though his body was bent out of bounds when he grabbed the ball, Santonio somehow kept both feet on the red paint. "All I did was stood up on my toes and extended my hands," he said. Replays confirmed the amazing catch, and Pittsburgh prevailed 27–23 for their record sixth Super Bowl victory.

"Was that a 60-minute game, or what?" exclaimed Steelers linebacker James Farrior. "It came down to the last play, and we made it."

Santonio Holmes somehow keeps two feet inbounds as he grabs Ben Roethlisberger's six-yard, game-winning touchdown pass with 35 seconds remaining. *Joe Rimkus Jr/Miami Herald/MCT via Getty Images*

As Arizona players close in, James Harrison leaps into the end zone to complete a 100-yard interception return for a touchdown in Super Bowl XLIII. *Al Bello/Getty Images*

Last-Chance Hero: James Harrison

If it weren't for a freak injury to Clark Haggans, the world might not know about James Harrison. After Haggans suffered a weight-lifting accident in the summer of 2004, the Steelers were desperate for another linebacker. They called Harrison, a player who had been written off time and time again.

If not for the Haggans injury, Harrison would admit, he would have retired from football and perhaps driven a truck for a living, like his father had. As it was, he bore down, studied his playbook and handwritten notes, and developed into a five-time Pro Bowler and Super Bowl hero.

The youngest of 14 children, Harrison was considered a head case in high school. He challenged coaches and opposing fans, and he was arrested for firing a BB gun in the school locker room. The major college programs stayed away, and after his productive career at Kent State (15 sacks in 2001), so did NFL teams. Undrafted, Harrison was cut three times by the Steelers and once by the Ravens. "He was a knucklehead that didn't know the plays," said Steelers linebacker James Farrior.

More dedicated in 2004, Harrison made the Steelers and wound up starting four games that year. It wasn't until November 5, 2007, his first year as a full-time starter, that he captured the nation's attention. Versus Baltimore on Monday night, Harrison logged 3.5 sacks, forced three fumbles, recovered a fumble, and intercepted a pass, earning the nickname "Mr. Monday Night." He also gained a reputation for late hits and running his mouth. "My rep is James Harrison," he said, "mean son of a bitch who loves hitting the hell out of people."

In 2008, Harrison amassed 93 total tackles, seven forced fumbles, and a Steelers-record 16 sacks, earning the AP NFL Defensive Player of the Year Award. He then capped his fairytale season with a 100-yard interception return in Super Bowl XLIII. Over the next three seasons, James rang up 29.5 sacks and returned to the Pro Bowl each year, including 2010 when he was named first-team All-Pro for the second time.

Harrison finally left the Steelers in 2013, although not to drive a truck. He continued his career with the Cincinnati Bengals.

2009

9–7   3rd place

Game-by-Game

9/10	**W,** 13–10 (OT), vs. Tennessee Titans
9/20	**L,** 14–17, at Chicago Bears
9/27	**L,** 20–23, at Cincinnati Bengals
10/4	**W,** 38–28, vs. San Diego Chargers
10/11	**W,** 28–20, at Detroit Lions
10/18	**W,** 27–14, vs. Cleveland Browns
10/25	**W,** 27–17, vs. Minnesota Vikings
11/9	**W,** 28–10, at Denver Broncos
11/15	**L,** 12–18, vs. Cincinnati Bengals
11/22	**L,** 24–27 (OT), at Kansas City Chiefs
11/29	**L,** 17–20 (OT), at Baltimore Ravens
12/6	**L,** 24–27, vs. Oakland Raiders
12/10	**L,** 6–13, at Cleveland Browns
12/20	**W,** 37–36, vs. Green Bay Packers
12/27	**W,** 23–20, vs. Baltimore Ravens
1/3	**W,** 30–24, at Miami Dolphins

Team Scoring

368 points scored
324 points allowed

"WIN OR WATCH"

It's the Latter, as Steelers' Late-Season Run Falls Short

A year after winning the Super Bowl, the Steelers broke down in 2009. Due to age, injuries, streaky play, and mental lapses, Pittsburgh finished at 9–7 and out of the playoffs.

All season long, the Steelers had fans reaching for their heart medicine. After beating Tennessee in overtime to start the season, Pittsburgh blew late leads against the Bears and Bengals, losing both battles. "We have to finish games," said offensive tackle Willie Colon. "We're not doing the little things, and it's catching up to us."

Pittsburgh followed with five straight wins—followed by five straight losses, two in overtime and three against bad teams. By that point, the 6–7 Steelers had dug themselves a deep hole. The only way they could reach the postseason would be to win their remaining three games and pray that other teams faltered.

On December 20 at Heinz Field, Pittsburgh survived a 37–36 heart-pounder against Green Bay, as Ben Roethlisberger hit Mike Wallace for a 19-yard touchdown pass on the final play of the game. "It was obviously pretty reminiscent of the Super Bowl," said center Justin Hartwig, referring to Santonio Holmes's catch.

Responding to coach Mike Tomlin's "Win or Watch" mantra, Roethlisberger threw for a team-record 503 yards the next week in a 23–20 nail-biter over Baltimore. The Steelers survived a late charge by Miami in the finale, but it still wasn't good enough, as two other 9–7 AFC teams made the playoffs. The Steelers may have won, but they still had to watch.

In a play reminiscent of Santonio Holmes's Super Bowl catch, Mike Wallace snatches this 19-yard Ben Roethlisberger pass as time expires to tie Green Bay 36–36. The extra point won it. *Gary Puskar/AP Images*

Coach Confidence:
Mike Tomlin

When Mike Tomlin told his mother he was going to try his luck at coaching instead of attending law school, she was shocked. But she shouldn't have been. Coaching was a perfect fit for the Hampton, Virginia, native. He had the brains (biology major at the prestigious William & Mary), the football acumen (all-conference receiver), and the personality and desire to coach the game.

"Confidence was never a problem with Mike," college teammate Darren Sharper told the *New York Times.* "He would talk trash not only to players, but to coaches. . . . He is always ready to go, trying to get guys to compete."

Tomlin coached wide receivers at Arkansas State in 1997 before, notably, switching to defensive back coach the following year. Defense would become his trademark. Tomlin guided the DBs for the Tampa Bay Buccaneers from 2001 to 2005, when he helped head coach Tony Dungy, his "life mentor," soar to become Super Bowl champions. Hailed as a rising star among the coaching community, Tomlin served one season as Minnesota's defensive coordinator (2006) before signing with the Steelers.

Tomlin entered the 2007 season with many of Bill Cowher's coaches, including defensive coordinator Dick LeBeau. Tomlin maintained team unity while injecting his own brand of competitive fire. Success was immediate. In his first five seasons, Tomlin won 55 games, took his team to two AFC championships, and prevailed in Super Bowl XLIII (2008 season)—becoming the youngest coach, at 36, to do so. By age 40, he had helped the Steelers lead the league in total defense four times.

The NFL Coach of the Year in 2008, Tomlin faced his first adversity a year later, as the Steelers needed to scramble late in the season to try to make the playoffs. "We will not go gently," Tomlin declared to the press. "We will unleash hell here in December, because we have to. We won't go in the shell. We will go into attack mode, because that is what is required."

That determination did not get the Steelers to the playoffs, but they did win their last three games, and a year later they were back in the Super Bowl. On July 24, 2012, the Steelers signed Tomlin to a contract extension that would keep him in Pittsburgh through the 2016 season.

"Steeler football is 60 minutes," Tomlin once said. "It's never going to be pretty. Throw style points out the window, but these guys will fight to the end." *George Gojkovich/Getty Images*

Team Leaders

(**Boldface** indicates league leader)

Scoring Leaders (Points)

2000: Kris Brown, 107
2001: Kris Brown, 124
2002: Hines Ward, 78
2003: Jeff Reed, 100
2004: Jeff Reed, 124
2005: Jeff Reed, 117
2006: Jeff Reed, 101
2007: Jeff Reed, 113
2008: Jeff Reed, 117
2009: Jeff Reed, 122

Passing Leaders

(Completions / Attempts / Yards)

2000: Kordell Stewart, 151 / 289 / 1,860
2001: Kordell Stewart, 266 / 442 / 3,106
2002: Tommy Maddox, 234 / 377 / 2,836
2003: Tommy Maddox, 298 / 519 / 3,414
2004: Ben Roethlisberger, 196 / 295 / 2,621
2005: Ben Roethlisberger, 168 / 268 / 2,385
2006: Ben Roethlisberger, 280 / 469 / 3,513
2007: Ben Roethlisberger, 264 / 404 / 3,154
2008: Ben Roethlisberger, 281 / 469 / 3,301
2009: Ben Roethlisberger, 337 / 506 / 4,328

Rushing Leaders

(Carries / Yards / TDs)

2000: Jerome Bettis, 355 / 1,341 / 8
2001: Jerome Bettis, 225 / 1,072 / 4
2002: Amos Zereoue, 193 / 762 / 4
2003: Jerome Bettis, 246 / 811 / 7
2004: Jerome Bettis, 250 / 941 / 13
2005: Willie Parker, 255 / 1,202 / 4
2006: Willie Parker, 337 / 1,494 / 13
2007: Willie Parker, 321 / 1,316 / 2
2008: Willie Parker, 210 / 791 / 5
2009: Rashard Mendenhall, 242 / 1,108 / 7

Receiving Leaders

(Receptions / Yards / TDs)

2000: Hines Ward, 48 / 672 / 4
2001: Hines Ward, 94 / 1,003 / 4
2002: Hines Ward, 112 / 1,329 / 12
2003: Hines Ward, 95 / 1,163 / 10
2004: Hines Ward, 80 / 1,004 / 4
2005: Hines Ward, 69 / 975 / 11
2006: Hines Ward, 74 / 975 / 6
2007: Hines Ward, 71 / 732 / 7
2008: Hines Ward, 81 / 1,043 / 7
2009: Hincs Ward, 95 / 1,167 / 6

Interceptions

(Number / Yards / TDs)

2000: Dewayne Washington, 5 / 59 / 0;
Chad Scott, 5 / 49 / 0
2001: Chad Scott, 5 / 204 / 2
2002: Joey Porter, 4 / 153 / 0;
Brent Alexander, 4 / 37 / 0
2003: Brent Alexander, 4 / 63 / 0
2004: Troy Polamalu, 5 / 58 / 1
2005: Chris Hope, 3 / 60 / 0
2006: Troy Polamalu, 3 / 51 / 0;
Bryant McFadden, 3 / 39 / 0
2007: Ike Taylor, 3 / 56 / 1
2008: Troy Polamalu, 7 / 59 / 0
2009: Troy Polamalu, 3 / 17 / 0;
Ryan Clark, 3 / 0 / 0

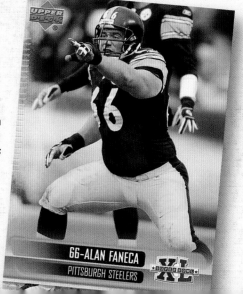

This McFarlane NFL 16 figure pays tribute to guard Alan Faneca, who represented Pittsburgh in seven straight Pro Bowls (2001–2007). *MVP Books Collection*

66-ALAN FANECA
PITTSBURGH STEELERS

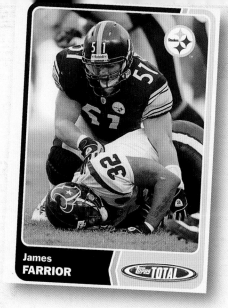

Showcased on this cover of a 2003 *Steelers Gameday*, middle linebacker James Farrior finished second in NFL Defensive Player of the Year balloting following the 2004 season. *MVP Books Collection*

Super Bowl XLIII set a record with 98.7 million American viewers. *MVP Books Collection*

First-Team All-Pros

2001: Alan Faneca, G
2001: Jason Gildon, LB
2002: Alan Faneca, G
2002: Joey Porter, LB
2004: Alan Faneca, G
2004: James Farrior, LB
2004: Jeff Hartings, C
2005: Alan Faneca, G
2005: Troy Polamalu, S
2006: Alan Faneca, G
2007: Alan Faneca, G
2008: James Harrison, LB
2008: Troy Polamalu, S

Pro Bowl Selections

2000: Jason Gildon, LB
2001: Kendrell Bell, LB
2001: Jerome Bettis, RB
2001: Alan Faneca, G
2001: Jason Gildon, LB
2001: Kordell Stewart, QB
2001: Hines Ward, WR
2002: Alan Faneca, G
2002: Jason Gildon, LB
2002: Joe Porter, LB
2002: Hines Ward, WR
2003: Alan Faneca, G
2003: Casey Hampton, NT
2003: Hines Ward, WR
2004: Jerome Bettis, RB

2004: Alan Faneca, G
2004: James Farrior, LB
2004: Jeff Hartings, C
2004: Troy Polamalu, S
2004: Joey Porter, LB
2004: Aaron Smith, DE
2004: Marvel Smith, DT
2004: Hines Ward, WR
2005: Alan Faneca, G
2005: Troy Polamalu, S
2005: Joey Porter, LB
2005: Casey Hampton, NT
2005: Jeff Hartings, C
2006: Alan Faneca, G
2006: Casey Hampton, NT
2006: Willie Parker, RB
2006: Troy Polamalu, S
2007: Alan Faneca, G
2007: Casey Hampton, NT
2007: James Harrison, LB
2007: Troy Polamalu, S
2007: Willie Parker, RB
2007: Ben Roethlisberer, QB
2008: James Farrior, LB
2008: James Harrison, LB
2008: Troy Polamalu, S
2009: Casey Hampton, DT
2009: James Harrison, LB
2009: Heath Miller, TE
2009: LaMarr Woodley, LB

1st-Round Draft Picks

2000: Plaxico Burress (8), WR, Michigan St.
2001: Casey Hampton (19), NT, Texas
2002: Kendall Simmons (30), G, Auburn
2003: Troy Polamalu (16), DB, Southern California
2004: Ben Roethlisberer (11), QB, Miami (Ohio)
2005: Heath Miller (30), TE, Virginia
2006: Santonio Holmes (25), WR, Ohio St.
2007: Lawrence Timmons (15), LB, Florida St.
2008: Rashard Mendenhall (23), RB, Illinois
2009: Evander Hood (32), DE, Missouri

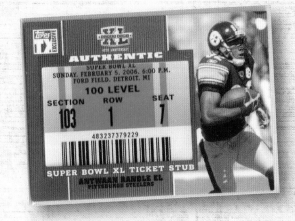

Topps offered collectors an authentic ticket stub from Super Bowl XL, this version featuring Antwaan Randle El. *MVP Books Collection*

THE 2010s

Polamalu, Steelers Nation, and Seventh Heaven

No matter their team's record, Steelers fans come out in droves—be it at Heinz Field, road games, or restaurants and bars around the world.

The Steelers missed out on their seventh Super Bowl title when Ben Roethlisberger threw four straight incompletions from his own 33-yard-line in the final two minutes. *MVP Books Collection*

By the second decade of the new century, the Steelers and their fans were like an old married couple—comfortable with each other, given to the occasional spat, but secure in the longevity of their relationship.

For Steelers Nation, it almost didn't matter who took the field. Not only would the fans outlast anyone in uniform, a Steelers game was *their* experience. The players were nearly incidental to the jerseys, Terrible Towels, trinkets, and tailgates.

In 2010, with hope running high, the team had another Lombardi in the making. But bad plays made XLV the team's second lost Super Bowl. A 2011 playoff loss was followed by two seasons out of the money.

"The Malone years," one fan grumbled, watching another sputtering season. Stagflation all around, ennui on and off the field. Even the great enmities—those mythic hatreds—were banked. No Ray Lewis–Joey Porter trash talking to get the blood boiling. No Hines Ward hitting anything that moved, grinning wickedly, being called every vile name imaginable. Even designated assassin James Harrison had moved on.

In the 2010s, when the once-hated Ravens come to town, they're just another football team. Heinz Field is oddly quiet. Not much to cheer or boo.

Yet for Steelers Nation, gear still abounds, from tangled Troy Polamalu manes to scruffy Brett Kiesel beards. Steelers jerseys remain *de rigueur*, including such classics as Franco and Rocky, Lambert and Swann.

Steelers Nation has grown globally, with some 1,500 coast-to-coast bars and restaurants identifying themselves with the team. And the fans who inhabit them remain uncounted and uncountable.

Wide receiver Mike Wallace (left) and cornerback Keenan Lewis celebrate Pittsburgh's 24–19 win over the Jets in the 2010 season's AFC Championship Game.
Gregory Shamus/Getty Images

"You go into sports bars in any city on game day," noted *USA Today*'s Gary Mihoces, a former Pittsburgher who's covered games in every NFL city. "There are six Bills fans. There are six Browns fans. And there are 300 Steeler fans. In every city. It's unbelievable."

It can also be overwhelming. It's not uncommon to have 30,000 very vocal, very jersey-wearing, Terrible Towel-waving Steelers fans come to a Giants-Steelers game. In New Jersey. That may be because for Steelers Nation it's inconceivable to change football allegiances. Even fans who've come to Pittsburgh for school or jobs remain Steelers fans for life.

"We take pride in our roots as Pittsburghers," said Pittsburgher Vince Laschied III, who's lived for four decades in Los Angeles. Added West Coast scholastic football coach T. J. Troup, "the Steelers are resilient, passionate, fight-to-the-end warriors—like Pittsburgh itself."

When Steelers Nation thinks warrior, one name comes to mind: Troy Polamalu.

Still the unbridled hero of the 2010s, the one-man highlight film fuels the fans' mythic imaginations. Stopping the run at the line of scrimmage; busting plays and belting receivers; clinging to ball carriers like some alien growth; anticipating the count, vaulting over the line at the snap, crushing the quarterback. . . . Polamalu keeps hope alive.

Steelers Nation casts its mind's eye back to the 2008 AFC Championship Game. Home against the Ravens, Steelers ahead 16–14, late in the fourth quarter, Polamalu pick-sixes to ice the 23–14 win. As one card-carrying Nation member said at the time, the roar was the loudest thing he'd ever heard.

It's that kind of sound—that elation—that Steelers Nation knows it will hear— and feel—again. Because winning is expected. If not this year, or even next, this team will win.

Clear a spot in the trophy case. The elusive Seventh Heaven—that coveted seventh Super Bowl title—will come.

It's only a matter of time.

—A. M.

Game-by-Game

9/12	W, 15–9 (OT), vs. Atlanta Falcons
9/19	W, 19–11, at Tennessee Titans
9/26	W, 38–13, at Tampa Bay Buccaneers
10/3	L, 14–17, vs. Baltimore Ravens
10/17	W, 28–10, vs. Cleveland Browns
10/24	W, 23–22, at Miami Dolphins
10/31	L, 10–20, at New Orleans Saints
11/8	W, 27–21, at Cincinnati Bengals
11/14	L, 26–39, vs. New England Patriots
11/21	W, 35–3, vs. Oakland Raiders
11/28	W, 19–16 (OT), at Buffalo Bills
12/5	W, 13–10, at Baltimore Ravens
12/12	W, 23–7, vs. Cincinnati Bengals
12/19	L, 17–22, vs. New York Jets
12/23	W, 27–3, vs. Carolina Panthers
1/2	W, 41–9, at Cleveland Browns

Playoffs

1/15	W, 31–24, vs. Baltimore Ravens
1/23	W, 24–19, vs. New York Jets
2/6	**Super Bowl:** L, 25–31, vs. Green Bay Packers

Team Scoring

375 points scored

232 points allowed

AGAINST ALL ODDS

Steelers Overcome Distractions, Storm to Super Bowl

Before it even began, the Steelers' 2010 campaign was shaping up as a disaster. Two assistant coaches were dismissed, two left voluntarily, and Santonio Holmes—coming off a 1,248-yard receiving season—was traded due to multiple brushes with the law and a forthcoming NFL suspension.

Most unsettling of all, the league suspended Ben Roethlisberger for the first six games (later reduced to four) for violating the NFL's personal-conduct policy. Roethlisberger had been accused of sexual assault in 2009 and again in 2010, with two different women, although no criminal charges were ever brought against him.

Though Big Ben's actions brought shame to Steelers Nation, his suspension did not hurt the team. Backup quarterbacks Charlie Batch and Dennis Dixon fared well in his absence, and a defense that would allow the fewest points in the league during the season kept Pittsburgh competitive in those first four games. Meanwhile, running back Rashard Mendenhall, en route to 1,273 rushing yards on the season, scored on a 50-yard run in overtime to win the season opener against Atlanta. The Steelers compiled a 3–1 record before Roethlisberger returned.

Big Ben came out gunning, throwing three touchdown passes in his first game back, a 28–10 cakewalk over the Browns. With their All-Pro quarterback, a formidable running game, and a defense that allowed just 1,004 rushing yards all year (3.0 per carry), the Steelers finished with a 12–4 record. Linebacker James Harrison (10.5 sacks) and strong safety Troy Polamalu (seven picks) were named first-team All-Pro, while linebacker Lawrence Timmons amassed 135 total tackles. The only losses under Roethlisberger came against top-tier opponents—Patriots, Jets, and Saints—and in eight games, Pittsburgh's foes scored 11 points or fewer.

That's not to say that all 12 wins were easy. In Miami, with the Steelers trailing 22–20 late in the game, Roethlisberger fumbled around the Dolphins' goal line. No one was sure who got the ball, but it was awarded to the Steelers, who kicked a game-winning field goal before

Wide receiver Antonio Brown eludes a Ravens tackler in their playoff encounter. On third-and-19 with 2:07 to go, Brown turned a long pass from Ben Roethlisberger into a 58-yard gain, setting up the winning touchdown. *Gregory Shamus/Getty Images*

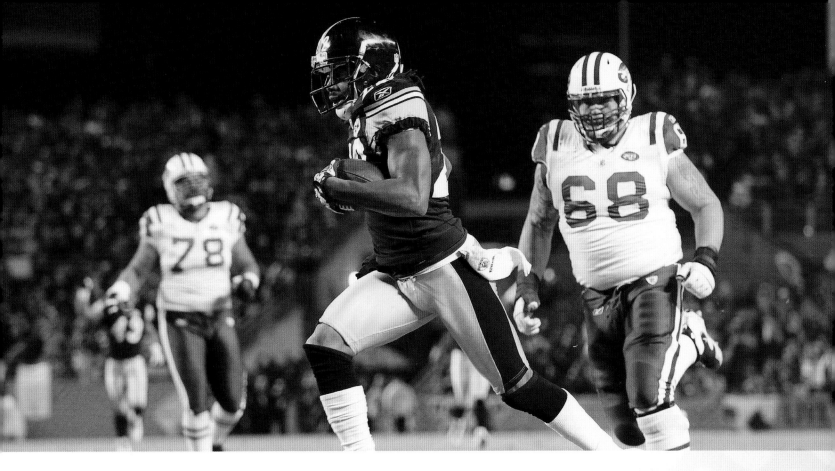

Defensive back William Gay returns a Mark Sanchez fumble 19 yards for a touchdown in the AFC Championship Game, putting the contest out of reach.
Ronald Martinez/Getty Images

bolting out of Dodge. "Make it quick," coach/comedian Mike Tomlin told reporters after the game. "We've got the buses warming up." In Buffalo, Bills receiver Stevie Johnson should have won the game in overtime. "I had the game in my hands and I dropped it," he said. Pittsburgh won that one when Shaun Suisham boomed a 41-yard, walk-off field goal.

The Steelers' luck continued at season's end, as they beat out 12–4 Baltimore for the AFC North title due to a tiebreaker. They also earned a No. 2 seed, which gave them a playoff bye. The Black and Gold needed their home-field advantage in their first postseason game, a dogfight against the rival Ravens. With the score tied 24–24 late in the game, the Steelers faced third-and-19 in their own territory.

"Let's just chuck it deep," Roethlisberger told offensive coordinator Bruce Arians. "If they pick it, it will be a pick way down there, just as good as a punt." As it turned out, it was Steelers rookie Antonio Brown who picked it out of the sky, for 58 yards. Mendenhall scored the winning touchdown with 1:33 to go.

The next week, the Steelers—playing in the AFC Championship Game for the eighth time in 17 years—hosted the Jets, who had won by dominating both sides of the line of scrimmage. But not this time. The mighty Pittsburgh D held New York to 70 yards rushing on 22 carries, and Mendenhall rushed for 121 yards. When William Gay returned a fumble 19 yards for a touchdown in the second quarter, the Steelers went ahead 24–0. A late Jets touchdown made the final 24–19.

Afterward, the storyline was how the Steelers had made it to the Super Bowl despite all the distractions entering the season. "We overcame a lot more obstacles this year than we have in the past," Polamalu said. "But we still got one more to go."

Super Bowl XLV: Driven to Tears

It had all the promise of the greatest show on earth: Packers versus Steelers—two of the NFL's marquee brands—at the new, $1.2 billion Cowboys Stadium. Two quarterbacks had something to prove. Ben Roethlisberger, suspended earlier in the year for personal misconduct, sought redemption. Aaron Rodgers, who long had lived under the shadow of Brett Favre, looked to forge his own identity. Rodgers hoped to become the second quarterback, following Big Ben, to lead a No. 6 seed to a Super Bowl victory.

The Super Bowl itself got off to a rough start. Snow fell off the stadium roof, injuring six people. More than a thousand temporary seats were deemed unsafe, frustrating ticket buyers. And Christina Aguilera muffed the words to the National Anthem.

But for Pittsburgh fans—who outnumbered their counterparts in the 103,000-seat stadium—the biggest botch of all was committed by Roethlisberger. With Green Bay up 7–0 in the first quarter, Nick Collins picked off a wayward pass and returned it 37 yards for a touchdown. From that pick-six to game's end, the Steelers were in crisis mode.

A Rodgers touchdown pass with 2:24 remaining in the half gave the Packers a 21–3 lead, although a Hines Ward scoring grab before intermission kept the Steelers in the game. Rashard Mendenhall's eight-yard touchdown run was the only scoring play of the third quarter, and Rodgers's third TD toss of the game made it 28–17 Green Bay. After Roethlisberger hit Mike Wallace for a 25-yard score, and the subsequent two-point conversion, the Steelers cut the deficit to 28–25 with 7:34 remaining. But that's as close as they got, as the Packers prevailed 31–25.

The Steelers outgained Green Bay 387 yards to 338, but three turnovers (including two interceptions) to the Packers' none did them in.

Afterward, no one felt worse about the defeat than Roethlisberger. "I feel like I let the city of Pittsburgh down—the fans, my coaches, and my teammates—and it's not a good feeling," he said. He later buried his head in a towel and cried.

Ben Roethlisberger pitches the ball to Antwaan Randle El on a two-point conversion following a fourth quarter touchdown. Randle El carried it into the end zone to put the Steelers within three points, 28–25, but Green Bay held on to win 31–25. *Joe Robbins/Getty Images*

PAINFUL TWISTS

Ben's Bad Ankle, Tebow's Miracle Doom Steelers

Blame it on Scott Paxson. With a potent offensive attack, a formidable running game, and the stingiest defense in the NFL in both yards and points, the Steelers looked to have another Super Bowl run in them. But when the Browns defensive lineman grabbed Ben Roethlisberger by the left leg in Pittsburgh's 13th game, the season took a painful twist. Big Ben writhed in pain, victim of a severely sprained ankle. He would miss the next contest and limp into the postseason, which lasted just one game.

Despite the injury, Roethlisberger threw for 4,077 yards, about half of which to his two Pro Bowl wide receivers, Mike Wallace and Antonio Brown. Rashard Mendenhall rushed for 928 yards, and Pro Bowl safeties Troy Polamalu and Ryan Clark were the top tacklers on a team that held five of its last six opponents under 10 points. Season highlights included a last-second, tiebreaking field goal to defeat the Colts, Big Ben's five TD passes versus Tennessee, and Mike Wallace's 95-yard touchdown reception against Arizona.

The Steelers and Ravens finished atop the AFC North at 12–4, but Pittsburgh lost the tiebreaker and was forced to open on the road against the 8–8 Broncos. Still limping, Roethlisberger completed just 22 of 40 passes with one touchdown, one interception, and five sacks. The TD toss, a 37-yarder to Jerricho Cotchery, came with 3:48 remaining in the fourth quarter, leading to a 23–23 tie. Counterpart Tim Tebow, who was short on talent but big on miracles, had one more left in him.

On the first play of overtime, Tebow hit Demaryius Thomas on a crossing pattern that turned into an 80-yard touchdown play. Just like that, the Steelers' season was over. Big Ben limped off the field in defeat.

In the opening playoff game at Denver, on the first play from scrimmage in overtime, Broncos receiver Demaryius Thomas turns a 20-yard Tim Tebow pass into an 80-yard touchdown play. *Doug Pensinger/Getty Images*

2011

12–4   2nd place

Game-by-Game

9/11	L, 7–35,	at Baltimore Ravens
9/18	W, 24–0,	vs. Seattle Seahawks
9/25	W, 23–20,	at Indianapolis Colts
10/2	L, 10–17,	at Houston Texans
10/9	W, 38–17,	vs. Tennessee Titans
10/16	W, 17–13,	vs. Jacksonville Jaguars
10/23	W, 32–20,	at Arizona Cardinals
10/30	W, 25–17,	vs. New England Patriots
11/6	L, 20–23,	vs. Baltimore Ravens
11/13	W, 24–17,	at Cincinnati Bengals
11/27	W, 13–9,	at Kansas City Chiefs
12/4	W, 35–7,	vs. Cincinnati Bengals
12/8	W, 14–3,	vs. Cleveland Browns
12/19	L, 3–20,	at San Francisco 49ers
12/24	W, 27–0,	vs. St. Louis Rams
1/1	W, 13–9,	at Cleveland Browns

Playoffs

1/8	L, 23–29 (OT),	vs. Denver Broncos

Team Scoring

325 points scored
227 points allowed

2012

8–8   3rd place

Game-by-Game

9/9	**L**, 19–31,	at Denver Broncos
9/16	**W**, 27–10,	vs. New York Jets
9/23	**L**, 31–34,	at Oakland Raiders
10/7	**W**, 16–14,	vs. Philadelphia Eagles
10/11	**L**, 23–26,	at Tennessee Titans
10/21	**W**, 24–17,	at Cincinnati Bengals
10/28	**W**, 27–12,	vs. Washington Redskins
11/4	**W**, 24–20,	at New York Giants
11/12	**W**, 16–13 (OT),	vs. Kansas City Chiefs
11/18	**L**, 10–13,	vs. Baltimore Ravens
11/25	**L**, 14–20,	at Cleveland Browns
12/2	**W**, 23–20,	at Baltimore Ravens
12/9	**L**, 24–34,	vs. San Diego Chargers
12/16	**L**, 24–27 (OT),	at Dallas Cowboys
12/23	**L**, 10–13,	vs. Cincinnati Bengals
12/30	**W**, 24–10,	vs. Cleveland Browns

Team Scoring

336 points scored
314 points allowed

NAIL-BITING MEDIOCRITY

Steelers Go 3–3 in "Walk-off" Games, 8–8 Overall

For a team that finished at 8–8, the Steelers sure put their fans through the wringer in 2012. Incredibly enough, six of their games were decided on the *very last play*—three wins, three losses.

All six of the games ended in field goals. Boots by Pittsburgh's Shaun Suisham defeated the Eagles, Chiefs (overtime), and Baltimore. However, walk-off three-pointers by the Raiders, Titans, and Cowboys (OT) were daggers to the hearts of the Steelers.

Considering Pittsburgh's 12–4 record a year earlier, and that the defense once again led the NFL in fewest total yards, the .500 record was extremely discouraging. The laundry list of explanations included: new offensive coordinator Todd Haley, who instituted a conservative passing offense and clashed with Ben Roethlisberger; problems on the offensive line; a draft class that offered little production; Mike Wallace's holdout; Rashard Mendenhall's injuries; a minus-10 takeaway deficit; and Big Ben's shoulder and rib injuries, which forced him to miss three late-season games, two of which were losses.

In one of those defeats, 20–14 at Cleveland, the Steelers turned the ball over eight times, with Charlie Batch throwing three interceptions. After narrowly defeating the Ravens the following week, Pittsburgh stood on the playoff cusp at 7–5. Though heavily favored in their next game against the Chargers, and with Roethlisberger back in the huddle, they lost 34–24. It was their fourth defeat of the season against a subpar team. "I have no clue [why we're inconsistent]," Roethlisberger said. "If I knew, I don't think we'd do it anymore. I thought we'd play better."

So did the fans.

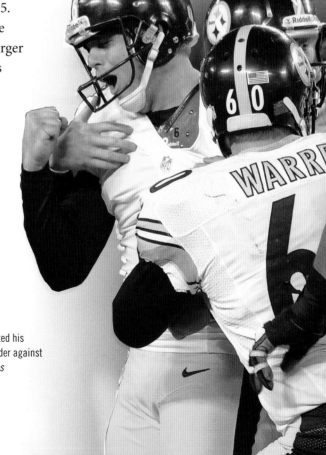

Kicker Shaun Suisham is swarmed by teammates after he booted his third game-winning field goal of the season, this one a 42-yarder against Baltimore on December 2. *Doug Kapustin/MCT via Getty Images*

REACHING FOR A MIRACLE

Steelers Almost Make the Playoffs After Woeful Start

Mike Tomlin's Steelers had dug themselves out of holes in previous years, but in 2013 they would have to emerge from a bottomless pit. Pittsburgh, for the first time since 1968, opened the season at 0–4 despite playing beatable opponents. A lack of a running attack hurt them against Tennessee and Cincinnati, and a minus-five takeaway game doomed them against Chicago. In London, in a battle of winless teams, the Steelers fell a touchdown short against the Vikings.

After a bye week, Pittsburgh looked sharper in a 19–6 win over the Jets. "The men in this locker room believe there's a chance that something great could come out of this if we all work toward it," defensive lineman Brett Keisel said after the game. A week later, Shaun Suisham booted a 42-yard field goal as time expired to defeat Baltimore, a loss that the Ravens avenged on Thanksgiving by preventing a two-point conversion with a minute to go in a 22–20 win.

The Steelers nearly pulled off a miracle against Miami, as Antonio Brown reached the end zone after a series of laterals on the final play. However, officials ruled that he stepped out of bounds before scoring, and Pittsburgh fell to 5–8. After barely escaping with a win at Green Bay, the Steelers entered the final weekend at 7–8.

Wearing a 1934-era throwback uniform, rookie running back Le'Veon Bell goes sky high to avoid a tackle against the Lions at Heinz Field on November 17. The second-round pick out of Michigan State gained a team-best 860 yards on 224 carries in his debut season. *Joe Sargent/ Getty Images*

To grab a wildcard berth, Pittsburgh needed to beat Cleveland while Miami, Baltimore, and San Diego lost. The first three scenarios came true, but San Diego ended up beating Kansas City in a late-afternoon game—in overtime. Had the Chiefs prevailed, the Steelers would have become the second of 189 0–4 NFL teams ever to make the playoffs.

2013

8–8   3rd place

Game-by-Game

9/8	L, 9–16, vs. Tennessee Titans
9/16	L, 10–20, at Cincinnati
9/22	L, 23–40, vs. Chicago Bears
9/29	L, 27–34, vs. Minnesota Vikings
10/13	W, 19–6, at New York Jets
10/20	W, 19–16, vs. Baltimore
10/27	L, 18–21, at Oakland Raiders
11/3	L, 31–55, at New England Patriots
11/10	W, 23–10, vs. Buffalo Bills
11/17	W, 37–27, vs. Detroit Lions
11/24	W, 27–11, at Cleveland Browns
11/28	L, 20–22, at Baltimore Ravens
12/8	L, 28–34, vs. Miami Dolphins
12/15	W, 30–20, vs. Cincinnati Bengals
12/22	W, 38–31, at Green Bay Packers
12/29	W, 20–7, vs. Cleveland Browns

Team Scoring

379 points scored
370 points allowed

The Greatest NFL Franchise?

When it comes to baseball, no one questions that the New York Yankees—with their 27 world titles—are the greatest franchise of all-time. But in football, fans from Green Bay and Chicago, Dallas and San Francisco, and even Cleveland and New York all challenge Pittsburghers' claims that the Steelers are the greatest franchise in NFL history.

The Steelers are the only team to win six Super Bowls, with the Cowboys and 49ers trailing at five apiece. The Packers and Giants have each won four. Of course, the Super Bowl era dates back only to 1967.

The Bears have won only one Lombardi Trophy, but they rank first in NFL history in both total wins (727) and winning percentage (.578). Their nine NFL championships are the second most ever. Surely, the Packers could claim top honors as well. They lead all teams with 13 NFL titles, and they place second behind Chicago with 695 total victories. The Browns (third all-time with eight NFL championships) and the Giants (third with eight titles, third with 657 wins, and third with four Super Bowl victories) are in the mix as well. Then there's Dallas: second in Super Bowl wins, second in all-time winning percentage.

Steelers fans can counter that the Packers, Bears, and Browns dominated during the league's early decades, when only a dozen teams competed including such ragtag clubs as the Frankford Yellow Jackets. Pittsburgh has flexed its muscle during far more competitive eras. In the old days, winning a championship required just winning one playoff battle—the NFL Championship Game. In recent decades, teams have needed to win three or four postseason games to hoist the Lombardi Trophy. The Steelers and Cowboys are tied for the most playoff-game victories in history with 33—as well as conference titles with eight.

It's not just about wins and titles. The Steelers have one of the NFL's largest and most loyal fan bases in Steelers Nation, a family that has owned the team since its inception, and a foundation so stable that only three men have coached the team since 1969.

Certainly, the Steelers can claim to be the greatest team of the Super Bowl era, at least until another team wins its sixth Lombardi Trophy. Then again, by that time, Pittsburgh may already have won its seventh.

With six Super Bowl trophies to display, the Pittsburgh Steelers can make a strong case for being the greatest NFL franchise of all time. *George Gojkovich/Getty Images*

THE 2010s
RECORD BOOK

Team (Boldface indicates league leader)

2010: Rashard Mendenhall, 78
2011: Shaun Suisham, 105
2012: Shaun Suisham, 118
2013: Shaun Suisham, 129

2010: Ben Roethlisberger, 240 / 389 / 3,200
2011: Ben Roethlisberger, 324 / 513 / 4,077
2012: Ben Roethlisberger, 284 / 449 / 3,265
2013: Ben Roethlisberger, 375 / 584 / 4,261

2010: Rashard Mendenhall, 324 / 1,273 / 13
2011: Rashard Mendenhall, 228 / 928 / 9
2012: Jonathan Dwyer, 156 / 623 / 2
2013: Le'Veon Bell, 244 / 860 / 8

2010: Mike Wallace, 60 / 1,257 / 10
2011: Mike Wallace, 72 / 1,193 / 8
2012: Heath Miller, 71 / 816 / 8
2013: Antonio Brown, 110 / 1,499 / 8

2010: Troy Polamalu, 7 / 101 / 1
2011: Troy Polamalu, 2 / 33 / 0;
    Ike Taylor, 2 / 29 / 0;
    William Gay, 2 / 12 / 0
2012: Lawrence Timmons, 3 / 80 / 1
2013: Ryan Clark, 2 / 50 / 0;
    Cortez Allen, 2 / 43 / 1;
    Troy Polamalu, 2 / 36 / 1;
    Lawrence Timmons, 2 / 26 / 0

2010: James Harrison, LB
2010: Troy Polamalu, S
2011: Maurkice Pouncey, C
2011: Troy Polamalu, S

2010: James Harrison, LB
2010: Brett Keisel, DE

Brett Keisel, featured here in bobblehead form, was a Pro Bowler at defensive end in 2010 as he made the opposition "fear the beard."
MVP Books Collection

2010: Troy Polamalu, S
2010: Maurkice Pouncey, C
2011: Antonio Brown, KR
2011: Ryan Clark, S
2011: James Harrison, LB
2011: Troy Polamalu, S
2011: Maurkice Pouncey, C
2011: Ben Roethlisberer, QB
2011: Mike Wallace, WR
2012: Heath Miller, TE
2012: Maurkice Pouncey, C
2013: Antonio Brown, WR
2013: Troy Polamalu, S

2010: Maurkice Pouncey (18), C, Florida
2011: Cameron Heyward (31), DT, Ohio St.
2012: David DeCastro (24), G, Stanford
2013: Jarvis Jones (17), LB, Georgia

the Pittsburgh Steelers All-Time Player Roster

Player	Position	Seasons	Games
Abercrombie, Walter	RB	1982–87	79
Adamchik, Ed	T	1967	2
Adams, Bob	TE	1969–71	42
Admas, Flozell	OT	2010	16
Adams, Mike	OT	2012–13	25
Adams, Mike	WR	1997	6
Agajanian, Ben	K	1945	5
Alban, Dick	E	1956–59	48
Alberghini, Tom	G	1945	1
Albrecht, Art	C/OT	1942	3
Alderton, John	E	1953	10
Alexander, Brent	S	2000–03	64
Allen, Chuck	LB	1970–71	24
Allen, Cortez	CB	2011–13	44
Allen, Jim	DB	1974–77	50
Allen, Lou	T	1950–51	24
Allen, Will	S	2010–13	58
Alley, Don	WR	1969	8
Allred, John	TE	2002	13
Alston, Lyneal	WR	1987	3
Andabaker, Rudy	G	1952, 1954	10
Anderson, Anthony	RB	1979	16
Anderson, Art	T	1963	13
Anderson, Chet	E	1967	14
Anderson, Fred	DE	1978	16
Anderson, Gary	K	1982–94	197
Anderson, Jesse	TE	1992	2
Anderson, Larry	DB	1978–81	52
Anderson, Melvin	WR	1987	2
Anderson, Ralph	DB	1971–72	21
Apke, Steve	LB	1987	3
Arndt, Al	G	1935	7
Arndt, Dick	T	1967–70	34
Arnold, David	CB	1989	15
Arnold, Jahine	WR	1996–98	12
Arnold, Jay	QB	1941	10
Asbury, Willie	B	1966–68	33
Askson, Burt	DE	1971	11
Atkinson, Frank	T	1963	14
August, Steve	OT	1984	5
Augusterfer, Gene	B	1935	1
Austin, Ocie	DB	1970–71	21
Avery, Steve	FB	1994–95	25
Aydelette, Buddy	OT/C	1987	12
B			
Badar, Rich	QB	1967	1
Bahr, Matt	K	1979–80	32
Bailey, Patrick	LB	2008–09	28
Bailey, Rodney	DE	2001–03, 2006	60
Baker, Conway	T	1944	9
Baker, Dallas	WR	2008	8
Baker, John	E	1963–67	62
Baker, Tim	WR	2001	3
Baldacci, Lou	B	1956	10
Ballman, Gary	B	1962–66	57
Balog, Bob	C	1949–50	16
Banaszak, John	DE/DT	1975–81	91
Bankston, Warren	RB	1969–72	39
Barbolak, Pete	T	1949	10
Barnes, Johnnie	WR	1995	3
Barnes, Reggie	LB	1993	16

Player	Position	Seasons	Games	Player	Position	Seasons	Games
Barnett, Tom	B	1959–60	24	**Brandt,** Jim	B	1952–54	33
Barry, Fred	DB	1970	9	**Bray,** Maurice	T	1935–36	24
Bartlett, Earl	B	1939	1	**Breedlove,** Rod	LB	1965–68	39
Basrak, Mike	C	1937–38	15	**Breen,** Gene	LB	1965–66	16
Bassi, Dick	G	1941	22	**Brett,** Ed	E	1936–37	18
Batch, Baron	RB	2011–12	12	**Brewster,** Pete	E	1959–60	21
Batch, Charlie	QB	2002–12	34	**Brister,** Bubby	QB	1986–92	61
Battaglia, Marco	TE	2002	1	**Britt,** Jessie	WR	1986	8
Battle, Arnaz	WR	2010–11	25	**Britt,** Ralph	TE	1987	3
Battles, Ainsley	S	2000, 2004	17	**Brooks,** Barrett	T	2003–05	21
Beachum, Kelvin	G	2012–13	22	**Broussard,** Fred	C	1955	6
Beams, Byron	T	1959–60	9	**Brovelli,** Angelo	QB	1933–34	13
Beasley, Tom	DE/DT	1978–83	79	**Brown,** Antonio	WR	2010–13	54
Beatty, Charles	DB	1969–72	30	**Brown,** Anthony	T	1999	16
Beatty, Ed	C	1957–61	54	**Brown,** Chad	LB	1993–96, 2006	65
Becker, Wayland	E	1939	2	**Brown,** Chris	CB/S	1984–85	22
Behning, Mark	OT	1986	16	**Brown,** Curtis	CB	2011–13	45
Bell, Kendrell	LB	2001–04	47	**Brown,** Dante	RB	2003–04	1
Bell, Le'Veon	RB	2013	13	**Brown,** Dave	DB	1975	13
Bell, Myron	S	1994–97, 2000–01	80	**Brown,** Dee	RB	2003	1
Bell, Richard	RB	1990	8	**Brown,** Ed	QB	1962–65	55
Bell, Theo	WR	1976, 1978–80	56	**Brown,** Ernie	DL	1999	3
Bentley, Albert	RB	1992	2	**Brown,** J. B.	DB	1997	13
Berger, Mitch	P	2008	13	**Brown,** John	T	1967–72	69
Bernet, Ed	E	1955	12	**Brown,** Kris	K	1999–01	48
Best, Greg	S	1983	13	**Brown,** Lance	CB	1998–99	32
Bettis, Jerome	RB	1996–05	145	**Brown,** Larry	TE/OT	1971–84	167
Bettis, Tom	LB	1962	11	**Brown,** Levi	T	2013	1
Billock, Frank	G	1937	2	**Brown,** Tom	E	1942	9
Bingham, Craig	LB	1982–84, 1987	32	**Bruder,** Henry	QB	1940	8
Binotto, John	B	1942	7	**Bruener,** Mark	TE	1995–03	12
Bishop, Don	B	1958–59	14	**Brumbaugh,** Boyd	B	1939–41	24
Bishop, Harold	TE	1998	7	**Brumfield,** Jim	RB	1971	14
Bivins, Charles	B	1967	2	**Brundage,** Dewey	E	1954	11
Blackledge, Todd	QB	1988–89	6	**Bruney,** Fred	B	1956–57	17
Blackwell, Will	WR	1997–01	47	**Bruno,** John	P	1987	3
Blake, Antwon	CB	2013	15	**Bryant,** Corbin	DE	2011	1
Blankenship, Brian	G	1987–91	61	**Bryant,** Fernando	CB	2008	2
Blankenship, Greg	LB	1976	6	**Bryant,** Hubie	WR	1970	14
Bleier, Rocky	RB	1968, 1970–80	140	**Bucek,** Felix	G	1946	11
Blount, Mel	CB	1970–83	200	**Buckner,** Brentson	DE	1994–96	35
Bohannon, Fred	S/CB	1982	7	**Buda,** Carl	G	1945	3
Boiman, Rocky	LB	2009	6	**Bukich,** Rudy	QB	1960–61	23
Bolkovac, Nick	T	1953–54	17	**Bulger,** Chester	T	1944	10
Bond, Randall	QB	1939	11	**Bullocks,** Amos	B	1966	8
Bonelli, Ernie	B	1946	3	**Burleson,** John	G	1933	3
Bono, Steve	QB	1987–88	5	**Burnett,** Joe	CB	2009	15
Booth, Clarence	B	1944	5	**Burnett,** Len	DB	1961	4
Botkin, Kirk	TE	1996–97	29	**Burnette,** Tom	B	1938	6
Boures, Emil	C/G	1982–86	35	**Burrell,** John	E	1962–64	42
Bova, Tony	E	1942, 1943–47	61	**Burress,** Plaxico	WR	2000–04, 2012–13	75
Bowers, R. J.	RB	2001	3	**Butler,** Bill	DB/KR	1961	10
Bowman, Bill	B	1957	5	**Butler,** Crezdon	CB	2010	4
Boyd, Sam	E	1939–40	14	**Butler,** Drew	P	2012	16
Boyle, Jim	OT	1987–88	9	**Butler,** Jack	B	1951–59	103
Bradley, Ed	LB	1972–75	49	**Butler,** Jim	B	1965–67	39
Bradshaw, Charles	T	1961–66	82	**Butler,** John	B	1943–44	12
Bradshaw, Jim	B	1963–67	62	**Bykowski,** Frank	G	1940	1
Bradshaw, Terry	QB	1970–83	168				
Brady, Jeff	LB	1991	16	**C**			
Brady, Pat	B	1952–54	36	**Cabrelli,** Larry	E	1943	10
Brandau, Art	C	1945–46	6	**Calcagni,** Ralph	T	1947	9

Player	Position	Seasons	Games	Player	Position	Seasons	Games
Caliguire, Dean	G/C	1991–92	7	**Colquitt,** Craig	P	1978–81, 1983–84	97
Call, John	B	1959	4	**Combs,** Chris	DE	2000–01	8
Calland, Lee	DB	1969–72	42	**Compagno,** Tony	B	1946–48	34
Calloway, Chris	WR	1990–91	28	**Compton,** Dick	E	1967–68	19
Calvin, Tom	B	1952–54	30	**Condit,** Merlyn	B	1940, 46	19
Cameron, Paul	B	1954	12	**Conley,** Steve	LB	1996–98	20
Campbell, Bob	RB	1969	14	**Conn,** Dick	DB	1974	12
Campbell, Don	T	1939–41	22	**Connelly,** Mike	C	1968	14
Campbell, Glenn	E	1935	1	**Conrad,** Chris	T	1998–99	17
Campbell, John	LB	1965–69	52	**Conti,** Enio	G	1943	10
Campbell, Leon	B	1955	12	**Coomer,** Joe	T	1941, 1945–46	26
Campbell, Ray	LB	1958–60	36	**Cooper,** Adrian	TE	1991–93	46
Campbell, Russ	TE	1992	7	**Cooper,** Marquis	LB	2006–07	5
Campbell, Scott	QB	1984–86	24	**Cooper,** Sam	T	1933	1
Canale, Rocco	G	1943	5	**Cordileone,** Lou	G	1962–63	26
Capers, Wayne	WR	1983–84	27	**Corley,** Anthony	RB	1984	14
Capp, Dick	E	1968	14	**Coronado,** Bob	E	1961	5
Cara, Dom	E	1937–38	19	**Cotchery,** Jerricho	WR	2011–13	42
Cardwell, Joe	T	1937–38	18	**Cotton,** Russell	B	1942	11
Carpenter, Preston	E	1960–63	52	**Courson,** Steve	G	1978–83	73
Carr, Gregg	LB	1985–88	57	**Cousino,** Brad	LB	1987	3
Carter, Chris	LB	2011–13	29	**Craft,** Russ	B	1954	11
Carter, Rodney	RB	1987–89	40	**Cregar,** William	G	1947–48	23
Carter, Tyrone	S	2004–09	89	**Crennel,** Carl	LB	1970	3
Cash, Keith	TE	1991	5	**Critchfield,** Larry	G	1933	11
Casper, Charles	QB	1935	9	**Croft,** Winfield	G	1936	9
Catano, Mark	DE/DT	1984–85	31	**Cromartie-Smith,** Da'Mon	S	2011–13	10
Cenci, John	C	1956	7	**Cropper,** Marshall	E	1967–69	16
Chamberlain, Garth	G	1945	3	**Cunningham,** Bennie	TE	1976–85	118
Chandnois, Lynn	B	1950–56	72	**Currivan,** Don	E	1944	10
Cheatham, Ernest	T	1954	4	**Curry,** Roy	B	1963	6
Cherry, Edgar	B	1939	2	**Cushing,** Matt	TE	1999, 2000–04	53
Cherundolo, Chuck	C	1941–42, 1945–48	63	**Cuthbert,** Randy	RB	1993–94	11
Christy, Dick	B	1958	12				
Cibulas, Joe	T	1945	5	**D**			
Ciccone, Ben	C	1934–35	23	**Dafney,** Bernard,	OL	1996	14
Cichowski, Gene	B	1957	12	**Daigle,** Anthony	RB	1994	1
Cifelli, Gus	T	1954	5	**Dailey,** Ted	E	1933	10
Cifers, Bob	QB	1947–48	22	**Daniel,** Willie	B	1961–66	75
Clack, Jim	C/G	1971–77	92	**Davenport,** Najeh	RB	2006–08	32
Clancy, Kendrick	NT	2000–04	52	**Davenport,** Charles	WR	1992–94	38
Clark, Jim	B	1933–34	19	**Davidson,** Bill	B	1937–39	28
Clark, Mike	K	1964–67	56	**Davidson,** Kenny	DE	1990–93	59
Clark, Reggie	LB	1994	5	**Davis,** Art	B	1956	9
Clark, Ryan	S	2006–13	111	**Davis,** Bruce	LB	2008	5
Clark, Spark	RB	1987	1	**Davis,** Carey	FB	2007–09	36
Clay, John	RB	2011	2	**Davis,** Charlie	DT	1974	14
Clayton, Harvey	CB	1983–86	57	**Davis,** Dave	WR	1973	2
Clement, Henry	TE	1961	14	**Davis,** Henry	LB	1970–73	56
Clement, John	B	1946–48	26	**Davis,** Lorenzo	WR	1990	4
Cline, Jackie	DE	1987	1	**Davis,** Paul	QB	1947–48	11
Cline, Tony	TE	1999	2	**Davis,** Robert	E	1946–50	55
Clinkscales, Joey	WR	1987–88	11	**Davis,** Russell	RB	1980–83	42
Cobb, Marvin	DB	1970	6	**Davis,** Sam	G	1967–79	168
Codie, Nakia	S	2000	6	**Davis,** Steve	RB	1972–74	39
Colclough, Ricardo	CB	2004–06	36	**Dawkins,** Tommy	DE	1987	2
Cole, Robin	LB	1977–87	150	**Davis,** Travis	S	1999	16
Cole, Terry	B	1970	10	**Dawson,** Dermontti	C	1988–00	184
Coleman, Andre	WR	1997–98	12	**Dawson,** Len	QB	1957–59	19
Collier, Mike	RB	1975	14	**DeCarbo,** Nick	G	1933	11
Collier, Reggie	QB	1987	2	**DeCarlo,** Art	B	1953	12
Colon, Willie	OT	2006–12	63	**DeCastro,** David	G	2012–13	12

Player	Position	Seasons	Games	Player	Position	Seasons	Games
Dekker, Jon	TE	2007–08	3	Evans, Jon	E	1958	1
Deloplaine, Jack	RB	1976–79	33	Evans, Ray	QB	1948	9
Demko, George	T	1961	1	Everett, Thomas	FS	1987–91	73
Dempsey, John	T	1934	1				
DePascal, Carmine	E	1945	1	**F**			
DePaul, Henry	G	1945	4	Faneca, Alan	G	1998–07	158
Derby, Dean	B	1957–61	49	Fangupo, Hebron	DT	2012–13	5
Dess, Darrell	G	1958	12	Farquhar, John	TE	1996	4
Dial, Buddy	E	1959–63	66	Farrar, Venice	B	1938–39	7
Dickey, Charlie	G	1987	1	Farrior, James	LB	2002–11	154
Didio, Mark	WR	1992	2	Farrell, Ed	B	1938	5
Dirden, Johnnie	WR	1981	6	Faumui, Ta'ase	DL	1994–95	8
Dixon, Dennis	QB	2008–11	4	Feher, Nick	G	1955	2
Dockery, John	DB	1972–73	16	Ferguson, Bob	B	1962–63	18
Dodrill, Dale	G	1951–59	103	Ferry, Lou	T	1952–55	47
Dodson, Les	B	1941	2	Fiala, John	LB	1998–02	75
Doehring, John	B	1935	2	Fife, Ralph	C	1946	10
Doering, Chris	WR	2003–04	19	Figures, Deon	CB	1993–96	61
Dolly, Dick	E	1941–45	19	Fike, Dan	OL	1993	3
Dolaway, Cliff	E	1935	4	Filchock, Frank	QB	1938	6
Donelli, Allan	B	1941–42	11	Finks, Jim	QB	1949–55	79
Donnalley, Rick	C-G	1982–83	21	Fisher, Doug	LB	1969–70	10
Dornbrook, Thom	G-C	1979	16	Fisher, Everett	B	1940	4
Douds, Forrest	T	1933–35	18	Fisher, Ray	T	1959	12
Dougherty, Bob	LB	1958	12	Fiske, Max	B	1936–39	29
Douglas, Bob	B	1938	2	Flanagan, Dick	G	1953–55	29
Doyle, Dick	B	1955	12	Flowers, Lee	DB	1995–02	112
Doyle, Ted	T	1938–44	74	Foggie, Fred	CB	1994	3
Drulis, Al	B	1947	10	Folkins, Lee	E	1965	8
Druschel, Rick	G-OT	1974	11	Foltz, Vernon	C	1945	4
Dudley, Bill	B	1942, 1945–46	26	Foote, Larry	LB	2002–08, 2010–13	158
Duffy, Roger	C-G	1998–01	52	Ford, Darryl	LB	1992	8
Dugan, Len	C	1939	1	Ford, Henry	B	1956	12
Duggan, Gil	T	1944	10	Ford, Moses	WR	1987	1
Duhart, Paul	B	1945	2	Fordham, Todd	T	2003	11
Dunaway, Craig	TE	1973	11	Foruria, John	B	1967–68	9
Dungy, Tony	DB	1977–78	30	Foster, Barry	RB	1990–94	62
Dunn, David	WR	1998	10	Foster, Ramon	T	2009–13	72
Dunn, Gary	DT-NT	1977–87	146	Fournet, Sid	G	1957	2
Dutton, Bill	B	1946	11	Fox, Keyaron,	LB	2008–10	45
Dwyer, Jonathan	RB	2010–13	36	Francis, Sam	B	1939	5
				Frank, Joe	T	1943	2
E				Frazier, Andre	LB	2005, 2007–09	48
Eason, Nick	DE	2007–10	55	Freeman, Lorenzo	NT/DT	1987–90	46
Eaton, Vic	QB	1955	12	French, Ernest	S	1972	3
Echols, Terry	LB	1984	4	Frketich, Len	T	1945	2
Edge, Shayne	P	1996	4	Fuamatu-Ma'afala, Chris	RB	1998–02	53
Edwards, Dave	S	1985–87	33	Fugler, Dick	T	1952	12
Edwards, Troy	WR	1999–01	46	Fuller, Randy,	DB	1995–97	39
Edwards, Glen	DB	1971–77	89	Fullerton, Ed	B	1953	1
Elder, Donnie	CB	1986	9	Fuqua, John	B	1970–76	87
Elliott, Jim	K	1967	14	Furness, Steve	DT	1972–80	97
Ellstrom, Marv	B	1935	3				
Elter, Leo	B	1953–54, 1958–59	38	**G**			
Emmons, Carlos	LB	1996–99	51	Gage, Bob	B	1949–50	22
Engebretsen, Paul	G	1933	9	Gagner, Larry	G	1966–69	52
Engles, Rick	P	1987	1	Gammon, Kendall	OL	1992–95	64
Erenberg, Rich	RB	1984–86	46	Gandy, Wayne	T	1999–02	63
Ernster, Paul	P	2008	3	Gaona, Bob	T	1953–56	48
Essex, Trai	T	2005–11	75	Garnaas, Wilford	B	1946–48	26
Euhus, Tim	TE	2006	1	Gardocki, Chris	P	2004–06	48
Evans, Donald	DE	1990–93	64	Garrett, Reggie	WR	1974–75	28

Player	Position	Seasons	Games	Player	Position	Seasons	Games
Garrity, Gregg	WR	1983	21	Hall, Delton	CB	1987–91	60
Garvin, Terence	LB	2013	15	Hall, Ron	B	1959	2
Gary, Keith	DE	1983–88	86	Haller, Alan	CB	1992–93	7
Gasparella, Joe	QB	1948, 1950–51	24	Ham, Jack	LB	1971–82	162
Gauer, Charles	E	1943	9	Hampton, Casey	NT	2001–12	173
Gay, William	CB	2007–13	96	Hanlon, Bob	B	1949	12
Geason, Cory	TE	2000–01	16	Hanneman, Craig	DE	1972–73	27
Gentry, Byron	G	1937–39	25	Hanratty, Terry	QB	1969–75	47
George, Matt	K	1998	1	Harkey, Lem	B	1955	4
Gerela, Roy	PK	1971–78	114	Harris, Bill	E	1937	1
Geri, Joe	B	1949–51	36	Harris, Franco	RB	1972–83	165
Gibson, Oliver	DT	1995–98	60	Harris, Lou	B	1968	14
Gilbert, Marcus	T	2011–13	35	Harris, Tim	RB	1983	14
Gildea, John	QB	1935–37	35	Harrison, Arnold	LB	2006–09	28
Gildon, Jason	LB	1994–03	158	Harrison, James	LB	2002–11	131
Gillespie, Scoop	RB	1984	14	Harrison, Nolan	DE	1997–99	30
Gilliam, Joe	QB	1972–75	20	Harrison Reggie	RB	1974–77	44
Gilreath, David	WR	2012	3	Harrison, Robert	LB	1964	11
Girard, Earl	B	1957	12	Hartings, Jeff	C	2001–06	91
Glamp, Joe	B	1947–49	32	Hartley, Howard	B	1949–52	45
Glass, Glenn	B	1962–63	21	Hartwig, Justin	C	2008–09	32
Glatz, Fred	E	1956	4	Haselrig, Carlton	G	1990–93	57
Glick, Gary	B	1956–59	34	Hastings, Andre	WR	1993–96	54
Goff, Clark	T	1940	11	Hawkins, Courtney	WR	1997–00	54
Golden, Robert	S	2012–13	31	Hawthorne, Greg	RB	1979–83	59
Gonda, George	B	1942	5	Hayduk, Henry	G	1935	8
Gonzalez, Pete	QB	1998–99	1	Hayes, Dick	LB	1959–60, 1962	28
Goodman, John	DE/DT	1981–85	64	Hayes, Jonathan	TE	1994–96	48
Goodson, John	P	1982	9	Haynes, Verron	RB	2002–07	61
Gorinski, Walt	B	1946	6	Hays, George	E	1950–52	35
Gothard, Preston	TE	1985–88	50	Hebert, Ken	E & K	1968	3
Gowdy, Cornell	CB	1987–88	29	Hegarty, Bill	T	1953	1
Graff, Neil	QB	1976–77	4	Held, Paul	QB	1954	8
Graham, Jeff	WR	1991–93	42	Heller, Warren	B	1934–36	36
Graham, Ken	DB	1970	3	Henderson, Jon	B	1968–69	23
Graham, Kent	QB	2000	14	Hendley, Dick	QB	1951	7
Gravelle, Gordon	OT	1972–76	54	Henry, Kevin	DE	1993–00	116
Graves, Ray	C	1943	10	Henry, Mike	LB	1959–61	34
Graves, Tom	LB	1979	11	Henry, Urban	T	1964	10
Gray, Sam	E	1946–47	16	Hensley, Dick	E	1952	11
Green, Bob	K	1960–61	26	Henson, Ken	C	1965	4
Green, Eric	TE	1990–94	62	Henton, Anthony	LB	1986, 1988	32
Greene, Joe	DT	1969–81	181	Hewitt, Bill	E	1943	6
Greene, Kevin	LB	1993–95	48	Heyward, Cameron	DE	2011–13	48
Greene, Tracy	TE	1995	16	Hickey, Howard	E	1941	1
Greeney, Norm	G	1934–35	12	Hill, Derek	WR	1989–90	32
Greenwood, L. C.	DE	1969–81	170	Hill, Harlon	E	1962	7
Griffin, Larry	CB/S	1987–93	86	Hill, Jim	B	1955	10
Grigas, John	B	1944	9	Hillebrand, Jerry	LB	1968–70	36
Grisham, Tyler	WR	2009–10	4	Hills, Tony	OT	2008–10	3
Gros, Earl	B	1967–69	38	Hilton, John	E	1965–69	66
Grossman, Randy	TE	1974–81	118	Hines, Glen Ray	OT	1973	14
Gunderman, Bob	B	1957	1	Hinkle, Bryan	LB	1982–93	163
Gunnels, Riley	T	1956–66	28	Hinkle, John	B	1943	10
				Hinnant, Mike	TE	1988–89	21
H				Hinte, Hal	E	1942	3
Hackney, Elmer	B	1941	11	Hinton, Chuck	T	1964–71	98
Haggans, Clark	LB	2000–07	107	Hipps, Claude	B	1952–53	17
Haggerty, Mike	G	1967–70	43	Hoague, Joe	B	1941–42, 1946	21
Haines, Byron	B	1937	5	Hoak, Dick	B	1961–70	135
Hairston, Russell	WR	1987	3	Hoel, Bob	G	1935	12
Haley, Dick	B	1961–64	49	Hoffmann, Dave	LB	1993	1

Player	Position	Seasons	Games	Player	Position	Seasons	Games
Hogan, Darrell	G	1949–53	60	Johnson, Malcolm	WR	1999–00	10
Hoge, Merril	RB	1987–93	109	Johnson, Norm	PK	1995–98	63
Hohn, Bob	B	1965–69	46	Johnson, Ron	CB	1978–84	91
Hoke, Chris	DT	2001–11	114	Johnson, Tim	DE/DT	1987–89	41
Holcomb, Bill	T	1937	7	Johnson, Troy	WR	1988	14
Holler, Ed	LB	1964	13	Johnson, Will	FB	2012–13	31
Holliday, Corey	WR	1995–97	17	Johnston, Chet	B	1939–40	18
Hollingsworth, Joe	B	1949–51	31	Johnston, Rex	B	1960	12
Holm, Bernard	B	1933	9	Jones, Aaron	DE/LB	1988–92	67
Holmer, Walt	B	1933	4	Jones, Art	B	1941, 1945	18
Holmes, Earl	LB	1996–01	81	Jones, Bruce	SS	1987	2
Holmes, Ernie	DT	1972–77	81	Jones, Donta	LB	1995–98	63
Holmes, Mel	OT	1971–73	29	Jones, Felix	RB	2013	16
Holmes, Santonio	WR	2006–09	60	Jones, Gary	S	1990–91, 1993–94	52
Hood, Frank	B	1933	3	Jones, George	RB	1997	16
Hood, Ziggy	DE	2009–13	80	Jones, Jarvis	LB	2013	14
Hope, Chris	S	2002–05	62	Jones, Landry	QB	2013	1
Hornick, Bill	T	1947	4	Jones, Mike	LB	2001–02	12
Howe, Garry	NT	1992	11	Jones, Victor	FB	1993–94	16
Howe, Glen	OT	1985	2	Jordan, Darin	LB	1988	15
Hubbard, Cal	T	1936	1	Jorden, Tim	TE	1992–93	31
Hubka, Gene	B	1947	1				
Huff, Alan	NT	1987	2	**K**			
Hughes, David	RB	1986	5	Kahler, Royal	T	1941	9
Hughes, Dennis	TE	1970–71	18	Kakasic, George	G	1936–39	37
Hughes, Dick	B	1957	1	Kalina, Dave	WR	1970	2
Hughes, George	G	1950–54	60	Kalis, Todd	G	1994	11
Hunter, Art	C	1965	9	Kapele, John	T	1960–62	32
Huntley, Richard	RB	1998–00	45	Kapinos, Jeremy	P	2010–11	12
				Karcis, John	B	1936–38	21
I				Karpowich, Ed	T	1936–39	36
Ilkin, Tunch	OT	1980–92	177	Karras, Ted	T	1958–59	24
Itzel, John	B	1945	10	Kavel, George	B	1934	1
Ivy, Corey	CB	2009	1	Keating, Tom	DT	1973	12
Ivy, Frank	E	1940	4	Keisel, Brett	DE	2002–13	144
Ivy, Mortty	LB	2011	6	Keith, Craig	TE	1993–94	17
Iwuoma, Chidi	CB	2002–06	60	Kelley, Jim	E	1964	6
Izo, George	QB	1966	4	Kellum, Marv	LB	1974–76	42
				Kelsay, Chad	LB	1999	6
J				Kelsch, Mose	B	1933–34	16
Jackson, Alonzo	LB	2003–04	9	Kemoeatu, Chris	G	2006–11	75
Jackson, Earnest	RB	1986–88	37	Kemp, Jack	QB	1957	4
Jackson, John	OT	1988–97	153	Kemp, Ray	T	1933	5
Jackson, Lenzie	WR	2001–02	11	Kenerson, John	G	1962	1
James, Dan	T	1960–66	91	Kerkorian, Gary	QB	1952	12
Janecek, Clarence	G	1933, 1935	11	Keys, Brady	B	1961–67	85
Jansante, Val	E	1946–51	65	Kichefski, Walt	E	1940–42, 1944	43
Jarvi, Toimi	B	1945	1	Kielbasa, Max	B	1946	2
Jecha, Ralph	G	1956	7	Kiesling, Walt	G	1937–38	12
Jefferson, Roy	E	1965–69	65	Kiick, George	B	1940, 1945	17
Jelley, Tom	E	1951	5	Killorin, Pat	C	1966	5
Jenkins, A. J.	LB/DE	1989–90	21	Kilroy, Frank	T	1943	9
Jenkins, John	S	1998	1	Kimble, Frank	E	1945	9
Jeter, Tony	E	1966, 1968	11	King, Carlos	FB	1998	1
Johnson, Bill	DE	1995–96	24	King, Phil	B	1964	8
Johnson, Brandon	LB	2012	14	Kirchner, Mark	OT	1973	3
Johnson, Charles	WR	1994–98	76	Kirk, Ken	LB	1960	14
Johnson, David	CB	1989–93	79	Kirkland, Levon	LB	1992–00	144
Johnson, David	TE	2009–11, 2013	52	Kirschke, Travis	DE	2004–09	92
Johnson, Jason	WR	1979	14	Kish, Ben	B	1943	10
Johnson, John Henry	B	1960–65	67	Kissell, Ed	B	1952–54	13
Johnson, Jovon	CB	2006	2	Klapstein, Earl	T	1946	9

Player	Position	Seasons	Games	Player	Position	Seasons	Games
Klein, Dick	T	1961	2	Lewis, Keenan	CB	2009–12	45
Klumb, John	E	1940	4	Liddick, Dave	T	1957	4
Knox, Darryl	LB	1987	3	Lind, Mike	B	1965–66	20
Kohrs, Bob	LB	1981–85	55	Lipps, Louis	WR/KR	1984–91	108
Kolb, Jon	OT	1969–81	177	Lipscomb, Gene	T	1961–62	28
Kolberg, Elmer	E	1941	4	Little, David	LB	1981–92	179
Kolodziejski, Chris	TE	1984	7	Littlefield, Carl	B	1939	11
Kondrla, John	T	1945	1	Lloyd, Greg	LB	1988–97	131
Kortas, Ken	T	1965–68	56	Lockett, Charles	WR	1987–88	27
Koshlap, Jules	B	1945	1	Logan, Charles	E	1964	14
Kotite, Dick	TE	1968	12	Logan, Mike	S	2001–06	73
Kottler, Martin	B	1933	3	Logan, Stefan	WR	2009	16
Kranchick, Matt	TE	2004–05	6	Long, Bill	E	1949–50	10
Kreider, Dan	FB	2000–07	113	Long, Terry	G	1984–91	105
Kresky, Joe	G	1935	1	Looney, Don	E	1941–42	12
Kriewaldt, Clint	LB	2003–07	74	Lott, John	C/G	1987	1
Krisher, Bill	G	1958	8	Love, Duval	G	1992–94	48
Kruczek, Mike	QB	1976–79	29	Lowther, Russ	B	1945	2
Krupa, Joe	OT	1956–64	110	Lucas, Jeff	OT	1987	3
Krutko, Larry	RB	1958–60	25	Lucente, John	B	1945	10
Kuhn, John	RB	2006	9	Luna, Bob	B	1959	12
Kurpeikis, Justin	LB	2001–02	9	Lusteg, Booth	K	1968	13
Kurrasch, Roy	E	1948	9	Lyons, Mitch	TE	1997–99	39
Kvaternik, Cvonimir	G	1934	1				
				M			
L				Mack, Red	B	1961–63, 1965	41
Lach, Steve	B	1946–47	23	Mack, Rico	LB	1993	8
LaCrosse, Dave	LB	1987	14	Mackrides, Bill	QB	1953	4
Ladygo, Pete	G	1952, 1954	24	Maddox, Tommy	QB	2001–05	43
Lajousky, Bill	G	1936	11	Madison, Anthony	CB	2006–11	59
Lake, Carnell	SS	1989–98	154	Magac, Mike	G	1965–66	22
Lamas, Joe	G	1942	8	Magulick, George	B	1944	9
Lambert, Frank	K	1965–66	28	Mahan, Sean	C	2007	16
Lambert, Jack	LB	1974–84	146	Maher, Francis	B	1941	2
Lantz, Montgomery	C	1933	10	Malkovich, Joe	C	1935	2
Lanza, Chuck	C	1988–89	27	Malecki, John	G	2012	1
Larose, Dan	T	1964	12	Mallick, Francis	T	1965	6
Lasse, Dick	LB	1958–59	24	Malone, Mark	QB	1980–87	60
Lattner, John	B	1954	12	Mandich, Jim	TE	1978	10
Laux, Ted	B	1943	4	Mansfield, Ray	C	1964–76	182
Law, Hubbard	C	1942, 1945	17	Manske, Edgar	E	1938	6
Lawrence, Ben	G	1987	1	Manuel, Rod	DE	1997–98	3
Layne, Bobby	QB	1958–62	55	Maples, Bob	C	1971	3
Lea, Paul	T	1951	9	Maras, Joe	C	1938–40	17
Leahy, Bob	QB	1971	1	Marchi, Basilio	C	1934	5
Leahy, Gerald	T	1957	1	Marchibroda, Ted	QB	1953, 1955–56	23
Lee, Bernard	B	1938	4	Marion, Jerry	B	1967	7
Lee, Danzell	TE	1987	13	Marker, Henry	B	1934	1
Lee, Greg	DB	1988	16	Markland, Jeff	TE	1988	1
Lee, Herman	T	1957	8	Marotti, Lou	G	1944	8
Lee, John	B	1939	5	Marsh, Curtis	WR	1997	5
Leftridge, Dick	B	1966	4	Martha, Paul	B	1964–69	75
Leftwich, Byron	QB	2008, 2010–12	8	Martin, John	B	1944	1
Legursky, Doug	C	2009–12	50	Martin, Tee	QB	2000–01	1
Lemek, Ray	G	1962–65	56	Martin, Vernon	B	1942	11
Lester, Tim	FB	1995–98	47	Mason, Grant	CB	2007	5
Letsinger, Jim	G	1933	1	Masters, Bob	B	1939, 1943	7
Levanti, Lou	G	1951–52	6	Masters, Walt	B	1944	33
Levey, Jim	B	1934–36	13	Mastrangelo, John	G	1947–48	23
Lewis, Frank	WR	1971–77	75	Matesic, Ed	B	1936	12
Lewis, Joe	T	1958–60	29	Matesic, Joe	T	1954	1
Lewis, Roy	CB	2008	1	Mathews, Ray	B	1951–59	108

Player	Position	Seasons	Games	Player	Position	Seasons	Games
Mathis, Terance	WR	2002	16	**Miner,** Tom	E	1958	12
Mattioli, Fran	G	1946	11	**Mingo,** Gene	K	1969–70	24
Matuszak, Marv	LB	1953, 1955–56	25	**Minter,** Michael	DT	1987	3
Maxson, Alvin	RB	1977–78	12	**Modzelewski,** Dick	T	1955	12
May, Ray	LB	1967–69	40	**Modzelewski,** Ed	B	1952	10
Mayhew, Hayden	G	1936–38	27	**Moegle,** Dick	B	1960	12
Mays, Alvoid	CB	1995	13	**Momsen,** Tony	C	1951	11
Mays, Lee	WR	2002–06	49	**Moore,** Bill	B	1933	5
Mazzanti, Jerry	E	1967	12	**Moore,** Mewelde	RB	2008–11	59
McAfee, Fred	RB	1994–98	64	**Moore,** Red	G	1947–49	36
McBean, Ryan	DE	2007	1	**Morales,** Gonzalo	B	1947–48	18
McBriar, Mat	P	2013	9	**Morey,** Sean	WR	2004–06	47
McCabe, Richie	B	1955, 1957–58	19	**Morgan,** Bob	B	1967–68	5
McCaffray, Art	T	1946	11	**Morgan,** Quincy	WR	2005	16
McCall, Don	RB	1969	13	**Moriarty,** Tom	S	1970	4
McCarthy, John	B	1944	7	**Morrall,** Earl	QB	1957–58	14
McClairen, Jack	E	1955–60	45	**Morris,** Bam	RB	1994–95	28
McClung, Willie	T	1955–57	36	**Morris,** John	B	1960	4
McConnell, Dewey	E	1954	9	**Morse,** Steve	RB	1985	16
McCoy, Jamie	TE	2012	1	**Moser,** Rick	RB	1978–79, 1981–82	43
McCullough, Hugh	B	1939, 1943	10	**Mosher,** Clure	C	1942	2
McDade, Karl	C	1938	6	**Mosley,** Norm	B	1948	5
McDonald, Ed	B	1936	5	**Moss,** Paul	E	1933	10
McDonough, Coley	QB	1939–41, 1944	19	**Motley,** Marion	B	1955	7
McDonough, Paul	E	1938	6	**Mott,** Norm	B	1934	1
McFadden, Bryant	CB	2005–08, 2010–11	80	**Moye,** Derek,	WR	2013	8
McFadden, Marshall	LB	2012	1	**Mularkey,** Mike	TE	1989–91	39
McFadden, Marv	G	1953, 1956	24	**Mulleneaux,** Lee	C	1935–36	19
McGee, Ben	E	1964–72	120	**Mullins,** Gerry	G/OT	1971–79	124
McGovern, Rob	LB	1991	15	**Mundy,** Ryan	S	2009–12	64
McGriff, Tyrone	G	1980–82	36	**Murley,** Dick	T	1956	2
McHugh, Sean	TE	2008–09	15	**Murray,** Earl	G	1952	11
McLendon, Steve	DT	2010–13	51	**Myslinski,** Tom	OL	1996–97, 2000	30
McMakin, John	TE	1972–74	36				
McNally, Johnny "Blood"	B	1934, 1937–39	24	**N**			
McNamara, Ed	T	1945	1	**Nagler,** Gern	E	1959	12
McPeak, Bill	E	1949–57	105	**Naioti,** John	B	1942, 1945	7
McWilliams, Tom	B	1950	10	**Nelsen,** Bill	QB	1963–67	32
Meadows, Ed	E	1955	12	**Nelson,** Darrell	TE	1984–85	16
Meeks, Bryant	C	1947–48	18	**Nelson,** Edmund	NT/DE	1982–87	72
Mehelich, Chuck	E	1946–51	59	**Nery,** Carl	G	1940–41	22
Meilinger, Steve	E	1961	4	**Newberry,** Tom	G	1995	16
Mendenhall, Rashard	RB	2008–12	57	**Newsome,** Harry	P	1985–89	76
Meredith, Jamon	G	2011	4	**Niccolai,** Armand	T/K	1934–42	97
Merkovsky, Elmer	T	1944, 1945–46	23	**Nichols,** Allen	B	1945	1
Merriweather, Mike	LB	1982–87	85	**Nickel,** Elbie	TE	1947–57	131
Messner, Max	LB	1964–65	21	**Nickerson,** Hardy	LB	1987–92	84
Meyer, Dennis	DB	1973	11	**Nicksich,** George	G	1950	12
Meyer, Ron	QB	1966	4	**Nisby,** John	G	1957–61	60
Michael, Bill	G	1957	3	**Nix,** Kent	QB	1967–69	25
Michaels, Ed	G	1943	10	**Nixon,** Mike	B	1935	3
Michaels, Lou	E	1961–63	42	**Nkwenti,** Mathias	OT	2001–03	2
Michalik, Art	G	1955–56	24	**Nobile,** Leo	G	1948–49	24
Middleton, Kelvin	SS	1987	2	**Nofsinger,** Terry	QB	1961–64	9
Midler, Lou	G	1939	11	**Noppenberg,** John	B	1940–41	13
Miles, Eddie	LB	1990	1	**Nosich,** John	T	1938	2
Miller, Heath	TE	2005–13	137	**Nutter,** Buzz	C	1961–64	56
Miller, Jim	QB	1995–96	5	**Nuzum,** Jerry	B	1948–51	45
Miller, Josh	P	1996–03	122				
Miller, Tom	E	1943	8	**O**			
Mills, Ernie	WR	1991–96	86	**O'Brien,** Fran	T	1966–67	29
Minarik, Henry	E	1951	11	**O'Brien,** John	E	1954–56	31

Player	Position	Seasons	Games	Player	Position	Seasons	Games
Odelli, Mel	B	1945	2	Popovich, John	B	1944 45	7
Odom, Henry	RB	1983	16	Porter, Joey	LB	1999–06	122
O'Donnell, Neil	QB	1990–95	66	Postus, Al	B	1945	2
Okobi, Chukky	C/G	2001–06	77	Poteat, Hank	CB	2000–02	41
Oehler, John	C	1933–34	23	Pottios, Myron	LB	1961–65	41
Oelerich, John	B	1938	3	Potts, Bill	B	1934	1
O'Leary, Dan	TE	2002	4	Pough, Ernest	WR	1976–77	28
Oldham, Chris	CB	1995–99	78	Pouncey, Maurkice	C	2010–13	46
Oldham, Ray	DB	1978	4	Pourdanesh, Shar	T	1999–00	9
Olejniczak, Stan	T	1935	6	Powell, Tim	E	1966	4
Oliver, Clarence	DB	1969–70	23	Powers, John	E	1962–66	44
Olsavsky, Jerry	LB	1989–97	108	Priatko, Bill	LB	1957	2
Olszewski, Al	E	1945	1	Putzier, Rollin	DT	1988	5
O'Malley, Joe	E	1955–56	22				
O'Neil, Bob	G	1956–57	24	**Q**			
Opfar, Dave	DE/NT	1987	3	Quatse, Jesse	T	1933–34	13
Orlando, Bo	S	1998	11	Quick, Jerry	OT/G	1987	1
Orr, Jim	E	1958–60	36	Quinn, Mike	QB	1997	11
Ortmann, Chuck	QB	1951	12				
O'Shea, Terry	TE	1989–90	32	**R**			
Oswald, Paul	C	1987	2	Raborn, Carroll	C	1936–37	21
Owens, Darrick	WR	1992	3	Rado, Alex	B	1934–35	8
				Rado, George	G	1935–37	24
P				Ragunas, Vince	B	1949	3
Palelei, Si'ulagi	G	1993	4	Rainey, Chris	RB	2012	16
Palmer, Mike	TE	2013	16	Rajkovich, Pete	B	1934	3
Palmer, Tom	T	1953–54	18	Randle El, Antwaan	WR	2002–05, 2010	80
Papach, George	B	1948–49	22	Rankin, Walt	B	1944	10
Parker, Frank	DT	1968–69	10	Rasby, Walter	TE	1994, 2004	6
Parker, Willie	RB	2004–09	79	Raskowski, Leo	T	1933	3
Parquet, Jeremy	OL	2007–08	2	Rasmussen, Randy	C-G	1984–86	31
Parrish, James	OL	1995	16	Ravotti, Eric	LB	1994–96	23
Pastin, Frank	G	1942	1	Raybon, Israel	DE	1996	3
Patrick, John	B	1941, 1945–46	18	Reavis, Dave	DT	1974–75	24
Patterson, Bill	QB	1940	11	Rechichar, Bert	B	1960	6
Paulson, David	TE	2012–13	32	Redman, Isaac	RB	2010–13	47
Pavkov, Stonko	G	1939–40	11	Reed, Jeff	K	2002–10	127
Paxson, Scott	DT	2008	1	Reeder, Dan	RB	1986–87	13
Peaks, Clarence	B	1964–65	22	Reese, Jerry	DE	1988	15
Pearson, Barry	WR	1972–73	13	Reger, John	LB	1955–63	104
Pearson, Preston	B	1970–74	62	Reid, Willie	WR	2006–07	7
Pegram, Erric	RB	1995–96	27	Renfro, Will	G	1960	26
Pense, Leon	QB	1945	10	Repko, Joe	T	1946–47	17
Perko, John	G	1937–40, 1944–47	75	Retkofsky, Jared	LS	2008–09	11
Perry, Darren	FS	1992–98	110	Reutershan, Randy	WR	1978	11
Perry, Lowell	B	1956	6	Reynolds, Billy	B	1958	12
Petchel, John	QB	1945	9	Reynolds, Jim	B	1946	2
Petersen, Ted	OT/C	1977–83, 1987	85	Rhodes, Don	T	1933	7
Peterson, Todd	K	2002	10	Ribble, Loran	G	1934–35	13
Petrella, John	B	1945	3	Richards, Perry	E	1957	7
Pierre, Joe	E	1945	10	Richardson, Huey	LB/DE	1991	5
Pillath, Roger	T	1966	6	Richardson, Terry	RB	1996	1
Pine, Ed	LB	1965	8	Richmond, Rock	DB	1987	2
Pinney, Ray	OT/G/C	1976–78, 1980–82, 1985–87	125	Ricketts, Tom	OT	1989–91	42
				Riemersma, Jay	TE	2003–04	22
Pirro, Rocco	G	1940–41	20	Rienstra, John	G	1986–90	42
Pittman, Mel	C	1935	2	Riffle, Dick	B	1941–42	21
Platukis, George	E	1938–41	38	Riley, Avon	LB	1987	3
Pokorny, Frank	WR	1985	4	Riley, Cameron	DB	1987	2
Polamalu, Troy	S	2003–13	146	Rivera, Gabe	DT	1983	6
Pollard, Frank	RB	1980–88	111	Roberts, John	B	1934	6
Pope, Leonard	TE	2012	16	Robinson, Adrian	LB	2012	10

Player	Position	Seasons	Games	Player	Position	Seasons	Games
Robinson, Ed	LB	1994	16	**Scott,** Jonathan	OT	2010–11	28
Robinson, Gil	E	1933	1	**Scudero,** Joe	B	1960	4
Robinson, Jack	T	1938	2	**Seabaugh,** Todd	LB	1984	16
Robnett, Marshall	C	1944	8	**Seabright,** Charles	QB	1946–50	56
Rodak, Mike	B	1942	5	**Seals,** Ray	DE	1994–95	29
Rodenhauser, Mark	LS/C	1998	16	**Searcy,** Leon	OT	1992–95	63
Rodgers, John	TE	1982–84	28	**Sears,** Vic	T	1943	10
Roethlisberger, Ben	QB	2004–13	143	**Sebastian,** Mike	B	1935	2
Rogel, Fran	B	1950–57	96	**Seigler,** Richard	LB	2006	2
Rogers, Cullen	B	1946	5	**Seitz,** Warren	TE	1986	16
Rorison, Jim	T	1938	6	**Semes,** Bernard	B	1944	8
Ross, Oliver	OL	2000–04	64	**Sepulveda,** Daniel	P	2007–11	52
Rossum, Allen	PR/KR/CB	2007	15	**Sexton,** Brent	DB	1977	11
Rostosky, Pete	OT	1984–86	35	**Shaffer,** George	B	1933	5
Rouen, Tom	P	2002	2	**Shanklin,** Ron	WR	1970–74	67
Rowley, Bob	LB	1963	3	**Sharp,** Rick	T	1970–71	17
Rowser, John	DB	1970–73	47	**Shaw,** Bobby	WR	1998–01	47
Royals, Mark	P	1992–94	48	**Sheffield,** Chris	CB	1986–87	15
Roye, Orpheus	DE	1996–99, 2008	67	**Shell,** Donnie	SS	1974–87	201
Rozzell, Aubrey	LB	1957	7	**Shelton,** Richard	CB	1990–93	41
Rucinski, Ed	E	1944	10	**Shepard,** Charles	B	1956	12
Ruff, Guy	LB	1982	2	**Sheriff,** Stan	LB	1954	12
Ruple, Ernie	T	1968–69	14	**Sherman,** Alex	QB	1943	9
Russell, Andy	LB	1963, 1966–76	168	**Sherman,** Bob	B	1964–65	25
Russell, Gary	RB	2007–08	15	**Shields,** Burrell	B	1954	6
Ryan, Ed	E	1948	9	**Shields,** Scott	S	1999–00	26
				Shiner, Dick	QB	1968–69	25
S				**Shipkey,** Jerry	B	1948–52	58
Sader, Steve	B	1943	2	**Shorter,** Jim	B	1969	14
Sadowski, Troy	TE	1997–98	6	**Shugarts,** Bret	DE	1987	2
Sample, John	B	1961–62	20	**Shurtz,** Hubert	T	1948	12
Samuel, Don	B	1949–50	6	**Shy,** Don	B	1967–68	27
Samuelson, Carl	T	1948–51	43	**Simerson,** John	T	1958	3
Sanchez, Lupe	CB/KR	1986–88	39	**Simington,** Milt	B	1942	11
Sandberg, Sigurd	T	1935–37	30	**Simmons,** Jason	CB	1998–01	49
Sandefur, Wayne	B	1936–37	9	**Simmons,** Jerry	WR	1965–66	17
Sanders, Chuck	RB	1986–87	19	**Simmons,** Kendall	G	2002–08	80
Sanders, Emmanuel	WR	2010–13	56	**Simms,** Bob	E	1962	3
Sanders, John	G	1940–42	30	**Simpson,** Jack	B	1961–62	21
Sandig, Curt	B	1942	11	**Simpson,** Tim	G/C	1994	4
Sandusky, Mike	G	1957–65	104	**Sims,** Darryl	DE	1985–86	32
Sapp, Theron	B	1963–65	35	**Sinkovitz,** Frank	C	1947–52	64
Saul, Bill	LB	1964, 1966–68	44	**Sirochman,** George	G	1942	2
Saumer, Sylvester	B	1934	3	**Sites,** Vince	E	1936–37	19
Saunders, Weslye	TE	2011	16	**Skansi,** Paul	WR	1983	15
Scales, Charles	B	1960–61	26	**Skladany,** Joe	E	1934	12
Scarbath, Jack	QB	1956	12	**Skorich,** Nick	G	1946–48	32
Scales, Charles	B	1960–61	26	**Skoronski,** Ed	E	1935–36	15
Scherer, Bernard	E	1939	9	**Slater,** Walt	B	1947	11
Schiechl, John	C	1941–42	6	**Small,** Fred	LB	1985	16
Schmidt, John	C	1940	1	**Smith,** Aaron	DE	1999–11	160
Schmitz, Bob	LB	1961–66	49	**Smith,** Anthony	S	2006–08	46
Schneck, Mike	LS	1999–04	92	**Smith,** Ben	E	1934–35	22
Schnelker, Bob	E	1961	8	**Smith,** Billy Ray	T	1958–60	30
Schuelke, Karl	B	1939	1	**Smith,** Bob	B	1966	8
Schultz, Eberle	G	1941–42, 1944	32	**Smith,** Dave	WR	1970–72	34
Schwartz, Elmer	B	1933	10	**Smith,** Jim	WR	1977–82	73
Schweder, John	G	1951–55	60	**Smith,** Kevin	S	1991	16
Scolnik, Glenn	WR	1973	1	**Smith,** Laverne	RB	1977	7
Scot, Wilbert	LB	1961	4	**Smith,** Marvel	OT	2000–08	112
Scott, Chad	CB	1997–04	91	**Smith,** Ron	QB	1966	9
Scott, Chris	OT	2010–11	2	**Smith,** Steve	E	1966	3

Player	Position	Seasons	Games
Smith, Stu	QB	1937–38	21
Smith, Truett	QB	1950–51	20
Snell, Ray	OT	1984–85	18
Snyder, Bill	G	1934–35	12
Sodaski, John	DB	1970	3
Soleau, Bob	LB	1964	14
Solomon, Ariel	G/OT	1991–95	45
Somers, George	T	1941–42	21
Sorce, Ross	T	1945	1
Sortet, Wilbur	E	1933–40	84
Souchak, Frank	E	1939	4
Spaeth, Matt	TE	2007–10	60
Spencer, Todd	RB	1984–85	23
Spinks, Jack	G	1952	10
St. Pierre, Brian	QB	2003–04, 2006–07	1
Staat, Jeremy	DE	1998–00	28
Staggers, Jon	WR	1970–71	26
Stai, Brenden	G	1995–99	68
Staley, Duce	RB	2004–06	16
Stallworth, John	WR	1974–87	165
Stanley, Ron	LB	2006	1
Stanton, John	B	1961	2
Stapleton, Darnell	G/C	2007–09	14
Stark, Rohn	P	1995	16
Starks, Max	T	2004–12	123
Starret, Ben	B	1941	4
Station, Larry	LB	1986	6
Stautner, Ernie	T	1950–63	173
Steed, Joel	NT	1992–99	115
Steele, Ernie	B	1943	10
Stehouwer, Ron	B	1960–64	68
Stenger, Brian	LB	1969–72	49
Stenn, Paul	T	1947	11
Stephens, Jamain	OT	1996–98	18
Stephens-Howling, LaRod	RB	2013	1
Steward, Dean	B	1943	6
Stewart, Kordell	QB	1995–02	114
Stock, John	E	1956	2
Stock, Mark	WR	1989	8
Stofko, Ed	B	1945	2
Stone, Dwight	WR/RB/KR	1987–94	124
Stoudt, Cliff	QB	1977–83	30
Stough, Glen	T	1945	10
Stowe, Tyronne	LB	1987–90	55
Strand, Eli	G	1966	8
Strom, Rick	QB	1989–93	10
Strugar, George	T	1962	1
Strutt, Art	B	1935–36	19
Stryzinski, Dan	P	1990–91	32
Strzelczyk, Justin	OT	1990–99	133
Stuvaints, Russell	S	2003–05	23
Suhey, Steve	G	1948–49	24
Sulima, George	E	1952–54	31
Suisham, Shaun	K	2010–13	55
Sullivan, Chris	DE	2000	15
Sullivan, Frank	C	1940	9
Sullivan, Robert	B	1947	3
Summers, Frank	RB	2009	2
Sutherin, Don	B	1959–60	10
Sutton, Ricky	DL	1993	7
Swain, John	CB	1985–86	20
Swann, Lynn	WR	1974–82	115

Player	Position	Seasons	Games
Sweed, Limas	WR	2008–10	20
Sweeney, Calvin	WR	1980–87	102
Sweeney, Jim	C/G	1996–99	46
Sydnor, Willie	WR/KR	1982	8
Sylvester, Stevenson	LB	2010–13	50
Szot, Walter	T	1949–50	23

T

Player	Position	Seasons	Games
Tanguay, Jim	B	1933	3
Tarasovic, George	E	1952–53, 1956–63	118
Tatum, Jesse	E	1938	5
Taylor, Ike	CB	2003–13	169
Taylor, Jim	LB	1956	12
Taylor, Mike	T	1968–69	23
Tepe, Lou	C	1953–55	34
Terry, Nat	CB	1988	6
Tesser, Ray	E	1933–34	23
Tharpe, Larry	OT	2000	12
Thigpen, Yancey	WR	1992–97	77
Thomas, Ben	DE/DT	1988	8
Thomas, Clendon	B	1962–68	96
Thomas, J. T.	CB/S	1973–77, 1979–81	116
Thomas, Shamarko,	S	2013	14
Thompson, Clarence	B	1937–38	17
Thompson, Donnel	LB	2000	8
Thompson, Leroy	RB	1991–93	43
Thompson, Tommy	QB	1940	11
Thompson, Weegie	WR	1984–89	92
Thornton, Sidney	RB	1977–82	74
Thurbon, Bob	B	1943–44	20
Tiller, Morgan	E	Denver 1945	10
Timmons, Lawrence	LB	2007–13	110
Tinsley, Sid	B	1945	9
Titus, George	C	1946	11
Titus, Silas	E	1945	9
Toews, Loren	LB	1973–83	149
Tomasetti, Lou	B	1939–40	21
Tomasic, Andy	B	1942–46	15
Tomczak, Mike	QB	1993–99	84
Tomlinson, Dick	G	1950–51	23
Tommerson, Clarence	B	1938–39	4
Tosi, John	B	1939	3
Totten, Erik	S	2002	1
Townsend, Deshea	CB	1998–08	183
Tracy, Tom	B	1958–63	60
Trout, Dave	PK	1981, 1987	19
Tsoutsouvas, Lou	C	1938	5
Tuggle, Anthony	CB/S	1985, 1987	4
Tuman, Jerame	TE	1999–06	120
Turk, Dan	C	1985–86	17
Turley, John	QB	1935–36	14
Tylski, Rich	G	2000–01	28
Tyrrell, Tim	RB	1989	7

V

Player	Position	Seasons	Games
Valentine, Zack	LB	1979–81	56
Van Dyke, Bruce	G	1967–73	95
Van Dyke, DeMarcus	CB	2013	11
Varrichione, Frank	T	1955–60	72
Vaughan, John	QB	1933–34	19
Veals, Elton	RB	1984	15
Veasey, Craig	DL	1990–91	23

Player	Position	Seasons	Games	Player	Position	Seasons	Games
Velasco, Fernando	G	2013	11	Williams, Don	G	1941	6
Victorian, Josh	CB	2012	4	Williams, Eric	S	1983–86	49
Vidoni, Vic	E	1935–36	13	Williams, Erwin	WR	1969	9
Vincent, Keydrick	G	2001–04	38	Williams, Gerald	NT/DE	1986–94	120
Vincent, Shawn	CB	1991	10	Williams, Jerrol	LB	1989–92	64
von Oelhoffen, Kimo	DL	2000–05	95	Williams, Joe	LB	1987	3
Voss, Lloyd	T	1966–71	82	Williams, Joe	B	1939	1
Vrabel, Mike	LB	1997–00	51	Williams, John L.	FB	1994–95	26
				Williams, Ray	CB	1987	1
W				Williams, Robert	S	1984	2
Wade, Bob	DB	1968	14	Williams, Sidney	LB	1969	7
Wade, Tom	QB	1964–65	5	Williams, Vince	LB	2013	15
Wager, Clint	E	1944	8	Williams, Warren	RB	1988–92	66
Wagner, Mike	S	1971–80	119	Williams, Willie	CB	1993–96, 2004–05	83
Walden, Bob	P	1968–77	138	Williamson, Fred	B	1960	11
Walker, Sammy	CB	1991–92	18	Willis, Keith	DE	1982–87, 1989–91	126
Wallace, Cody	C	2013	10	Wilson, Bill	E	1938	4
Wallace, Mike	WR	2009–12	63	Wilson, Cedrick	WR	2005–07	47
Wallace, Ray	RB	1989	9	Wilson, Frank	TE	1982	1
Wallace, Rian	LB	2005–06	16	Wilson, Kion	LB	2013	7
Walsh, Bill	C	1949–55	72	Winfrey, Carl	LB	1972	1
Ward, Hines	WR	1998–11	217	Wingle, Blake	G	1983–85	34
Warren, Buist	B	1945	8	Winston, Dennis	LB	1977–81, 1985–86	99
Warren, Greg	LS	2005–13	133	Withycombe, Mike	C	1991	2
Warren, Xavier	DE/DT	1987	2	Witman, Jon	FB	1996–01	85
Washington, Anthony	CB	1981–82	25	Wolf, Jim	DE	1974	11
Washington, Clarence	DT	1969–70	27	Wolfley, Craig	G/OT	1980–89	129
Washington, Dewayne	CB	1998–03	96	Wolford, Will	G/T	1996–98	45
Washington, Nate	WR	2005–08	49	Womack, Joe	B	1962	11
Washington, Robert	OT	1987	3	Woodard, Ken	LB	1987	7
Washington, Sam	CB	1982–85	41	Woodley, David	QB	1984–85	16
Watkins, Tom	B	1968	1	Woodley, LaMarr	LB	2007–13	94
Watson, Allen	K	1970	4	Woodruff, Dwayne	CB	1979–85, 1987–90	157
Watson, Sid	B	1955–57	35	Woods, Al	DE	2011–13	28
Webster, Elnardo	LB	1992	3	Woods, Donovan	LB	2008–09	6
Webster, George	LB	1972–73	18	Woods, Rick	S/CB	1982–86	66
Webster, Mike	C	1974–88	220	Woodson, Marv	B	1964–69	67
Weed, Thurlow	K	1955	6	Woodson, Rod	DB/KR	1987–96	134
Weinberg, Henry	G	1934	8	Woolford, Donnell	CB	1997	15
Weinstock, Izzy	B	1937–38	13	Worilds, Jason	LB	2010–13	57
Weisenbaugh, Henry	B	1935	5	Worley, Tim	RB	1989–91, 1993	33
Wells, Billy	B	1957	10	Woudenberg, John	T	1940–42	29
Wendlick, Joe	E	1941	10	Wren, Lowe	B	1960	12
Wenzel, Ralph	E	1942	6	Wukits, Al	C	1943–45	23
Wenzel, Ralph	G	1966–70	43	Wydo, Frank	T	1947–51	60
Westfall, Ed	B	1933	6				
Wetzel, Damon	B	1935	9	**Y**			
Wheaton, Markus	WR	2013	12	Young, Al	WR	1971–72	15
Wheeler, Ernie	B	1939	5	Young, Dick	B	1957	11
Whelan, Tom	B	1933	1	Young, Theo	TE	1987	12
Whimper, Guy	T	2013	10	Young, Walter	WR	2006	2
White, Byron	B	1938	11	Younger, Paul	B	1958	12
White, Dwight	DE	1971–80	126	Yurchey, John	B	1940	1
White, Paul	B	1947	11				
Wiehl, Joe	T	1935	3	**Z**			
Wiggins, Paul	OT	1997	1	Zaninelli, Silvio	B	1934–37	44
Wilburn, J. R.	WR	1966–70	58	Zereoue, Amos	RB	1999–03	66
Wilcots, Solomon	S	1992	16	Zgonina, Jeff	DL	1993–94	21
Wiley, Jack	T	1946–50	57	Zimmerman, Leroy	QB	1943	10
Wilkerson, Eric	RB/WR	1989	1	Zombek, Joe	E	1954	9
Williams, Albert	LB	1987	3	Zoppetti, Frank	B	1941	4
Williams, Dave	WR	1973	1				

INDEX